FAMILY LAW AND PRACTICE

FAMILY LAW AND PRACTICE

Nancy Duffield BA, Solicitor (Hons)

Jo Theobald BA, Solicitor

JORDANS

2001

Published by
Jordan Publishing Limited
21 St Thomas Street
Bristol BS1 6JS

British Library Cataloguing-in-Publication Data
A catalogue record for this book is available from the British Library.

ISSN 1353–3614
ISBN 0 85308 683 4

Printed in Great Britain by Hobbs The Printers Ltd of Southampton

PREFACE

Family law is a dynamic subject, constantly changing, and a challenge to everyone involved with it. We have taken on the challenge in preparing this Resource Book. Our main aim has been to prepare a book which provides the legal background for students on the Legal Practice Course run by The College of Law. It will be the springboard for students to use to practise the skills learned during the Legal Practice Course. We hope it will also be of use to trainees and newly qualified solicitors who are using these skills for the first time in the real world.

Throughout the book, for uniformity, we have generally referred to the client and the solicitor as 'he'. In reality, it is usually the female who initiates proceedings on the breakdown of the relationship, and in some places, for example domestic violence, we have changed the sex of the client to reflect the more usual situation.

The Family Law Act 1996 was intended to introduce radical reforms to divorce law. At the time of writing, it is unclear whether these reforms will be introduced. Therefore, we have not changed the divorce law section of this book.

We would like to acknowledge with great thanks the contribution made to this book by Dawn O'Toole and Imogen Burton and Ian Jones who are unfortunately unable to continue as authors.

We would also like to thank Henry Brown, solicitor, for his help and advice in producing the original section on mediation and family practitioners. We would also like to thank our colleagues at The College of Law who have helped us with this book and, finally, thanks and sympathy to our long-suffering families and friends who have endured its rebirth.

Unless otherwise mentioned, the law is stated as at 1 September 2000.

NANCY DUFFIELD
JO THEOBALD
The College of Law

CONTENTS

TABLE OF CASES

References in the right-hand column are to paragraph numbers.

TABLE OF STATUTES

References in the right-hand column are to paragraph numbers.

TABLE OF STATUTORY INSTRUMENTS

References in the right-hand column are to paragraph numbers.

TABLE OF EUROPEAN LEGISLATION

References in the right-hand column are to paragraph numbers.

TABLE OF ABBREVIATIONS

ABWOR	assistance by way of representation
AI	assessable income
BDR	basic deduction rate
CA 1989	Children Act 1989
CAA 1984	Child Abduction Act 1984
CACA 1985	Child Abduction and Custody Act 1985
CAFCASS	Child and Family Court Advisory and Support Service
CGT	capital gains tax
CPR 1998	Civil Procedure Rules 1998
CSA 1991	Child Support Act 1991
CSAT	Child Support Appeal Tribunal
DPMCA 1978	Domestic Proceedings and Magistrates' Courts Act 1978
FDR	Financial Dispute Resolution
FLA 1996	Family Law Act 1996
FLBA	Family Law Bar Association
FMA	Family Mediators Association
FPR 1991	Family Proceedings Rules 1991
HRA 1998	Human Rights Act 1998
I(PFD)A 1975	Inheritance (Provision for Family and Defendants) Act 1975
LPA 1925	Law of Property Act 1925
LR	Legal Representation
MCA 1973	Matrimonial Causes Act 1973
MR	maintenance requirement
NFM	National Family Mediation
PHA 1997	Protection from Harassment Act 1997
PPO	periodical payment order
SFLA	Solicitors Family Law Association
TLATA 1996	Trusts of Land and Appointment of Trustees Act 1996

Chapter 1

INTRODUCTION: THE FAMILY PRACTICE

1.1 THE FAMILY CLIENT

There is a wide range of reasons why a client would wish to discuss family problems with a solicitor. The most common reason is that a marital relationship has permanently broken down. Some clients, however, may seek advice because they are encountering temporary difficulties and have no wish to terminate the relationship formally. Yet others may have some domestic problem which they need to resolve but are undecided and unclear as to the future of the relationship.

Whether or not a client has made a firm decision about the relationship, she will usually be reasonably clear about her more immediate problems which prompted her to seek legal advice. The three most common problem areas concern money and property (see Chapters 4 to 10), children (see Chapters 12 and 13) and protection from violence (see Chapter 14). How these problems are to be dealt with depends in the first place on whether the couple are married. The problems and concerns of unmarried couples are virtually indistinguishable from those of married ones; the legal remedies, however, are by no means the same and are more limited for unmarried couples. The unmarried family is considered in detail in Chapter 15, although comparison between the position of cohabitants and spouses is made throughout this book.

In the case of married couples, there is a broad range of solutions to the key problems. The skill of the family lawyer is to match the appropriate solution to the needs of the individual client. Which measures are to be taken will depend on whether the client has made the decision to end the marriage or whether a more temporary solution is favoured. The marriage may be terminated formally by divorce (or nullity) or the couple may separate formally by judicial separation (these options are considered in Chapter 3). Alternatively, the client may not wish to make any final decision about the relationship itself but merely wish to seek advice on a particular problem, for example, a wife may be anxious about her position in the matrimonial home or a father may be being denied contact with his children.

It is worthwhile pausing to consider some of the likely issues and concerns facing a family client. Whilst there is no such thing as a 'typical' family client (and it would be a mistake to assume that there was), there are certain concerns which are common to many families.

Example
Beverley is a mother with two young children. She has been married to Colin for the last 10 years but is seeking a divorce because Colin has recently begun to be violent towards her and on one occasion to her son. She does not work and has no savings. She has fled the family home and her main worry is to be able to return to the home in safety.

One of the first issues for the solicitor to consider is how the client will pay for the legal advice. This will also be high on the client's list of concerns. The question of costs including public funding are considered in context throughout this book and in Chapter 2. A private client should be advised about the costs policy of the firm and will usually be asked to make a payment on account. As with most contentious work, it is difficult to give an estimate of costs in the initial interview as so much depends on the attitude of the other party and indeed of the client himself. In this example, Beverley is likely to be eligible for public funding.

Beverley's primary need is to seek protection from the violence and to be able to return home. It will be necessary, therefore, to take instructions to prepare for proceedings for a non-molestation and occupation order under the Family Law Act 1996 (FLA 1996) (see Chapter 14). As she wishes to obtain a divorce, the solicitor will also need to obtain the information and prepare the documentation required to institute divorce proceedings (see Chapter 3). Since the order under the FLA 1996 will provide only a temporary solution to Beverley and the children's housing needs, the solicitor must also discuss the future arrangements in relation to the former matrimonial home (see Chapter 8). Although it will be some time before this can be dealt with, the solicitor needs to think ahead and obtain public funding in good time to commence ancillary proceedings. The solicitor should also be aware of the need to protect his client's interest in the matrimonial home. He will, therefore, need to establish how the property is held between the parties and make any necessary registrations against the title. In addition, Beverley should be advised to make (or alter) a will. Further, there may be a problem regarding the mortgage as Colin may stop paying the mortgage if he is ordered to leave the home (although, if an occupation order is made, provision can be included instructing Colin to continue to pay the mortgage). It will probably be necessary, therefore, to advise Beverley regarding maintenance and possibly to write to the lender to explain any short-term difficulties which there may be in relation to the mortgage. The procedure for obtaining financial orders is considered in Chapter 9 and their enforcement and variation is considered in Chapter 10.

As it will be some time before any application for maintenance for Beverley can be considered in detail, she should be advised of her entitlements to welfare benefits (see Chapter 6) and for maintenance for the children under the Child Support Act 1991 (see Chapter 7).

The other important consideration is, of course, the children (see Chapters 12 and 13). At an early stage, it is likely to be necessary to raise the question of the children's contact with their father. As with the other issues, this may be agreed upon between the parties (after negotiation) but in Beverley's case, in view of her husband's violence towards her son, she may well object to any contact. If Colin wished to pursue this, it would involve further proceedings (and an extension of any Legal Representation certificate).

It will not always be appropriate to discuss all of these issues at the initial interview but the solicitor will need to be aware of the wider picture from the outset. He will need to raise the various issues at an appropriate stage and encourage his client to confront the future and make informed decisions. The topics covered in this book deal with all of the problems faced by Beverley in the example above. Of necessity, the book takes each issue in turn but it is important to appreciate from the beginning that all the issues are strongly interrelated and that several disputes and difficulties can occur concurrently.

1.2 THE FAMILY PRACTITIONER

1.2.1 Professional conduct

Family solicitors owe the same duties towards their clients as those of any other solicitor. The solicitor may not act for both parties no matter how amicable their separation. Confidentiality towards clients' affairs must also be observed, for example a client's address cannot be disclosed without his consent.

1.2.2 Adviser – not decision-maker

There are certain special considerations to be borne in mind when dealing with a family matter. Family clients are likely to be more vulnerable than other clients. They may have only recently (or are even yet to) come to terms with the breakdown of their relationship and the consequent breakup of their home and family. They will invariably face many problems, be presented with a bewildering array of options, and be called upon to make many important decisions. It is hardly surprising, therefore, that such clients may be tempted to pass the responsibility to make these decisions on to their solicitor. However, it is important that the family solicitor is able to distinguish between advising the client of his choices and influencing the client's decisions or even assuming certain choices on the client's behalf. However much a client's marriage appears to the solicitor to be irredeemably lost, the solicitor must be careful to advise the client fully of all the options and not to push the client prematurely down the route to divorce. If the solicitor is in any doubt as to what the client really wants to do about his relationship, he should pause to allow the client time to make a free and firm decision. Many clients will find the initial interview an emotional and stressful experience and, bearing in mind that many important and complex matters will have been discussed in the interview, it is sensible to confirm advice given and to set out the options in a letter following the interview. This enables the client to absorb the advice and reflect upon it before embarking upon a particular course of action.

1.2.3 Objectives

A further important consideration for the family solicitor is to keep sight of the client's overall long-term objectives. If a relationship has finally broken down, it is fair to assume that a family client's ultimate objective is to be able to unravel the legal ties of that relationship and to begin life afresh with the minimum of pain and bitterness. This will apply particularly where children are involved. There will be times when a client may be so involved in the detail of a particular dispute that he loses sight of this wider aim. It is here that the good family practitioner can make a positive contribution; by maintaining a sufficiently detached viewpoint the professional may enable a client to refocus on his goal and to regard matters in the round.

In pursuing these long-term objectives the good family solicitor has a very positive role to play. The approach taken by the solicitor can significantly influence a client's response. If a solicitor takes an aggressive stance, advising in terms of 'winning' and 'losing' and 'fighting' and 'giving in' then this is likely to serve to stir up bitterness and lead a client to set his face against compromise. Conversely, the solicitor who attempts to defuse tensions, concentrating on important issues rather than petty matters and talks in terms of arriving at fair solutions and compromise is likely to find that his client is more willing to follow this lead. It is important to address the advantages of a negotiated settlement whilst at the same time assuring the client that, where appropriate, a firm stance will be taken to protect his interests. The people most likely to come through the trauma of a divorce or separation successfully are those who have been involved in reaching agreement about important issues. A party is also much more likely to abide by such an agreement than by an arrangement imposed by the court. Most important of all is the benefit of reducing the impact of the disputes on any children who are at risk of being caught in the cross-fire. For further consideration of these matters, see the Solicitors Family Law Association Code of Practice (SFLA) (set out in the Appendix) which advocates a conciliatory approach in family matters and sets out helpful reminders in dealing with the client, other solicitors, the other party (if he is unrepresented) and children. The SFLA has a membership of approximately 4500 family law solicitors and is one of the largest groupings outside The Law Society. Its Code of Practice is endorsed by The Law Society and supported by the President of the Family Division and many senior members of the judiciary (see, for example, *Dutfield v Gilbert Stephens & Sons* [1988] Fam Law 473). The Code is essential reading for anyone working in this area.

In order to achieve these objectives, the family practitioner must acquire negotiating skills; he must know when and how to achieve a settlement (see LPC Resource Book *Skills for Lawyers* (Jordans)). Having successfully negotiated a settlement, the family solicitor must use his drafting skills to draw up a clear and enforceable agreement (see LPC Resource Book *Skills for Lawyers* (Jordans)). This document may take the form of a consent order (see Chapter 8) or a separation agreement (see Chapter 10).

If a negotiated settlement cannot be achieved, the matter must be determined in court. Since most proceedings will be dealt with in chambers in the county court the family solicitor will have rights of audience. This will call for the use of advocacy skills (see LPC Resource Book *Skills for Lawyers* (Jordans)).

If the solicitor's approach to family work is a conciliatory one then this is likely to encourage clients to take advantage of conciliation and mediation services offered by other agencies (see **1.3**). Conversely, if the solicitor takes a more antagonistic approach and, in particular, is openly cynical about conciliation and mediation then this will hardly encourage the client to take advantage of these options.

1.2.4 Interviewing skills

The success of the solicitor–client relationship in family cases is to a large extent dependent upon the impression created in the first interview. The practitioner may be in the privileged position of being the first person with whom the client has discussed his relationship difficulties. The client will be sensitive to the atmosphere in that interview and it is of crucial importance that the solicitor attempts to create the right environment and to adopt an appropriate tone for the interview.

Preparation for the interview is vital. Thought should be given to the length of the interview and its venue as well as to the information which should be obtained from, and given to, the client. In family matters the interview could also be complicated by the fact that the client may bring her children with her or have chosen to bring a friend for support. This field of interviewing is a hugely important subject in itself which cannot be considered in detail here, but reference should be made to the section on Interviewing in the LPC Resource Book *Skills for Lawyers* (Jordans). Use of a checklist or instruction sheet will ensure that the information required is obtained. However, care must be taken when using such aids to explain their use to the client and to ensure that the interview does not become too formal or narrow.

Although family practitioners may have a special relationship with their clients, it is important to be able to recognise the boundaries of the practitioner's role and the limitations of their skills. Although the practitioner should consider the possibility of reconciliation for his client, he cannot himself undertake this role. Similarly, the solicitor will wish to facilitate compromise but cannot act as mediator between the parties. Instead, the family practitioner will be familiar with the local agencies and services which are more suitable and capable of performing these roles.

1.2.5 Awareness and balance

When a marriage is in crisis, each party may experience a wide range of feelings. These will inevitably vary between individuals, but may variously include disappointment, anger and blame, hurt, sadness, self-doubt, loss, guilt, uncertainty and anxiety. For some time, there may be a sense of relief that an unhappy situation is being addressed. Sometimes, there may be worry and concern for the other spouse. It is not uncommon for people in this crisis situation to move inconsistently from one feeling to another. There is no standard reaction to marriage breakdown, and family solicitors need to be aware of the sensitivity of the situation in which they are intervening.

Most clients need, and are entitled to have, solicitors who will advise and support them in these difficult times. Their solicitors may have to act as their champions, protecting their rights and position. However, while maintaining awareness of these legitimate expectations, the family solicitor also needs to be aware that supporting the client can sometimes mean helping him or her to understand and come to terms with unpalatable consequences or seeking compromises which the client may prefer not to make. Parents may be able to keep their children's best interests in mind, but in that situation those interests may sometimes blur with the client's own preferences, antagonisms or strength of feeling; and here again the solicitor may have a role in helping the client to be aware of the children's needs and interests as well as the client's.

The family solicitor accordingly has to maintain a balance between the supportive partisan role, and the need to confront the client's perceptions where appropriate. As previously stated, an objective view, sympathetically but not patronisingly expressed, may be necessary to help the client make necessary shifts. The solicitor must also appreciate the extent to which his or her actions and approach can have an effect, whether helping or damaging, on the client and on the relationship between the parties and their children. Communications with the other side can always be courteous and sensitive, even where tough positions are being stated. Opportunities for dialogue can be established early on and maintained even when confrontation is indicated. This is all consistent with having a sympathetic and effective relationship with the client. The Solicitors Family Law Association encourages the development of these skills in a number of ways, for example by issuing guides to good practice in various areas of family law – service correspondence, disclosure, acting for children, and domestic violence and working with the Bar in family cases – and by holding seminars and workshops on understanding the emotional aspects of family life and of the personal consequences which may follow any change, and increasing members' self-awareness as well as training in 'black letter' family law.

1.3 OTHER FAMILY AGENCIES

There is a wide (and somewhat confusing) array of agencies whose work complements that of the family practitioner. Principally, the roles they perform fall into two categories: counselling and mediation.

1.3.1 Counselling

Counselling takes different forms and may have different aims. It may involve working with an individual, the couple, members of the family or the whole family together. It may be relatively short term or may involve longer-term marital or family therapy; and there are different theoretical perspectives.

One of the aims of counselling may be to try to save the marriage where it is under stress or to establish a reconciliation where it has already broken down. Another may be to explore whether there is any basis for continuing with the relationship, and if so what has to happen to make this possible. Not uncommonly, a couple may disagree about the future of the marriage; one wishing to end it and the other to continue with it. Counselling may assist them to come to their own conclusion, whether this proves to be preserving the relationship or bringing it to an end. Counselling may therefore help a couple to accept the ending of their relationship if that is appropriate.

Organisations which can assist in providing counselling, and in exploring possibilities of reconciliation if required, are:

- Relate
- National Marriage Guidance
- Jewish Marriage Council
- Catholic Marriage Advisory Council
- Institute of Family Therapy

The local Citizens Advice Bureau will have the addresses of local branches of these organisations. It is a good idea for the practitioner to compile his own list of local services and individual counsellors.

1.3.2 Mediation

In family mediation the couple engage the assistance of one or two impartial mediators, who have no authority to make any decisions for them, but who use certain skills to help them to resolve their issues by negotiated agreement without adjudication.

The mediator (or co-mediators) will usually meet the parties together (although, in some circumstances, may see them separately) and will try to help them to clarify and resolve their issues on a basis which they find mutually acceptable. Depending on the issues, this may involve obtaining all relevant facts including, where appropriate, financial data, exploring alternative settlement options and their acceptability and viability, and generally helping the couple to communicate and make decisions. The mediator may give information, but will not advise the couple what terms they should agree, this being a matter for them; and may help them to examine different solutions but will not try to press the one which the mediator may prefer.

Mediation does not aim to save the marriage, but to help parties deal by agreement rather than through the courts with the consequences of its breakdown.

Historically, the mediation process in UK family work was called 'conciliation' and this term is still used, although increasingly these terms are being used interchangeably. 'Mediation' is now more commonly used (possibly because 'conciliation' is often mistakenly confused with 'reconciliation').

Mediation has been welcomed as a valuable process for the avoidance of litigation by the Lord Chancellor, The Law Society, the Solicitors Family Law Association and the Bar. It has now received statutory backing, for example, s 29 of FLA 1996, which provides that public funding in family matters will be refused unless the applicant has first attended a meeting with a mediator to assess whether mediation is suitable for the dispute.

There are a number of facilitation, communication and management skills which mediators should have and which generally necessitate special training. Mediators should also work to a Code of Conduct which regulates the ethical and practical approach which they adopt. Many solicitors have undergone training as mediators and may belong to the British Association of Lawyer Mediators. Family mediators are also drawn from other ranks including social workers, probation officers, court welfare officers, psychotherapists, counsellors and other mental health professionals.

A solicitor cannot act as a mediator for his own client and would need to refer to an outside organisation or individual mediator.

There are a number of types of mediation services available. A primary distinction is between in-court and out-of-court services.

In-court schemes exist at divorce county courts and family proceedings courts throughout the country. However, there is no uniform system and many local variations exist. The best-known scheme is the one at the Principal Registry in London which deals with children issues only. In contested children cases the first appointment takes place before a district judge sitting with a court welfare officer. The parties who are present with their legal advisers, will be encouraged to settle their dispute by negotiation and, if necessary, the appointment can be adjourned to enable the matter to be resolved.

Out-of-court services have existed for a number of years and are staffed by trained mediators. The advantage of these services is that they are more informal and flexible and, since they are not sited within the court, have a more relaxed atmosphere, all of which not only encourages people to use the services but also makes an agreement more likely. They can also be used before proceedings have been started, and so introduce the idea of resolving issues far sooner.

Apart from the services provided directly through the courts, there are three main organisations offering family mediation in England and Wales. One organisation is National Family Mediation (NFM) which was established in 1981 as the National Family Conciliation Council to provide a national framework and to ensure that certain uniform standards were maintained by independent services. It originally dealt virtually exclusively with children issues only, and its Code of Practice was agreed with The Law Society. The second organisation is the Family Mediators Association (FMA) which was established in 1988 with Law Society support to provide mediation on all issues arising on separation and divorce, including property, finance, children and the divorce itself ('comprehensive mediation'). The FMA model pairs a family solicitor with another professional experienced in family dynamics, such as a counsellor or social worker, to work as co-mediators, both trained as such; but they are also exploring the use of sole mediation for experienced mediators. Both the FMA and NFM, who now share the same Code of Practice, offer comprehensive mediation as well as specific issue resolution. The FMA, NFM and Family Mediation Scotland have set up the UK College of Family Mediators which was officially launched in September 1997. The aims of the College are to establish standards, to monitor and regulate professional practice and to ensure that mediators receive the best possible training and continuous professional development. Membership of the College is open to all individuals who can meet its standards. The third organisation is the Solicitors Family Law Association which also offers comprehensive mediation and was the first training planned entirely by family lawyer mediators to train experienced family solicitors in mediation skills. The SFLA subscribes to The Law Society Code of Practice on mediation and is a UK College of Family Mediators-approved body.

The Family Law Bar Association (FLBA) has an out-of-court mediation scheme aimed at resolving financial disputes between couples. A barrister will act as an adjudicator and make written recommendations.

A few points may be noted about mediation.

- It is, in essence, an assisted form of negotiation, leaving responsibility for decision-making in the hands of the parties.
- It is not the same as solicitors adopting a conciliatory approach in traditional negotiation, because of the added dynamic of a skilled impartial third party facilitating communication and resolution.
- Solicitors acting for the parties do not ordinarily participate directly in the mediation process, but can and generally do provide advice to their clients outside of the mediation before any decisions are finalised. In some models they may participate directly in some stages.
- Mediation may be used for couples who are co-operative through to those in a very high state of conflict and distress; and those who have limited finances and struggle to bridge their financial shortfall, through to those involving substantial and complex financial, business, property and trust issues.
- Mediation is not a panacea suitable for all cases, but rather an additional resource which complements or replaces traditional processes where the couple cannot reach agreement themselves or through solicitors' negotiating. It may be used at any stage of the matter, and may precede, run parallel with or follow other formal procedures. Discussions during mediation are undertaken on a totally or substantially privileged basis, with a reservation of rights. If mediation is unsuccessful, the parties are free to use conventional adjudication/litigation.

1.4 THE FAMILY COURTS

The family practitioner must not only be able to identify the client's needs and determine the correct approach to meet these, but must also decide in which court the remedies will be sought and, if a choice of venue exists, which will be the most appropriate. Often proceedings can be brought in either the county court, the High Court or the family proceedings court. The jurisdiction of the courts to make orders under the Children Act 1989 is more complicated and is outlined in Chapters 12 and 13.

1.4.1 County court

All actions under the Matrimonial Causes Act 1973 (ie for divorce, judicial separation or nullity) begin in a divorce county court. This is a county court which has jurisdiction to deal with matrimonial causes (conferred by the Matrimonial and Family Proceedings Act 1984, s 33). In London, the Principal Registry acts also as a divorce county court. Most work is carried out by the district judge from whom appeal may be made to a county court judge. A judge is required to try most defended actions.

1.4.2 The High Court

Generally, actions are only dealt with in the family division of the High Court if the nature of the issues involve facts or arguments which are complex, difficult or grave. Cases may be transferred down to the county court or referred up by the latter to the High Court. If, for example, a financial dispute involved substantial sums of money invested in complex assets, perhaps coupled with allegations of non-disclosure or misappropriation, the county court might prefer to decline jurisdiction and transfer the case to the High Court. Certain applications in relation to children (eg wardship) must be brought in the High Court as must cases seeking a declaration of incompatability under the Human Rights Act 1998, s 4 (or where an issue in any case may lead to the court considering making such a declaration).

1.4.3 The family proceedings court

Magistrates, when dealing with domestic matters, sit as a family proceedings court. The magistrates (including at least one man and one woman) are selected from the family panel and receive special training to deal with family matters. The hearing is entirely different from criminal proceedings in magistrates' courts and there are restrictions on those who may be present.

Magistrates have no jurisdiction to deal with divorce, nullity or judicial separation proceedings. They can deal with orders for periodical payments and lump sums for married applicants during the marriage, they can also deal with protection orders and children orders.

1.4.4 A family court?

For many years now there have been calls to rationalise family litigation through a single comprehensive family court. A unified family court would end the confusing disparity in procedure, terminology, law and personnel which currently exists in the plethora of family courts. There appears, however, to be little immediate prospect of such a development, although some encouragement may be drawn from the unified approach adopted in the Children Act 1989 which requires the same orders and principles to be applied in all courts dealing with applications under that Act. A similar approach has also been adopted under FLA 1996 in relation to domestic violence.

1.5 HUMAN RIGHTS ACT 1998

The Human Rights Act 1998 (HRA 1998) incorporated the European Convention on Human Rights into the law of England and Wales with effect from 2 October 2000. It provides a scheme whereby domestic legislation must be read and given effect so as to be compatible with the rights and freedoms guaranteed by the Convention as far as is possible. If a Convention right is infringed, then an application for judicial review, or proceedings against the appropriate public body for failure to act compatibly with the Convention, may be appropriate. The most relevant of the Convention Rights for the purposes of family law would seem to be Article 8 (right to respect for family and private life), which provides:

> '1. Everyone has the right to respect for his private and family life, his home and his correspondence.
>
> 2. There shall be no interference by a public authority with the exercise of this right except such as is in accordance with the law and is necessary in a democratic society in the interests of national security, public safety or the economic well-being of the country, for the prevention of disorder or crime, for the protection of health or morals, or for the protection of the rights and freedoms of others.'

Public law relating to children (see Chapter 13) is an obvious example of an area of UK law where this article will need to be taken into account.

If interference with this right is established, the State must show that the interference is justified. There are four underlying principles which justify such interference.

(1) It must be in accordance with the domestic law.
(2) It must serve a legitimate aim.
(3) It must be necessary (ie correspond to a social need and be proportionate to the aim pursued).
(4) It must not be discriminatory.

Other Convention Rights which could give rise to litigation and, potentially, changes in UK law are Article 3 (prohibiting inhuman or degrading treatment); Article 5 (the right to liberty and security of person); Article 6 (right to a fair hearing) and Article 14 (prohibiting discrimination on any ground, including sex, birth or other status). The significance of these Articles will be considered in more detail in the relevant chapters of this book.

A case seeking a declaration of incompatability under HRA 1998, s 4 must be brought in the High Court, as must any case which raises an issue which may lead to the court considering making such a declaration (*Practice Direction (Human Rights Act 1998)* (24 July 2000) [2000] Fam Law 670).

1.6 FAMILY LAW ACT 1996

FLA 1996 sets out wide-ranging reforms to several areas of family law.

FLA 1996, Part I came into force in March 1997 and lays down some general guidelines for individuals and the courts to consider when implementing the Act. These are that:

- the institution of marriage is to be supported;
- parties to a marriage breakdown are to be encouraged to take all practicable steps (including marriage counselling) to save the marriage;
- marriages which have irretrievably broken down should be brought to an end:
  - with minimum distress to the parties and children;
  - with questions dealt with in a manner designed to promote as good a continuing relationship between the parties and children as is possible in the circumstances; and
  - without costs being unreasonably incurred;

- any risk of violence to one of the parties and children should as far as practicable be removed or diminished.

FLA 1996, Part IV totally reformed the law relating to domestic violence and came into force in October 1997. Part IV of FLA 1996 is dealt with in detail in Chapter 14.

Part III of FLA 1996 deals with reforms to public funding. Section 26 makes public funding available for mediation, not only in divorce proceedings, but also in proceedings involving domestic violence and children. Section 29 provides that, except in domestic violence or public children applications, applicants for public funding will not be granted representation unless they have first attended a meeting with a mediator to determine whether mediation appears suitable to the dispute. The Legal Services Commission will take into account the outcome of this meeting in deciding whether it is reasonable to grant Legal Representation to take proceedings or whether mediation would be a suitable alternative.

Part II of FLA 1996 is intended to totally reform the law and procedure of divorce. The new law is based on the Government White Paper 'Mediation and the ground for divorce' (Cmnd 2799).

The new procedure has been piloted in various areas around the country. These pilots appear not to have been very successful and, on 17 June 1999, the Lord Chancellor announced that FLA 1996, Part II would not be brought into force during 2000. Thus it is not clear when, if ever, Part II will be brought into force. None the less, we set out below a brief summary of the major changes proposed.

Under Part II of FLA 1996, the sole ground for divorce will be the irretrievable breakdown of the marriage without the need to evidence that breakdown with one of the five facts (see **3.4**).

Before a divorce order can be granted, the following conditions must be met.

(1) The applicant must attend a one-to-one information meeting. In this meeting, the applicant will be given general information about divorce and its consequences and details of marriage guidance, mediation and costs. Details of the procedure will be determined by regulations. The meeting will not involve a solicitor. The applicant will be encouraged to use marriage counselling.

(2) Three months after the information meeting, the applicant can lodge at the court a statement that the marriage has broken down.

(3) There must then be a wait of 9 or 15 months before the divorce order can be made. This is called the period of consideration and reflection. The 15-month

period will apply if there are children under 16 or if the other party wants further time for reflection. The court can waive this longer period if there has been domestic violence or if the wait would be detrimental to the children's welfare. It is not possible to reduce the period below 9 months.

(4) No divorce can be granted until the court is satisfied about arrangements for any children and also financial and property matters. This will involve producing to the court evidence that matters have been resolved, for example a court order dealing with financial matters or a negotiated agreement. There are some exceptions to this covering situations where the other party has been obstructive or where it is impossible to sort things out due to the ill-health or disability of either party or a child. If arrangements are not settled within a year after the consideration and reflection period, the whole divorce process must start again.

There has been a mixed reaction to FLA 1996, Part II. 'No fault' divorce is generally welcomed and also the constructive use of mediation but there is concern that mediation may be used as a substitute for legal advice rather than as complementary to it. Hardship may be caused by the fact that divorce will take longer. Recently married couples will have to wait at least 2 years from the date of the marriage as the current one-year bar to divorce is to be retained. Couples with children will have to wait at least 18 months. However, conversely, there are groups who see the time as much too short.

1.7 CONCLUSION

The problems facing a family client are as diverse as families themselves. The challenge facing the family practitioner is to steer a client through those problems on to a new life. This requires the practitioner to fit the appropriate solution from a diverse range of remedies to meet the specific needs of each individual client. To succeed in this, the family solicitor must acquire a firm grasp of a broad range of law and develop a variety of legal skills. A healthy measure of common sense and a sense of humour are also invaluable. Thus equipped, the family practitioner can look forward to a highly interesting and rewarding career.

1.8 CHAPTER SUMMARY

- The family client will usually want advice on money and property, children and protection from violence.
- The family practitioner will need to consider professional conduct, the need to advise but not take decisions for a client and the need to keep in mind long-term objectives.
- Outside agencies can also help a client, for example counselling and mediation services.
- The courts that generally deal with family matters are the county court (all divorces start here), the High Court (which deals with complex matters) and the family proceedings court (which has no divorce jurisdiction but which deals with finance within marriage and other family matters).

1.9 FURTHER READING

Clout *The Matrimonial Solicitor* (Family Law, 1992)

Hodson and Dunmall *The Business of Family Law* (Family Law, 1992)

Parker *Know-How for Family Lawyers* (FT Law & Tax, 1993)

Brown and Marriott *ADR Principles and Practice* (Sweet & Maxwell, 1999)

Parkinson *Family Mediation* (Sweet & Maxwell, 1997)

MacFarlane *Rethinking Disputes: The Mediation Alternative* (Cavendish, 1997)

Bird and Cretney *Divorce – The New Law* (Family Law, 1996)

Bishops, Hodson et al *Divorce Reform: A Guide For Lawyers and Mediators* (FT Law & Tax, 1996)

Burrows *Family Law Act 1996 – A Practitioner's Guide* (CLT Ltd, 1996)

Chapter 2

PUBLIC FUNDING

2.1 INTRODUCTION

At the first interview, one of the client's major concerns may be how he is going to pay for legal advice. A solicitor cannot enter a conditional fee agreement with a client in relation to family proceedings. However, where the client is of modest means, public funding may be available. The Access to Justice Act 1999 (AJA 1999) has radically reformed public funding for legal services. It provides that funding in civil cases (including family cases) will be provided through the Community Legal Service. AJA 1999 also establishes the Legal Services Commission which administers funding. Section 8 of AJA 1999 establishes the Funding Code which sets down criteria for the funding of individual cases.

This chapter provides an outline of public funding in relation to family work. The AJA 1999, Regulations made under it and the Funding Code (plus guidance on the Code) should be consulted if more detail is needed. A further source of reference is the *Legal Services Commission Manual* which consists of three loose-leaf volumes and is published by Sweet & Maxwell.

2.2 FRANCHISING AND CONTRACTING

Since October 1993, it has been possible for a firm of solicitors to apply for a franchise to carry out publicly funded work. To obtain a franchise, a firm must satisfy practice management standards set by the Legal Services Commission. In particular, the Commission requires that franchise holders handle all relevant cases in accordance with quality assurance standards specified by the Commission. In addition, each franchise holder must satisfy the Commission that it has within its staff a member qualified to recognise and fulfil the need for welfare benefit advice for each publicly funded client requiring advice within a franchised category of work.

From 1 January 2000, family law solicitors may undertake publicly funded work only if their firm has a contract with the Legal Services Commission. Only those solicitors' firms who already have (or are in the process of applying for) a franchise will be eligible to apply for a contract.

2.3 LEVELS OF SERVICE

The Funding Code sets down various 'levels of service'. Those which are relevant to the family practitioner are Legal Help, General Family Help, Help with Mediation and Legal Representation.

Legal Help is Controlled Work. The remainder are all Licensed Work.

2.4 CONTROLLED WORK

This is carried out under the firm's contract and does not require separate applications to be made to the Legal Services Commission at the outset of each case. Instead, under the terms of its contract, each firm will be given a maximum number of new cases (or 'new matter starts') to be undertaken during the period of the contract. Legal Help is Controlled Work.

2.4.1 Legal Help

Legal Help enables people who satisfy the means and merits test to obtain advice from a solicitor. It can cover advice on any question of English law or procedure and can, therefore, include correspondence, negotiating or drafting documents for a client. It cannot cover any step in court proceedings (with the exception of undefended divorce (see **3.9.1**)) and, therefore, if litigation follows, Legal Representation (or General Family Help) will have to be obtained.

Financial eligibility

A client must come within the financial limits for both capital and income. The capital limit is very low (at present £1,000). If the client is in receipt of income support or income-based jobseeker's allowance, he will automatically qualify in terms of income, otherwise the solicitor will need to calculate his disposable income. If the client is eligible, he will not have to pay a contribution, but the statutory charge (see **2.6**) may apply.

Sufficient benefit test

Legal Help may only be provided where there is sufficient benefit to the client, having regard to the circumstances, to justify work being carried out. The question to ask is 'would a reasonable privately paying client of moderate means pay for this as legal advice?' Thus Legal Help will not be provided if the claim is clearly hopeless, vexatious or would be an abuse of the process or the client is seeking advice on non-legal matters.

Procedure for obtaining advice under Legal Help

The solicitor will need to ensure that the client is both financially eligible and satisfies the sufficient benefit test. The former can be done by completing the Controlled Work 1 Form. Appropriate warning must be given of the impact of the statutory charge (see **2.6** below). If the client is happy to proceed, he must sign the Controlled Work 1 Form.

Initial financial limit

Once a Controlled Work 1 Form has been completed and signed, the solicitor can do 3 hours' work if advising the petitioner in a divorce and preparing the petition, or 2 hours for general advice on other matters or if consulted by the respondent. The hourly rate is fixed. These fixed amounts include disbursements but are exclusive of VAT.

Extensions

If the initial time-limit is insufficient to cover the work done, a franchised firm has the power to set a new financial limit without having to obtain prior authority from the Legal Services Commission up to an 'upper financial limit' (which is set by the Legal Services Commission). If extensions above this upper financial limit are required, a further extension will need to be applied for from the Legal Services Commission before the upper financial limit is reached.

Limit to number of Controlled Work 1 Forms

The rule in divorce proceedings is that all matters arising from or connected with the divorce must be treated as the same matter so that only one Controlled Work 1 Form is available for all the proceedings. Thus, if a client fills in a Controlled Work 1 Form initially for her undefended divorce, the original form, with necessary extensions, must be used for any subsequent advice given to her relating to ancillary financial matters, non-molestation and occupation orders, or orders relating to the children. General Family Help or Legal Representation are available for matters other than the undefended divorce so, in these cases, the Controlled Work 1 Form will be needed only for the initial advice and the time spent making the application for General Family Help or Legal Representation. A solicitor cannot generally provide Legal Help where the client has already received Legal Help in the same matter from another solicitor within the previous 6 months (unless, for example, the client has reasonable cause to be dissatisfied with the service provided by the first solicitor).

Payment

When the work is completed, the bill on the Controlled Work 1 Form must be completed by the firm and kept on file for audit purposes. The firm will receive a regular monthly payment from the Legal Services Commission, the amount depending on the number of new matter starts specified in the contract.

2.5 LICENSED WORK

This is also carried out under the firm's contract, but an application must be made to or registered with the Legal Services Commission in each case. The Legal Services Commission will assess whether the client is eligible for funding. There are both financial and merits tests. Financial eligibility is assessed by reference to the appropriate regulations. The merits of a case are assessed by applying the criteria set out in the Funding Code. Legal Representation, General Family Help and Help with Mediation are Licensed Work.

2.5.1 Mediation

In private law children cases and proceedings for financial provision (apart from under the Matrimonial Causes Act 1973, s 37 (see **8.6.2**)), General Family Help or Legal Representation will be refused unless the case is first referred to a mediator who determines whether mediation is suitable in the circumstances for the dispute and the parties.

Certain cases are exempt from this requirement:

(1) urgent cases;

(2) where no recognised mediator is available;

(3) where the client is the grandparent or other extended family member in private law children proceedings;

(4) where proceedings are already in existence and the client is the respondent who has been given a court hearing date within the next 3 months;

(5) where the applicant has a reasonable fear of violence or significant harm from his/her partner or former partner.

Funding is available for mediation of a family dispute for couples who qualify financially. In such cases, Family Mediation will pay the mediator's costs.

2.5.2 Help with Mediation

This covers legal advice given to support Family Mediation, for example, drawing up a financial agreement reached by way of mediation and confirming it as a court order.

Financial eligibility

If the client receives funding for Family Mediation, he will automatically qualify for Help with Mediation in respect of the same mediation. Alternatively, if the client is in receipt of income support or income-based jobseeker's allowance, he will automatically qualify. In other cases, both his capital and income must come within the current financial limits. No contribution is payable and the statutory charge (see **2.6**) will not apply.

Sufficient benefit test

Help with Mediation may only be provided where there is sufficient benefit to the client to justify the work being carried out. This is the same test as applies in relation to Legal Help. Thus, an agreement should only be confirmed in a court order in circumstances where a privately paying client would be advised to do so.

Financial limit

The solicitor can do up to £150-worth of work where mediation relates to children-only issues, up to £250-worth of work where mediation relates to financial-only issues and up to £350-worth of work for all-issues mediation. These limits can be extended where necessary provided the authority of the Legal Services Commission is obtained in advance of exceeding the limit.

2.5.3 General Family Help

This covers helping people negotiate and obtaining disclosure of information from their partner with a view to resolving family disputes before going to court. It includes services covered by Legal Help, for example, giving advice or drafting documents. It also covers obtaining a consent order following settlement and related conveyancing work.

Financial eligibility

If the client is in receipt of income support or income-based jobseeker's allowance, he will qualify automatically on financial grounds without having to pay a contribution. In other cases, both his capital and income must come within the current financial limits. A contribution may be payable from capital or income depending on resources. It is essential that the solicitor explains to the client the effect of the statutory charge (see **2.6**)

Sufficient benefit test

The test is the same as for Help with Mediation and Legal Help (ie there must be sufficient benefit to the client to justify the work being carried out). The likely cost of achieving the benefit must be proportionate to the benefit sought. So, for example, where the solicitor receives an offer of settlement from the other party, he must carefully consider whether the additional costs of further negotiation to improve on that offer would be proportionate to any improvement likely to be gained.

Financial limit

The standard costs limitation is £1,500-worth of work. It is possible to extend this by application to the Legal Services Commission, but if there is little immediate prospect of resolution of the issues it may be more appropriate to apply for Legal Representation instead.

2.5.4 Legal Representation

This covers representation in court. An application for Legal Representation will be refused unless the case has first been referred to a mediator (see **2.5.1**) and it can be shown that a genuine attempt has been made to resolve the dispute by way of negotiation and this attempt has failed. This rule does not apply in public law children cases or cases of domestic violence. Often, therefore, negotiations will initially have been carried out under General Family Help. When it becomes clear that there is no reasonable prospect of settlement, it will be appropriate to apply for Legal Representation. This can be done by applying to amend the General Family Help certificate to cover Legal Representation. It is not essential, however, for negotiations to have been carried out under General Family Help. It may be the case that this test can be satisfied by negotiations carried out using Legal Help. In such a case, there will be no need to apply for General Family Help and the solicitor can instead immediately apply for Legal Representation.

Financial eligibility

This is the same as for General Family Help. Special rules apply to public law children proceedings where funding is available without reference to means for certain people (see **13.11.4**).

Sufficient benefit test

The test will differ depending on the type of case involved.

Private children proceedings and financial proceedings

Legal Representation will be refused unless the likely benefits to be gained from the proceedings for the client justify the likely costs, such that a reasonable privately paying client would be prepared to take or defend the proceedings in all the circumstances.

In addition, in cases for financial provision, Legal Representation will be refused if the prospects of success are:

(a) borderline (ie where it is not possible to say that prospects of success are better than 50 per cent) unless the case has overwhelming importance to the client or a significant wider public interest; or

(b) poor (less than 50 per cent).

In private children cases, Legal Representation will be refused if the prospects of success are poor.

Public law children proceedings

Legal Representation for children, parents and those with parental responsibility will generally be granted without reference to prospects of success or reasonableness.

Domestic violence proceedings

Legal Representation will be refused unless the likely benefits to be gained from the proceedings for the client justify the likely costs, having regard to the prospects of obtaining the order sought and all other circumstances.

In addition, Legal Representation will be refused if the prospects of success are poor.

Financial limit

There is no standard financial limit for Legal Representation.

Emergency representation

Emergency applications can be made for Legal Representation in appropriate cases, for example, in cases of domestic violence.

2.5.5 Procedure for application

The solicitor will need to complete the appropriate application form for the type of funding required (eg, CLSAPP3 for General Family Help and Legal Representation, CLSAPP4 for Help with Mediation). He will also need to ask the client to complete the relevant means form. This should then be sent to the regional office of the Legal Services Commission. The regional office will assess whether the client qualifies financially and also decide whether the application passes the merits test.

If a certificate is to be granted and the client has a contribution to pay, an offer of funding is sent out direct to the client, with a copy to the solicitor. The client accepts by signing the offer and sending the required contribution to the regional office of the Legal Services Commission. The contribution may be from capital or income or both. A contribution from capital must normally be paid in full immediately. A contribution from income is normally payable by instalments. If no contribution is payable, the certificate is sent out straight away.

Effect of legal aid

(1) Duty to notify the court and other parties

Immediately upon receipt of the certificate or, if proceedings have not yet commenced when they do, the solicitor must file the original public funding certificate at court and must inform all other parties of the fact that the client is publicly funded by serving upon them a notice of issue of funding.

(2) Relationship between solicitor and client

The solicitor will continue to owe the normal solicitor/client duties to a publicly funded client. In addition, the solicitor will owe duties to the Legal Services Commission. If the client acts unreasonably (eg refuses a reasonable offer of settlement), the solicitor must report this to the Legal Services Commission. This duty to the Legal Services Commission overrides the solicitor's usual duty of confidentiality to his client.

(3) Costs

If a publicly funded party loses, it is possible for him to be ordered to pay the winning party's costs. However, the Access to Justice Act 1999, s 11 provides that an order for costs against an unsuccessful publicly funded party cannot exceed the amount (if any) which is a reasonable one for him to pay having regard to all the circumstances, including the means of the parties and their conduct in relation to the dispute. This will often mean that the publicly funded party will be ordered to pay no costs. However, where the publicly funded party had to pay a contribution under his certificate, the court may well order him to pay a similar amount by way of costs to the winning party. But what about the winning party? If this is the applicant, then they will have no recourse – they could have chosen not to take proceedings in the first place. However, if the winner is the respondent they have no choice but to defend the proceedings. In this situation, the court has power under reg 5 of the Community Legal Service (Cost Protection) Regulations 2000 to order that the respondent's costs be paid from the Community Legal Service Fund. It may do so only if satisfied that it would have made an order for costs if both parties were fee-paying, that the respondent would suffer severe financial hardship unless it makes the order and that it is just and equitable in all the circumstances to do so.

Payment of solicitor's costs

Once the client is in receipt of public funding, the solicitor will receive payment of his costs from the Legal Services Commission. Just as with a private client, it is possible for the solicitor to receive payment on account of costs and disbursements from the Legal Services Commission.

2.6 THE STATUTORY CHARGE

The statutory charge is relevant to all types of public funding except Help with Mediation (see **2.5.2**).

The solicitor is obliged to explain the effect of the statutory charge when his client applies for public funding. It is vital that the client fully understands the charge and he should be reminded of it throughout the action. Clients should also be advised periodically as to the approximate costs accumulated.

Once a certificate has been issued the Legal Services Commission will be responsible for paying the assisted party's legal costs. Those costs will be subject to detailed assessment. The Commission will attempt to recoup these costs where possible. In order to do so, it first claims any money paid pursuant to an order for costs made in favour of the assisted party. Secondly, if a shortfall remains, it will retain any contribution paid by the assisted party under the terms of the offer of public funding. Any surplus will be returned to the assisted party. Thirdly, if there is still a deficit to the fund, the statutory charge will apply (AJA 1999, s 10(7)). The effect of this is that any property (including money) 'recovered or preserved in the proceedings' may be applied to make up the shortfall.

When is property 'recovered or preserved in the proceedings'? It was said in the case of *Hanlon v Law Society* [1980] 2 All ER 199:

> '... property has been recovered or preserved if it has been in issue in the proceedings: recovered by the claimant if it has been the subject of a successful claim, preserved by the respondent if the claim fails ... .'

The Legal Services Commission will determine from the statements of case, correspondence and order what the issues of the case were.

The statutory charge may even apply where the ownership of the property has not been in dispute but proceedings were brought to determine what should happen to the property, ie whether it is to be sold, transferred or retained (see *Curling v Law Society* [1985] 1 All ER 705 and, similarly, *Parks v Legal Aid Board* [1997] 1 FLR 77, CA).

The charge applies to the costs incurred in all proceedings, meaning the entire cause or matter and not just the ancillary proceedings. Typically, it will include the Legal Help costs of the divorce suit and any costs incurred in a dispute over the children.

The costs are not limited to property obtained as a result of contested proceedings. Whilst a settlement will reduce the overall costs of the case, s 10(7) of AJA 1999 ensures that a settlement will not avoid the effect of the statutory charge. The charge also applies to compromises arrived at to avoid bringing or continuing the proceedings. Indeed, where there has been a compromise the property does not need to have been in issue for the statutory charge to apply. For example, if the parties were arguing over the matrimonial home and a compromise was reached which instead transferred a holiday home (which had not been in issue) from the husband's sole name to the wife, the statutory charge can apply to the holiday home (see *Van Hoorn v The Law Society* [1984] 3 WLR 199).

Some property recovered or preserved will be exempt from the charge (reg 44 of the Community Legal Service (Financial) Regulations 2000). The following are not subject to the statutory charge:

(1) periodical payments;
(2) the first £2,500 of the money or property recovered or preserved by an order under, inter alia, MCA 1973, ss 23, 24 and 24A;
(3) payments on or after the making of an occupation order under FLA 1996, Part IV; and
(4) lump sums or property adjustment orders made after divorce in substitution for spousal maintenance under MCA 1973, s 31(7A) or (7B).

To facilitate collection of the charge, the assisted party's solicitor is required to pass any money payable to the assisted party under an agreement or court order to the Legal Services Commission. In addition, the solicitor must notify the regional office of the Legal Services Commission of any property recovered or preserved by his client. The solicitor will usually send a copy of the court order or agreement to the regional office of the Legal Services Commission. If a party receives a lump sum well in excess of the anticipated statutory charge, the solicitor may apply to the regional office of the Legal Services Commission for authority to release some of the money to the client provided sufficient sums are retained to cover the firm's costs. In all cases, once the solicitor's costs have been finally determined and the statutory charge has been satisfied, any balance is sent to the assisted party.

There is no discretion to waive the statutory charge but the Legal Services Commission can agree to postpone enforcement of the charge where it is charged on either:

(1) property which is expressly stated (in the order or agreement) to be used as a home by the assisted person or his dependants; or

(2) a lump sum which is agreed or ordered with the express purpose of it being used to purchase a home (the purchase to be made within one year).

In both cases, before agreeing to postponement, the Commission will need to be satisfied that the property represents adequate security for the charge.

The charge will be protected by registration against the title of the property and simple interest will accrue. The interest rate applied is a commercial one, currently 8 per cent. This may influence a client's decision to pay or postpone the charge. In most cases, the charge and interest will be enforced when the home is sold. However, it is possible for the charge to be transferred to a substitute property provided, first, that the consent of the regional office of the Legal Services Commission is obtained before the charged property is sold and, secondly, that the substitute property represents adequate security.

Where an assisted party recovers both a lump sum and property, the Legal Services Commission will look to take their charge from the money first, only attaching the charge to property as a last resort.

2.7 HUMAN RIGHTS

The Legal Services Commission is a public body and therefore it cannot act in a way that is incompatible with Convention rights under the Human Rights Act 1998.

Article 6 of the European Convention of Human Rights provides that 'everyone is entitled to a fair and public hearing within a reasonable time by an independent and impartial tribunal established by law.'

One of the Article 6 rights is thus for effective access to the courts. In *Airey v Ireland* (1979) 2 EHRR 305, a wife wanted to bring proceedings for judicial separation. She could not afford legal representation and her application was complex but she was refused legal aid. The European Court held that Article 6 might sometimes compel the State to provide legal assistance if such assistance was indispensable for effective access to court. The court said that complexity of procedure, complicated points of law, the need to call expert witnesses or the emotional involvement of the parties might all result in a requirement that legal assistance be provided. In *Airey*, for access to be effective, the wife required legal representation which, in her case, meant granting legal aid.

The European Commission on Human Rights has attempted to confine the application of the *Airey* principles. It recognised that, due to limited resources, States might legitimately restrict the grant of legal aid, provided the decision whether or not to grant legal aid was not taken arbitrarily.

Under the Human Rights Act 1998, the Legal Services Commission may be liable to challenge if it fails to grant public funding in circumstances that result in a litigant being unable to have effective access to the court. The Funding Code specifically states that legal assistance must be provided in accordance with Article 6. Yet the Funding Code also restricts public funding in most family cases until after the parties have been referred to mediation. This in itself may be open to challenge.

Arguments for public funding will be stronger when a Convention right is in issue. So, family cases dealing with, for example, Article 8 rights will arguably have a greater call on State resources than cases involving breach of contract. Equally, cases which raise Article 3 issues, such as those concerning child abuse or serious domestic violence, will need serious consideration and have greater entitlement to legal assistance.

2.8 CHAPTER SUMMARY

(1) Where a client is of modest means, public funding may be available to enable them to pay for legal advice and representation.

(2) Family law solicitors can undertake publicly funded work only if their firm is franchised and has a contract with the Legal Services Commission.

(3) There are various 'levels of service' which may need to be provided by the family law solicitor:

- – Legal Help
- – Help with Mediation
- – General Family Help
- – Legal Representation.

(4) Except in public law children cases, the client will need to satisfy both means and merits test to be eligible for public funding.

(5) Public funding is not 'free' and will need to be repaid from any property 'recovered or preserved' (with some exceptions) – the statutory charge.

2.9 FURTHER READING

Legal Services Commission Manual (Sweet & Maxwell, 2000)

Chapter 3

DIVORCE LAW AND PROCEDURE

3.1 INTRODUCTION

3.1.1 General

Over 165,000 couples divorce each year in England and Wales. This is the highest divorce rate in Europe. By comparison, relatively few proceedings for judicial separation and nullity are brought. This chapter, therefore, deals in detail with the law relating to divorce and contains an outline of the law relating to judicial separation and nullity.

The chapter also deals with the procedure for divorce. Since less than one per cent of all divorces are defended, only the undefended procedure is dealt with in detail. A checklist summarising the undefended divorce procedure is given at **3.12.2**.

The grounds on which a divorce can be obtained is a controversial subject and is regularly the subject of review. The latest reforms are contained in FLA 1996 (see **1.5**), but it is unclear whether these will ever be brought into force.

3.1.2 Human rights

Article 12 of the Convention on Human Rights gives 'men and women of marriageable age the right to marry and found a family according to the national laws governing the exercise of that right'. Marriage is the only relationship that is given special treatment under the Convention. The protections of Article 12 are limited to unions between members of the opposite sex and Article 12 has no application to same-sex relationships.

By way of contrast, there is no similar right to divorce, whether this is to re-marry or for any other reason (*Johnston v Ireland* (1987) 9 EHRR 203).

3.2 ONE-YEAR RULE

A petition for divorce cannot be presented to the court before the end of a period of one year from the date of the marriage (Matrimonial Causes Act 1973, s 3 (MCA 1973)). The reason for this restriction is to discourage over-hasty decisions to end such short marriages.

The rule cannot be waived in any circumstances. However, provided that grounds for divorce can be satisfied, a petition may be presented after one year based on matters which occurred during this time; for example, the respondent's adultery or other unreasonable behaviour during the first year of marriage can form the basis of a petition as soon as the year has expired. A solicitor should also bear in mind the alternative solutions which exist to protect a client with matrimonial problems, even during the first year. A decree of nullity or judicial separation is not affected by the one-year rule (see **3.6** and **3.7**). Maintenance can be applied for in the divorce county court (MCA 1973, s 27) or in the family proceedings court (Domestic Proceedings and Magistrates' Courts Act 1978, s 2 (DPMCA 1978)). A spouse could be protected from violence by using Part IV of FLA 1996 (see Chapter 14).

3.3 JURISDICTION OF THE ENGLISH COURTS TO HEAR SUITS FOR DIVORCE

3.3.1 General

The English courts do not have the right to deal with a person's matrimonial affairs merely because that person is a British citizen or is present in this country. The English courts have jurisdiction to hear a divorce suit only if either party is:

(1) domiciled in England and Wales on the date when the proceedings are begun; or
(2) was habitually resident in England and Wales throughout the period of one year ending with that date (Domicile and Matrimonial Proceedings Act 1973, s 5).

No simple definition of domicile is possible and, if issues arise in this respect, reference should be made to textbooks on private international law.

Broadly, a person is said to be domiciled in a territory having a single legal system if he has his permanent home there.

Everyone has a domicile and can only have one operative domicile at any one time. However, a person's domicile may alter as his circumstances change throughout his life. A person may acquire, and lose, any of three types of domicile. Each is described in outline below.

3.3.2 Domicile of origin

A person acquires domicile of origin at birth. In the case of a child whose parents are married, it is the father's domicile. In the case of a child whose parents are not married, it is the mother's domicile. It is therefore irrelevant where the child was born.

A domicile of origin is never lost and even though it may not be operative for any period during which the person acquires a domicile of choice, it will revive if the domicile of choice is lost until another domicile of choice is acquired. For example, a woman may have a domicile of origin in Spain. If she comes to England and marries, she might acquire a domicile of choice in England. If the marriage broke down and she decided to leave this country and abandon her domicile of choice, her Spanish domicile would revive and would last until another domicile of choice was acquired.

3.3.3 Domicile of choice

Every person aged 16 or over may acquire a domicile of choice. This requires, first, residence in a country other than the domicile of origin and, secondly, an intention to remain there permanently. This intention may be shown by becoming a citizen of that country, by the purchase of a home or by the length of time spent in that country. No single factor will be decisive.

3.3.4 Domicile of dependence

A child can only acquire an independent domicile at 16 years of age or on marriage under that age. If he is under 16 years and unmarried, his domicile will follow his father's domicile if his parents are married or his mother's if his parents are not married. If married parents separate, the child will acquire the domicile of the parent with whom he lives. For example, if the father has a different domicile from the mother, the child will take the father's domicile while the parents are living together; if they separate and the child lives with the mother, the child will take the mother's domicile.

3.3.5 Habitual residence

The term 'habitual residence' is not defined in MCA 1973. In *Kapur v Kapur* [1984] FLR 920, it was held that this expression meant the same as ordinary residence, ie voluntary residence with a degree of settled purpose. There must be a regular physical presence which must last for some time. Temporary absences (eg on holiday), will not prevent someone from establishing habitual residence. For the English courts to have jurisdiction, a person must be habitually resident for at least one year before filing the petition.

3.3.6 Choice of forum

In many cases, it will be clear that the divorce will take place in England and Wales. In other cases, for example where the couple (or one of them) has been habitually resident in England for the past year but either party has a domicile other than England and Wales, it may be possible to choose whether to start proceedings in England and Wales or elsewhere. Such a choice will be governed by a number of factors, such as convenience and the law of the other jurisdiction(s) involved. Where choice of forum is an issue, the solicitor must contact a lawyer in the other jurisdiction as soon as possible for advice on the legal position should a divorce be started there. Speed will normally be of the essence, since usually proceedings will continue in the jurisdiction where they were first started, any which commence later in an alternative jurisdiction being stayed.

3.3.7 Recognition of foreign decrees by the English courts

A relevant factor when dealing with foreign marriages is to check that the English courts recognise a foreign decree; for example, of divorce. If the English courts recognise the foreign decree, then the parties are free to remarry in England and Wales, and no English divorce is necessary or, indeed, possible. However, in these circumstances, the English courts can make ancillary financial orders. If, on the other hand, the foreign decree is not recognised, then the parties are still married and they will have to petition for a divorce through the English courts, in which case ancillary orders can be made in the normal way. The law is set out in the Family Law Act 1986 and reference should be made to this, and to relevant textbooks, should an international aspect arise.

3.4 THE GROUND FOR DIVORCE

3.4.1 General

There is only one ground on which a petition for divorce may be presented to the court by either party to the marriage; that is, that the marriage has broken down irretrievably (MCA 1973, s 1(1)). However, the court cannot hold that the marriage has broken down unless the petitioner satisfies the court of one or more of the five facts specified in MCA 1973, s 1(2). There is no need for there to be a causal relationship between the fact and the breakdown. Therefore, it is no defence to a divorce suit that, for example, the respondent committed adultery after having left the petitioner because the marriage had broken down; the fact does not have to precede and cause the breakdown, but can follow and merely evidence it.

If the court is satisfied that a fact is proved, it must grant the decree nisi unless it is satisfied that the marriage has not broken down (MCA 1973, s 1(4)). This could occur if the parties began living together again before the divorce was granted.

3.4.2 Fact A: adultery and intolerability

> 'That the respondent has committed adultery *and* the petitioner finds it intolerable to live with the respondent' (MCA 1973, s 1(2)(a)).

There are two elements to this fact which must both be proved to the court.

Adultery

Adultery is voluntary sexual intercourse between two persons of the opposite sex, one or both of whom is married but not to each other.

Adultery may be proved or inferred from the following.

(1) Birth of a child to the wife on proof that the husband was not the father.
(2) Circumstantial evidence showing both guilty purpose and the opportunity to gratify it, for example, an enquiry agent's report which shows that the respondent and a member of the opposite sex are cohabiting.
(3) Conviction of the respondent in a criminal court of an offence entailing adultery, for example, rape (Civil Evidence Act 1968, s 11).
(4) A finding of adultery against the respondent in an earlier case in the High Court or county court (Civil Evidence Act 1968, s 12). If the petitioner had already been granted a decree of judicial separation on the grounds of adultery, the court can treat the judicial separation decree as sufficient proof of the adultery (MCA 1973, s 4(2)).
(5) A confession of adultery by the respondent. This is the method often used in undefended divorces. Proof can either be by way of a separate confession statement signed by the respondent or by the respondent answering 'yes' to a question in the Acknowledgement of Service form which is served on the respondent with the petition. If this method is to be used, the Acknowledgement must be returned to court signed by the respondent personally.

enquiry agent

Intolerability

Intolerability must be proved as well as the adultery but this element rarely causes any problem. First, because the petitioner does not have to show that it was in consequence of the adultery that she found it intolerable to live with the respondent.

She could say, for example, that she found it intolerable to live with him because of his treatment of the children or because of some behaviour of the respondent other than the adultery. Secondly, the test of intolerability is subjective. The petitioner has merely to convince the court that she finds it intolerable to live with the respondent.

The intolerability can be proved by an assertion of intolerability in an affidavit sent to the court as part of the divorce proceedings. In practice, in undefended cases, courts do not even require the petitioner to state the reason why she finds it intolerable to live with the respondent.

The co-respondent

The person with whom the respondent committed adultery can be made a party to the divorce proceedings and is called the co-respondent. However, even if the co-respondent is made a party, it is not necessary to obtain an admission of adultery from the co-respondent if the respondent admits the adultery because the fact requires only evidence that the respondent has committed adultery.

The Family Proceedings Rules 1991 (FPR 1991) enable a petitioner, if she wishes, not to name the co-respondent in the petition, in which case it will not be necessary to make the co-respondent a party to the divorce. This is an important point to bear in mind as it could persuade a respondent who is reluctant to involve the co-respondent to admit the adultery and enable the divorce to be undefended. It is wise to make a co-respondent a party in a defended divorce as this could make proving adultery easier.

The SFLA Code of Practice (see Appendix) recommends that solicitors should discourage a petitioner from *naming* a co-respondent unless there is a compelling reason to do so. It would therefore seem that, unless a divorce is defended, a solicitor taking a conciliatory approach when drafting the petition should not include the name of the co-respondent or make him a party. Doing this will help to reduce animosity between the parties, and will not prejudice the petitioner in an undefended divorce.

Effect of cohabitation

ADULTERY

The petitioner is not entitled to rely on adultery committed by the respondent if the parties cohabit for a period, or periods together, exceeding 6 months after the petitioner has discovered the adultery (MCA 1973, s 2(1)).

The purpose behind this provision is to allow the parties a reasonable length of time in which to achieve a reconciliation without prejudicing their ground for divorce.

The time begins to run when the petitioner discovers the adultery. It is not relevant how long ago the adultery was actually committed. The 6 months can be made up of a number of periods of cohabitation, it need not be a continuous period. If the respondent has committed adultery on several occasions, time will not begin to run until after the petitioner learns of the last act of adultery.

INTOLERABILITY

Where the parties have lived together for a period or periods not exceeding 6 months in total after the petitioner knew of the adultery, the court must disregard the cohabitation when considering whether the petitioner finds it intolerable to live with the respondent (MCA 1973, s 2(2)).

This is another attempt to encourage the parties to attempt reconciliation. Without it, any cohabitation after discovery of the adultery could be used by the respondent as evidence that the petitioner did not in fact find it intolerable to live with the respondent.

3.4.3 Fact B: behaviour

'That the respondent has behaved in such a way that the petitioner cannot reasonably be expected to live with the respondent' (MCA 1973, s 1(2)(b)).

Behaviour

The phrase 'cannot reasonably be expected to live with the respondent' lays down an objective test. The court must make a value judgement about the respondent's behaviour and its effect on the petitioner. In contrast to the test for intolerability, the petitioner's word alone is not enough. However, the court must have regard to the history of the marriage as well as to the personalities of the individual spouses. In the case of *O'Neill v O'Neill* [1975] 1 WLR 1118, the respondent, after retiring, bought a flat for himself, his wife and teenage daughter. He then personally began extensive renovation, involving mixing cement in the living room and leaving the toilet without a door for 8 months, embarrassing his wife and daughter. After 2 years of the upheaval the wife left and was entitled to a decree using this fact.

In the case of *Birch v Birch* [1992] 1 FLR 564, CA, the wife's main complaint against the husband was that he was dogmatic and dictatorial with nationalistic, male chauvinistic characteristics which she had resented for many years. The court granted the divorce and acknowledged that the wife's sensitive nature made it unreasonable for her to go on living with him.

It is a question of fact in each case whether the behaviour is such as to entitle the petitioner to a decree; it does not have to be grave and weighty behaviour. There is also no need to prove that the respondent had any intention to inflict misery on the petitioner.

In practice, in the absence of violence, in an undefended divorce the court will look for three to six examples of behaviour. A further guide to follow in drafting a behaviour petition is 'first, worst and last'. This will ensure that the length of time that the behaviour has been suffered will be established, the major incidents included and when the latest example occurred.

The sort of conduct that can be included will always depend on the particular circumstances of the case, but relevant matters include physical violence, verbal abuse (which could include insults, threats, nagging), demanding sexual intercourse too often or not agreeing to intercourse at all, intimate relationships with people of the same or opposite sex (even if it falls short of sexual acts), cruelty and failure to provide money or food as well as failure to provide affection or attention. However, the mere fact that the petitioner has become bored with the marriage or that the parties are simply incompatible will not be sufficient.

Effect of cohabitation on behaviour

The fact that the petitioner and respondent have lived with each other for a period or periods not exceeding 6 months in total after the last incident of behaviour relied on must be disregarded in deciding whether the petitioner can reasonably be expected to live with the respondent (MCA 1973, s 2(3)). This is to encourage the parties to consider reconciliation as cohabitation will not immediately prevent a divorce.

If the parties have lived together for longer than 6 months, this will not be an absolute bar to a petition being granted. However, the court will take the length of the cohabitation into account in determining whether the petitioner can reasonably be expected to live with the respondent. The longer the cohabitation, the less likely it will be that the court will grant the petition. It would always be open to the petitioner to show a good reason why the cohabitation continued. In *Bradley v Bradley* [1973] 1 WLR 1291, the wife had continued to cohabit but proved to the court that she had no choice but to do so as she had seven children, nowhere else to go and was frightened that unless she went on sleeping with the husband and looking after the house he would seriously injure her.

3.4.4 Fact C: desertion

> 'That the respondent has deserted the petitioner for a continuous period of at least two years immediately preceding the presentation of the petition' (MCA 1973, s 1(2)(c)).

Desertion

The elements needed to constitute the fact of desertion are as follows.

(1) There must be a separation. In calculating the period of separation, the date of separation will not be included. In most cases the parties are living apart, but people who are living under the same roof can be separated in law if the common home and the common life have ceased altogether. The petitioner must establish that there are, in fact, two separate households under the same roof (see *Hopes v Hopes* [1948] 2 All ER 920). The court will examine the extent to which the parties share domestic life; whether they cook for each other, eat together and sleep together will all be relevant considerations.

(2) There must be an intention to desert, ie to bring the matrimonial union permanently to an end.

(3) The petitioner must not consent or agree to the separation.

(4) The respondent must not have a just cause for leaving. This could apply if the respondent were away on business or if his leaving was because of the wife's adultery.

(5) The desertion must be continuous. Normally, several periods of separation cannot be added together to form the 2-year period.

(6) The desertion must immediately precede the presentation of the petition, ie the date when it is filed.

In practice, desertion is rarely cited in a petition because it is so technical and because other facts can usually be cited where the parties are living separately.

Effect of cohabitation on desertion

In considering whether a period of desertion has been continuous, no account is to be taken of a period or periods not exceeding 6 months in total during which the parties cohabited (MCA 1973, s 2(5)).

However, any period of cohabitation cannot be counted as part of the period of desertion. Therefore, if a husband first deserted the wife exactly 2 years ago and during this time they have had two attempts at reconciliation which has meant that in total they have lived together for a period of 4 months, the cohabitation will not prevent the wife petitioning on the ground of desertion, but she cannot file the petition until a period of 2 years and 4 months has expired since the husband first deserted.

3.4.5 Fact D: two years' separation and consent

> 'That the parties to the marriage have lived apart for a continuous period of at least two years immediately preceding the presentation of the petition *and* the respondent consents to a decree being granted' (MCA 1973, s 1(2)(d)).

The elements which are necessary for this fact are, first, separation and, secondly, the respondent must consent to the decree.

Separation

Two years' separation is necessary. The spouses are treated as living apart unless they are living with each other in the same household (MCA 1973, s 2(6)). The test is similar to the test of separation in desertion cases; accordingly, people can be living apart even though living under the same roof if they are living completely separate lives. The actual date of separation will not be included when calculating the period of separation.

A physical separation does not of itself constitute living apart. There must also be a mental element, ie one of the spouses must regard the marriage as a mere shell, never intending to live with the other spouse again (*Santos v Santos* [1975] 2 All ER 246, CA). This intention does not necessarily have to be communicated to the other spouse and the petitioner could, in theory, rely on the respondent's intention. However, in practice, it is almost always the petitioner's intention that is relied on and the standard-form divorce documents are drafted on this basis.

Consent

The respondent must consent to the divorce. This consent can be given at the hearing (if any) or before it. If the respondent wishes to indicate his consent before the hearing, he must do so by giving the district judge notice to that effect signed personally by him (FPR 1991, r 2.10). In practice, in an undefended divorce, this is given in the Acknowledgement of Service form returned by the respondent to the court following service of the petition on him. All a respondent has to do is answer 'yes' to one of the standard questions and sign the form personally.

The respondent may give notice to the court at any time before decree nisi that he does not consent or that he withdraws consent already given. No reason for this is needed (FPR 1991, r 2.10).

Even after the decree nisi has been granted, the court has discretion to rescind the decree nisi on the respondent's application if satisfied that the petitioner misled the respondent (whether intentionally or unintentionally) about any matter which he took into account in deciding to give his consent (MCA 1973, s 10(1)). This could apply in a situation where the respondent was misled about a financial or property matter, but could also apply where the respondent was misled about the petitioner's intentions to remarry. However, in many cases the court will use its discretion to grant the decree absolute even though the respondent has been misled by the petitioner so long as this does not have serious consequences.

Effect of cohabitation on separation

Section 2(5) of MCA 1973 applies to the continuity of separation in the same way as it does to desertion (see **3.4.4**). Therefore, in deciding whether the living apart has been continuous, a period not exceeding, or periods together not exceeding, 6 months will be ignored. However, they must be added to the total period of separation so that the time that the parties have actually lived apart is at least 2 years.

Financial position of the respondent (MCA 1973, s 10(2))

If the only fact found is Fact D (or Fact E, see **3.4.6**) the respondent may apply to the court for a consideration of his financial position following the divorce (MCA 1973, s 10(2)).

If such an application is made, the court must consider all the circumstances and will not make the decree absolute unless satisfied that:

(1) the petitioner should not be required to make any financial provision for the respondent; or

(2) the financial provision made is fair and reasonable or the best that can be made in the circumstances (MCA 1973 s 10(3)).

The court may proceed without observing the above requirements if it is satisfied that the circumstances make it desirable that the decree should be made absolute without delay *and* that the court has obtained a satisfactory undertaking from the petitioner that he will make such financial provision for the respondent as the court may approve (MCA 1973, s 10(4)).

In practice, s 10 is rarely used, but it can sometimes be of use to a respondent if the petitioner is anxious to obtain the divorce and the threat of a s 10 application will persuade him to agree to a more favourable financial settlement. It is not a defence to the divorce but, in such circumstances, a useful negotiating mechanism. The court has no power under this section actually to make financial orders, so it will generally insist that a court order is obtained in ancillary proceedings under MCA 1973 before the decree absolute is granted.

If the court exercised its discretion under s 10(4) to enable the decree absolute to be granted without satisfactory provision being made (it might do so, eg if the petitioner's new partner was about to have his child and he urgently wanted to marry her), it would still insist on detailed provisions being included in any undertaking given by the petitioner.

3.4.6 Fact E: five years' separation

> 'That the parties to the marriage have lived apart for a continuous period of at least five years immediately preceding the petition' (MCA 1973, s 1(2)(e)).

After 5 years' separation, there is no need for the petitioner to obtain the respondent's consent to the divorce and either party can petition. Living apart has the same meaning as in Fact D (see **3.4.5**).

There is no defence to a Fact E petition except to deny the separation or to prove grave hardship under MCA 1973, s 5 (see below).

The decree may also be delayed by the respondent asking for his financial position to be considered under MCA 1973, s 10(2) (see **3.4.5**).

Grave hardship

It is a defence to proceedings for divorce, where the only fact found is Fact E, that the dissolution of the marriage would result in grave financial or other hardship to the respondent *and* in all the circumstances it would be wrong to dissolve the marriage (MCA 1973, s 5(1)).

In deciding whether s 5 applies, the court must take account of all the circumstances, including the parties' conduct, the interests of the parties and the interests of any children or other persons concerned (MCA 1973, s 5(2)).

In *Talbot v Talbot* (1971) 115 SJ 870, the husband left his wife for another woman and ceased maintaining his wife and children. He obtained a divorce under Fact E. The court held that the s 5 defence did not apply as his wife's hardship arose from the breakdown of the marriage and not from the prospective divorce. Accordingly, granting the decree would not add to it. The court may also grant the decree even though grave hardship does result provided it is satisfied that it is not wrong to grant it. In *Brickell v Brickell* [1973] 3 All ER 508, the Court of Appeal looked at the surrounding circumstances, including the conduct of the parties, and concluded that the husband was entitled to a decree, even though the wife would suffer grave financial hardship, because the wife had behaved so badly during the marriage.

The grave hardship most commonly pleaded is financial; this will include the loss of the chance of acquiring any benefit which the respondent might acquire if the marriage were not dissolved (MCA 1973, s 5(3)). If, for example, the husband was contributing to an occupational pension scheme his wife could be faced with grave financial hardship if he obtained a divorce because she would then cease to be entitled to a widow's pension under his pension scheme (*Julian v Julian* (1973) 116 SJ 763). However, the defence would not succeed if the petitioner could show that the hardship was not grave because, for example, the wife was entitled to her own occupational pension, or the husband could compensate her for the loss with, say, a deferred annuity or by 'earmarking' the pension or 'splitting' it (see **4.7**). In practice, this defence is usually used by the respondent to persuade the petitioner to make satisfactory financial provision.

Grave hardship may take other forms and may necessitate examination of hardship caused by religious censure or social ostracism. In practice, it is very difficult to establish that such other hardships are grave enough to warrant refusing a decree.

Distinction between MCA 1973, s 5 and MCA 1973, s 10(2)

Section 5 is a complete defence, therefore, if the defence succeeds, the couple remain married. Section 10(2) merely delays the decree absolute. Section 5 requires the respondent to establish 'grave' financial or other hardship, whereas under s 10(2) the respondent must merely show that the provision is not fair and reasonable. It is easier to establish that s 10(2) applies, but its effect is less drastic.

Effect of cohabitation on separation

The effect of cohabitation on Fact E is the same as on Fact D (see **3.4.5**).

3.5 PROTECTION OF CHILDREN: MATRIMONIAL CAUSES ACT 1973, s 41

Although children are not parties to the divorce, it is accepted that they suffer most on a breakdown of marriage. Therefore, the welfare of the children must be considered before a divorce is finalised.

3.5.1 Child of the family

The MCA 1973 requires the court to consider the welfare of any child who is a 'child of the family'. A child of the family is a child who is either:

(1) a child of both parties to the marriage; or
(2) any other child (not having been placed with the parties as foster parents by the local authority or voluntary organisation) who has been treated by both parties as a child of the family (MCA 1973, s 52(1)).

The definition, therefore, applies to all natural children of both parties, but can apply to a wide variety of more distantly related or unrelated children, for example, step-children or adopted children.

3.5.2 Protection of children on divorce under MCA 1973, s 41

In any proceedings for a decree of divorce or judicial separation the court must consider:

(1) whether there are any children of the family to whom s 41 applies. The section will apply to any child of the family who, at the date when the court considers the case, is under 16 or any other child of the family of 16 and over to whom the court directs that s 41 shall apply. This could cover a child still in full-time education or who is suffering from a disability; and
(2) where there are any such children, whether in the light of the arrangements which have been, or are proposed to be, made for their upbringing or welfare it should exercise any of its powers under the Children Act 1989 with respect to any of them (eg that the child resides with a particular parent or that the child has contact with a parent).

By r 2.39 of FPR 1991, if no application for a Children Act 1989 order is pending, this function will normally be carried out by the district judge. He will usually decide on the papers alone without any hearing. In such a case, the court is unlikely to wish to exercise any of its powers under the Children Act 1989 (for the detailed procedure, see **3.9.1**).

3.5.3 Power to delay decree absolute

The court is given the power to delay the grant of the decree absolute if:

(1) the circumstances of the case require it, or are likely to require it, to exercise any of its powers under the Children Act 1989 with respect to any such child; and

(2) it is not in a position to exercise that power without giving further consideration to the case; and

(3) there are exceptional circumstances which make it desirable in the interests of the child that the court should give a direction under this section.

In reality, this power is rarely exercised. However, it could apply, for example, where the court considers that there is a problem with the arrangements for the children, it asks the parents to attend court to explain the circumstances but the parents fail to co-operate and do not attend the appointment. By delaying the decree the court might force the parents to address themselves to the problems and to work out satisfactory arrangements.

3.6 NULLITY

This section gives an outline of the decree of nullity which can, in certain circumstances, be sought as an alternative to a decree of divorce. In comparison with divorce, relatively few decrees of nullity are sought.

3.6.1 General

A decree of nullity may declare that a marriage is either void from the outset, in which case it is treated as never having existed at all, or voidable, in which case it will be treated as being valid and subsisting until the decree is obtained.

3.6.2 Void marriages

A marriage will be void in situations which include the following:

(1) where the parties are too closely related to each other; or
(2) either party was under 16 years of age at the time of the ceremony; or
(3) either party was already lawfully married (MCA 1973, s 11).

If a marriage is void, it never existed. Therefore, a decree is not needed to end it. However, since a decree is needed if ancillary financial orders are required, it is usually obtained.

3.6.3 Voidable marriages

A marriage will be voidable in situations which include the following:

(1) non-consummation, either due to incapacity of one party or wilful refusal; or
(2) lack of consent, for example, due to duress; or
(3) one party was suffering from a mental disorder such as to make them unfit for marriage.

A voidable marriage exists until such time as a decree of nullity is obtained. A bar to obtaining a decree can exist if the respondent, first, satisfies the court that the petitioner, knowing that the marriage could be ended, behaved in such a way as to lead the respondent reasonably to believe that he would not seek to do so and secondly, that it would be unjust to the respondent to grant the decree (MCA 1973, s 13(1)).

Generally, the petitioner must apply for the decree within 3 years of the date of the marriage. This does not apply to non-consummation cases and, in any event, the court also has a discretion to extend the time-limit (MCA 1973, s 13(4)).

3.6.4 Consequences of a decree of nullity

Ancillary orders

The parties to a suit for nullity are entitled to apply for all those orders in relation to children, property and finance as are available on divorce.

Children

Children born to parents who subsequently obtain a decree of nullity are automatically legitimate if the parents' marriage is voidable, because the marriage existed up to the time of the decree. If the marriage is void, the children will be legitimate if, at the time of conception (or the celebration of the marriage if this is later), both or either of the parents reasonably believed the marriage was valid and the father was domiciled in England and Wales at the time of the birth or, if he died before the birth, was so domiciled immediately before his death (Legitimacy Act 1976, s 1).

Wills

A voidable marriage will revoke a previous will, whereas a void marriage, as it never existed, does not have this effect.

When a decree of nullity is granted, whether in respect of a void or voidable marriage, it will have the same effect on a will as a decree of divorce. This means that the former spouse is to be treated as having died on the date of the decree.

Neither spouse will be able to claim in the event of the other's intestacy.

3.6.5 Divorce or nullity?

In some cases, there can be grounds for both divorce and nullity. It is generally better for clients to apply for divorce in these circumstances as only in divorce is there a procedure known as the 'Special Procedure' available for undefended suits which is cheap and simple. There is no equivalent for nullity cases and every case must be held in open court which adds to the cost and publicity. However, Legal Representation is available, subject to financial eligibility and merits (eg Legal Representation will not be granted if divorce would be a reasonable alternative), even for undefended nullity proceedings. As nullity can be obtained in the first year of marriage and as there can be religious reasons for wanting to have the marriage declared non-existent, rather than dissolved, nullity is sometimes preferred.

3.7 JUDICIAL SEPARATION

An alternative to a decree of divorce is a decree of judicial separation. It does not dissolve the marriage but can be used, for example, if religious beliefs forbid divorce.

3.7.1 Grounds for judicial separation

The grounds on which a decree of judicial separation can be obtained are the same as the facts that need to be proved to obtain a divorce (MCA 1973, s 1(2)) (see **3.4.2–3.4.6**). This means that MCA 1973, s 2 will apply regarding periods of reconciliation and cohabitation and s 41 will apply in relation to any children of the family. However, the parties do not need to show irretrievable breakdown (MCA 1973, s 17(2)). The Special Procedure available in undefended divorces applies to undefended petitions for judicial separation, although in contrast to divorce, there is only one stage to the decree. The public funding position on judicial separation is the same as for divorce, ie it is not normally available for an undefended main suit.

3.7.2 Effect of decree of judicial separation

When a decree of judicial separation has been obtained, the parties are still married as the decree does not dissolve the marriage but only releases the parties from the duty to live together.

3.7.3 Reasons for seeking judicial separation

Reasons for seeking judicial separation include the following.

(1) Judicial separation can be sought at any time after the marriage, so this could assist a spouse who separates within the first year who cannot start divorce proceedings.
(2) The same financial and other ancillary orders can be obtained on judicial separation as on divorce.
(3) Some clients have religious or moral objections to divorce and so this decree offers an alternative.
(4) The fact used in the judicial separation proceedings can subsequently be used as proof of a fact in later divorce proceedings (MCA 1973, s 4(1)).

Note that judicial separation does not affect existing wills and advice should be given to clients recommending that they review their wills in the light of their separation. If, subsequently, a spouse dies intestate, his or her property will devolve as if the other spouse was already dead, so the surviving spouse will not benefit.

3.8 PRESUMPTION OF DEATH AND DISSOLUTION OF MARRIAGE

If the respondent has disappeared in circumstances where it is reasonable to suppose he is dead, the petitioner can apply under MCA 1973, s 19 for a presumption of death and dissolution of marriage. There is a presumption that, after 7 years' continuous absence, during which time the petitioner has had no reason to believe that the respondent was alive, the respondent is dead.

3.9 DIVORCE PROCEDURE

3.9.1 Legal Help and Legal Representation

On marriage breakdown, it is usual for both spouses to seek legal advice. A solicitor must be able to assess whether a client is eligible for State assistance towards his legal costs and advise him accordingly.

An outline of public funding is provided in Chapter 2. This section highlights some points of particular relevance to the divorce suit itself.

Legal Representation is not available for undefended divorces because Legal Help is intended to cover the whole of the divorce, including the drafting of the divorce documents. If a client is eligible, Legal Help enables 2 or 3 hours' work to be undertaken at a fixed rate.

Solicitor not acting

Where a solicitor advises under Legal Help, he is not treated by the court as 'acting' for the client and so the solicitor's name will not appear on the court record. The client is a litigant in person which means that all procedural documents in the divorce must be signed by the client personally.

If Legal Representation is subsequently obtained (eg for an ancillary financial claim), the solicitor must place his name on the court record for that matter by filing a Notice of Acting with the court and serving any other party with a copy. However, so long as the divorce remains undefended, the client will remain a litigant in person in the divorce.

Legal Representation

Legal Representation is available for defended divorces but will only be granted extremely rarely.

It is possible for Legal Representation to be obtained in an undefended suit, but only where the matter is transferred to open court, for example, for a jurisdictional point to be resolved or, where by reason of physical or mental incapacity, it is impracticable for the applicant to proceed without representation.

3.9.2 The first interview

The first interview is of crucial importance. It is the first meeting with the client and gives the opportunity for the solicitor to obtain information needed from the client as well as to give advice and plan what is to be done (for general advice on interviewing, see **1.2.4**).

When a client seeks advice on his marriage, it is important to discover what the client wants. Does he want a divorce or are the parties hoping for a reconciliation?

Assuming that the client wants to obtain a divorce, the following areas will need to be covered in the interview. Appropriate use of a checklist or instruction sheet will help to obtain the information. For example:

(1) general advice on divorce and alternatives, for example, grounds, timing, mediation;

(2) information sufficient to fill in the divorce petition and the supporting documents;

(3) general advice on costs as well as filling in the Controlled Work 1 Form if appropriate;

(4) financial matters, for example, property and maintenance principles and orders that could be made;

(5) children, for example, advice on general principles and orders available;

(6) welfare benefits if client has no income;

(7) public funding: statutory charge. If the client is eligible for public funding for ancillary matters, advice must be given on the effect that the statutory charge will have on any order obtained (for a more detailed explanation, see **2.6**);

(8) injunction law and procedure. If the client has problems with domestic violence, appropriate advice should be given (see Chapter 14).

A file note of the interview should be made as soon as possible after the interview. A letter should be written to the client reminding him of what happened at the interview and what advice was given, as well as reminding the client of any action he has asked for. Any advice given on costs, especially public funding, should be repeated.

3.9.3 The petition

The FPR 1991 provide that every divorce must be begun by petition. The FPR 1991 also contain a list of the information to be contained in a petition. In practice, standard form petitions are available from law stationers or via computer software packages that are specifically drafted to suit each Fact and to enable the solicitor to insert the prescribed information. This is as follows.

(1)   Names of the parties and date and place of the marriage. This information should be copied exactly from the marriage certificate.

(2)   The last address where the parties lived as husband and wife.

(3)   The ground on which it is alleged that the court has jurisdiction. The standard form documents assume that the court will have jurisdiction as the petitioner will be domiciled in England and Wales. If this is not the case, the form must be amended and the grounds on which jurisdiction is claimed must be stated. If habitual residence is being used, the addresses of places of residence and the dates and periods of residence must be included.

(4)   Present occupations and residences of the parties. There are provisions enabling the petitioner's address to be concealed if this is necessary for the protection of the petitioner, for example, where there is a fear of violence from the respondent.

(5)   Information about the children of the family. The full names and dates of birth of all children of the family under 18 years must be given and where there are children of the family of over 18 years their names should be given together with the words 'over 18 years'. If any child is over 16 the petition must include details of any further education or training being undertaken.

(6)   Information about any other living child born to the wife during marriage. This will cover any children born to the wife who are not children of the family, for example, children from an extramarital relationship. Details of

their full names and dates of birth must be given as above.

(7)   Information about any other court proceedings relating to the marriage or to any children of the family or between the parties regarding any property of either or both. If there have been any earlier proceedings, full details must be given, including any order made and, if the proceedings related to the marriage, whether the parties have lived together since any order was made.

(8)   Information about whether any proceedings have been taken in the Child Support Agency relating to any children of the family must be given. If an application has been made, details must be given, including the amount awarded.

(9)   Information about any continuing proceedings outside England and Wales relating to the marriage. It is important for the court to be aware of any foreign proceedings relating to the marriage. In some circumstances, the court can adjourn the divorce proceedings until the outcome of the foreign proceedings is known.

(10)   Whether or not any agreement between the parties has been made or is proposed for the support of any party or any child of the family. This statement is needed only if the petition is based on 5 years' separation (Fact E). It is required in these cases because of the grave financial hardship defence (see **3.4.6**). The court, therefore, needs to know about any existing arrangements or proposals.

(11)   Statement that the marriage has irretrievably broken down.

(12)   Statement of the Fact under MCA 1973, s 1(2) relied upon together with particulars of the incidents relied on but not the evidence by which these will be proved.

(13)   The petition must end with a prayer for the following:

(a)   dissolution of the marriage;

(b)   any claim for ancillary financial relief which is required. It is important that the petitioner makes an application for all forms of ancillary relief which might be needed in the petition. If this is not done, leave of the court will be required for a later application. The petitioner could also be prejudiced as orders for periodical payments can only be backdated to the date of application which will be the date of the petition unless leave of the court is needed for a later application when it will be the date of actual application. If the petitioner remarries, she will be prevented from making a claim for a lump sum or property adjustment order. If she had applied in the prayer, ie before remarriage, a hearing could take place after remarriage. There is provision on the standard form to claim ancillary relief for any children of the family. If a CSA application is to be made, the court will not usually have jurisdiction to grant periodical payments. However, other forms of ancillary relief, for example a lump sum order, could be applied for;

(c)   a claim for costs if required. In a divorce under Legal Help, costs will only be those of a litigant in person and, therefore, it is not usual to ask for costs, especially as there is a risk that if costs are sought the respondent might be sufficiently annoyed to defend the petition.

When the petition is drafted, it is not certain whether the proceedings will be defended or not, therefore practitioners often draft the prayer for costs in such a way as to ask for costs only if the petition is defended. Where the petitioner is paying privately, costs may be claimed in relation to fault-based divorces. The costs being sought in the prayer will only cover costs incurred in dissolving the marriage. Costs for ancillary matters, for example, financial orders will be sought separately during the ancillary proceedings;

(d)   it is generally inappropriate to apply in the petition for any order under CA 1989, s 8 for the children of the family. The arrangements proposed for the children will be set out in a separate document, Form M4 (see **3.9.4**) and will usually be agreed with the respondent before filing the petition. If, however, the parties are in serious dispute over, for example, where the children should live following the divorce an application can be made for a s 8 order at this stage.

The petition will be signed by the petitioner personally if advice is being obtained under Legal Help, because the petitioner is treated as a litigant in person. If the petitioner is not obtaining advice under Legal Help, the petition may be signed by the solicitor either in his own name or in the firm's name or if, unusually, counsel drafted the petition, by counsel.

The remainder of the petition lists the names and addresses of persons to be served with the petition and the petitioner's address for service. Here, although the petitioner receiving advice under Legal Help should strictly add her personal address, a concession enables the name of her solicitors to appear provided the address is stated to be 'care of' the solicitors. This ensures that court documents are sent direct to the solicitors rather than to the petitioner. If there is a co-respondent in a Fact A petition, the co-respondent must be served with the petition, and her address must be added.

Amendments

If an error or omission is discovered in a petition, for example, the prayer does not include an application for ancillary financial relief or the petitioner's domicile is stated incorrectly, it will have to be amended. The petition can be amended without leave of the court before directions for trial are made, unless an answer has been filed in which case leave is required. After directions for trial, leave of the court will generally be needed for amendments (FPR 1991, r 2.11(1)).

Leave can be given without notice if the respondent agrees to the amendment. If the respondent does not agree, an on notice application to the district judge will have to be made. Whenever a petition is amended after service, the amended petition will have to be served on the respondent (and co-respondent).

In practice, very minor amendments, for example an incorrect date of birth of a child or incorrect occupation of a party, can be corrected by referring to the error in the petitioner's affidavit (Form M7). The district judge can then give leave for the petition to stand as corrected without the need for re-service.

3.9.4   The supporting documents

The following additional documents must be prepared and filed with the petition.

Statement relating to the proposed arrangements for any children of the family (Form M4)

Form M4 is a standard form which gives details of the children of the family. It provides the court with the information which it needs in order to consider the arrangements for the children under MCA 1973, s 41.

Form M4 covers accommodation, education, child-care arrangements, health, maintenance and arrangements which have been made or which are proposed for contact with the parent with whom the child does not live full time. If the child is disabled or has a medical problem, Form M4 will have to give details of this and, where necessary, be supported by a medical report or doctor's letter giving details of the problem and its likely effect on the child. The petitioner must always sign this form personally even if paying privately.

If practicable, Form M4 should be agreed with the respondent (FPR 1991, r 2.2). This should be attempted by sending the completed and signed Form to the respondent before filing the petition. The Form enables the respondent to add his agreement and signature before returning it to the petitioner. If the respondent's agreement has not been, or cannot be, obtained, then the petitioner can still file the petition. In these circumstances, it would be sensible to file with Form M4 a letter explaining the situation to the court.

Marriage certificate

If the client cannot produce the original marriage certificate, a certified copy can be obtained on payment of a small fee either from the Superintendent Registrar of Marriages for the district where the marriage took place, or from the General Register Office. If the marriage certificate is in a foreign language, an authenticated translation must also be obtained and filed with the divorce documents.

Certificate relating to reconciliation (Form M3)

Where a solicitor is acting for a client, there is an obligation to file a certificate in Form M3 which states whether or not the solicitor has discussed with the petitioner the possibility of a reconciliation and given him details of agencies which are qualified to help effect a reconciliation (FPR 1991, r 2.6(3)).

There is no duty on a solicitor to discuss reconciliation in every case in which he acts. This is left to his discretion and, if he decides not to discuss this matter, he will inform the court of this on Form M3.

The obligation to file this form does not arise if a client is receiving advice under Legal Help as the client is then acting in person. However, this does not prevent a solicitor from advising a client who is receiving advice Legal Help on reconciliation if appropriate.

Service copies of the petition and Form M4

It is necessary to file the original petition plus one copy for each party who is to be served. One copy will be sufficient unless a co-respondent is involved in a Fact A petition, in which case two service copies will be needed.

Form M4 is served on the respondent, even if he has already signed the form and agreed to the arrangements; therefore, the original plus one copy of this form should be filed. It is never served on a co-respondent.

Fee or application for exemption from fees

A fee is payable on filing the petition. If the client is receiving advice under Legal Help or is receiving income support or family credit, she is exempt from the fee. However, a form applying for exemption must be completed and filed at court.

3.9.5 Filing

The petition and the appropriate additional documents and fee can be filed at any divorce county court (or the Divorce Registry in London).

3.9.6 Service of the petition

The petition and other appropriate documents must be served on the respondent and any co-respondent (FPR 1991, rr 2.9(1) and 2.24).

Usual method of service

The court will usually serve the petition by sending it by first-class post to the address given in the petition.

The court attaches the following to each service copy of the petition.

(1) A Notice of Proceedings (Form M5). This is a general explanation to the respondent of the divorce procedure with detailed instructions on completing and returning the Acknowledgement of Service.

(2) An Acknowledgement of Service (Form M6). This is an important procedural document which could furnish proof of service of the petition or of the fact relied on as well as other useful information, for example, whether the respondent intends to defend (see **3.9.7**).

(3) A copy of the statement as to the arrangements for the children (Form M4). This is attached only to the respondent's copy of the petition. The respondent may have already seen and signed this document because a copy will have already been sent to him by the petitioner.

If the respondent then completes and returns the Acknowledgement of Service to the court, this is proof of service (FPR 1991, r 2.9(5)). When the court receives the Acknowledgement from the respondent, it will send a copy to the petitioner's solicitors.

Alternative methods of service

If postal service by the court is unsuccessful or inappropriate, alternative methods of service are available and proof of service will depend on which method is used.

PERSONAL SERVICE

By court bailiff

The petitioner can request bailiff service by lodging the appropriate form. A fee is payable unless the petitioner has filed an exemption form. A description of the respondent, normally a photograph, must also be lodged in order to enable the bailiff to identify the respondent.

The bailiff will then serve the documents personally and file a certificate of service. If the Acknowledgement of Service is then returned by the respondent, this will be proof of service; if not, the bailiff's certificate will be used.

Service through the petitioner

The petitioner can request that service is carried out through her under FPR 1991, r 2.9(2)(b). A process server will be instructed or the petitioner's solicitors will themselves serve the documents. The Rules prohibit the petitioner herself from serving the documents on the respondent (FPR 1991, r 2.9(3)). Proof of service in these cases will be by affidavit of service by whoever served the documents.

DEEMED SERVICE

If the respondent does not return the Acknowledgement of Service to the court, the petitioner can apply for deemed service if she can satisfy the court that the respondent has in fact received the petition (FPR 1991, r 2.9(6)).

An application without notice should be made to the district judge supported by an affidavit showing why the petitioner is of the view that the respondent has received the petition. This can be done by using evidence from a third party, or, for example, even from the petitioner herself that the respondent read the petition and then threw it away, or a letter from solicitors instructed by the respondent to act for him referring to the petition.

SUBSTITUTED SERVICE

Substituted service will be relevant when all the petitioner's efforts to serve by post and personal service have failed and there is insufficient evidence to apply for deemed service.

An application without notice should be made to the district judge supported by an affidavit setting out the grounds on which the application is made (FPR 1991, r 2.9(9)).

If the order is granted, it will specify the alternative method to be used. This could be by advertisement if there is a reasonable likelihood that it will come to the respondent's notice, for example, by placing it in a newspaper which he is known to read regularly. Another method that could be specified is service on another person, for example, a relative whom he visits regularly or a person with whom he lives or works.

DISPENSING WITH SERVICE

Dispensing with service is only used as a last resort where all other methods have failed and the district judge is of the opinion that it is impracticable to serve the petition or for other reasons it is necessary or expedient to dispense with service (FPR 1991, r 2.9(11)). It is treated by the court very seriously as, by granting the order, the respondent can find that he is divorced without knowing that a divorce petition had been filed and having had no opportunity to defend. An application without notice should be made to the court supported by an affidavit setting out the grounds for the application (ie why there is a problem and what has been done to trace the respondent). The district judge can require the petitioner to attend to give evidence. Service will be dispensed with only where the petitioner can show that every effort has been made to trace the respondent.

Other problems with service

FINDING THE RESPONDENT

If the petitioner does not know the whereabouts of the respondent, enquiries must be made so that postal or personal service can be used. If particular difficulty is encountered, reference should be made to the *Practice Direction of 13 February 1989* [1989] 1 All ER 765. This enables the court to request a search for the respondent's address in the records of the DSS or the Passport Office. If the respondent is in the Armed Services the relevant service department can be asked for the respondent's address.

SERVING ON THE CO-RESPONDENT

The petition must also be served on any co-respondent. The co-respondent is not served with a copy of the statement of arrangements for the children. The same methods of service are available as for the respondent.

Service of the petition must also be proved and this will normally be done by the co-respondent returning the completed Acknowledgement of Service to the court. If this is not done, an alternative method of proving service will have to be used, for example, an affidavit of service following bailiff service or personal service. Otherwise an order for deemed service, substituted service or, as a last resort, an order dispensing with service will have to be obtained.

SERVICE OUTSIDE ENGLAND AND WALES

Rule 10.6 of FPR 1991 allows the divorce petition to be served outside England and Wales by post, personally or by substituted service without leave. Alternatively, the standard methods for such service in the High Court or county court can be used (see CPR 1998, Pt 6).

SERVICE ON A PARTY UNDER A DISABILITY

The court cannot serve the petition if the respondent is a minor (under 18 years of age) or a mental patient. Reference should be made to FPR 1991, r 9.2 and r 9.3.

3.9.7 Return of the Acknowledgement of Service

The respondent is required to complete and return the Acknowledgement of Service to the court within 7 days of service of the petition (FPR 1991, r 10.8(2)(a)).

The respondent is given guidance as to how to complete this form in the Notice of Proceedings (Form M5). He may also have instructed his own solicitors. When the court sends a copy of the Acknowledgement of Service to the petitioner, the replies to the straightforward questions it contains may reveal the following information.

(1) Proof of service (see **3.9.6**).
(2) Whether the respondent intends to defend the petition. Since the reply is not binding on the respondent, he can later change his mind.
(3) Whether the respondent is satisfied with the proposed arrangements for the children set out in Form M4. Again, he is not bound by his reply and can commence an application under the Children Act 1989 even if he has not indicated this in his reply.
(4) Whether he has admitted adultery or consented to the decree. If the petition is based on Fact A, the respondent can admit the adultery and, provided he has

signed the form personally, this will be sufficient proof of his adultery. If the petition is based on Fact D and the respondent has given his consent in this form, this will be proof of his consent, provided he has signed the form personally.

3.9.8 Requesting directions for trial

Provided the respondent has not given notice of intention to defend and a period of 7 days after service of the petition has expired, the next step is for the petitioner's solicitors to lodge a request for directions, which asks for the cause to be put on the Special Procedure list (for undefended divorces), together with an affidavit containing proof of the fact relied on and other essential matters. If the respondent has given a notice of intention to defend, the petitioner must wait 28 days from service of the petition to file a request for directions.

3.9.9 Petitioner's affidavit in support of the petition

The petitioner's affidavit in support of the petition is filed with the request for directions. The Rules provide standard form affidavits to suit each Fact (see FPR 1991, Appendix 1, Form M7(a) to (e)). The affidavit is in question and answer form. The main matters which are dealt with are as follows.

(1) The petitioner must confirm that the contents of her petition are true and that no amendments or alterations are required.
(2) If the parties have cohabited since the date of the incidents relied on, the affidavit requires the petitioner to give details of the periods of cohabitation to ensure that the fact is not barred by MCA 1973, s 2.
(3) Any corroborative evidence (FPR 1991, r 2.24(3)). For example, a medical report to confirm the injuries alleged in a Fact B petition. The Acknowledgement of Service will need to be exhibited if the petitioner is relying on it as proof of service, or if it has been signed by the respondent to admit adultery (Fact A), or to consent to the divorce (Fact D).
(4) The petitioner must confirm that the contents of the Statement of Arrangements (Form M4) are still correct and identify the signature of the respondent on that form.

3.9.10 Directions for trial

Before the district judge can give directions, he has to check the following:

(1) that the petition has been served. The district judge will check that proof of service is evident from the documents lodged. If the petitioner is relying on return of the Acknowledgement and it is a case where this has been signed personally by the respondent, he will check that the petitioner's affidavit identifies the respondent's signature;
(2) that the case is undefended. The case will be undefended if:

   (a) the respondent has told the court that he does not intend to defend (usually in the Acknowledgement of Service); or
   (b) no notice of intention has been given and 7 days have elapsed since service of the petition; or
   (c) the respondent has filed a notice of intention to defend but the time-limit for filing the answer has expired. Rules 2.12(1) and 2.24(1) of FPR 1991

provide that this time-limit is 28 days from the date of service of the petition;

(3) if the petition relies on Fact D, that the respondent's consent has been given. Consent can either be given in the Acknowledgement of Service or in a separate document (FPR 1991, r 2.24(3)).

If all the above matters are satisfied, the district judge will direct that the case be set down in the Special Procedure list (see **3.9.11**).

3.9.11 Special Procedure

Special Procedure is the standard procedure for all undefended divorces.

As soon as practicable after the case has been set down in the Special Procedure list, the district judge will consider the evidence of the petitioner. He will study the court file and in particular the petition, Form M4, the Acknowledgement of Service, the petitioner's affidavit and any exhibits (FPR 1991, r 2.36).

If the district judge is satisfied that the petitioner has proved her case, he will do the following:

(1) complete and file a certificate to this effect;
(2) fix a day for the decree nisi to be read out in open court by a judge or district judge;
(3) if there is a prayer for costs in the petition, make an order for costs if he considers that the petitioner is entitled to them. If he considers that he cannot make an order for costs without further information, he can require the respondent to file a written statement of his reasons for objecting to paying the costs or, refer the matter of costs to the judge or district judge who pronounces the decree nisi. In this case, he will notify the respondent that he must attend court on the date that the decree nisi is to be pronounced to argue his case. If he fails to attend that hearing an order for costs in favour of the petitioner will almost certainly be made;
(4) consider any children to whom s 41 of MCA 1973 applies (see **3.9.12**).

The court will then send a copy of the district judge's certificate and the notice of the date on which the decree nisi will be granted to both parties (FPR 1991, r 2.36(2)).

If the district judge is not satisfied that the petitioner has proved her case, he can:

(1) ask the petitioner to supply further evidence. This could clarify, for example, an uncertainty revealed in the petition relating to domicile or habitual residence or an ambiguity in the petitioner's affidavit relating to any period during which the petitioner cohabited with the respondent;
(2) remove the case from the Special Procedure list.

If there is a problem which cannot be resolved by supplying further information, for example, a question of whether there was sufficient behaviour to amount to grounds for a Fact B divorce or a complex domicile issue, there will be a hearing in front of the judge in open court to resolve the problem. If the problem is resolved and the ground for divorce is proved, the decree nisi will be made at the hearing. If not, the petition will be dismissed. Legal Representation is available for this hearing so the necessary application must be made.

3.9.12 Section 41 certificate

When the district judge grants a certificate that the petitioner has proved her case, he will consider the question of the arrangements for children to whom s 41 of MCA 1973 applies (see **3.5**).

Where there is no pending application for an order under the Children Act 1989

If there has been no application under the Children Act 1989 made by either party, there being no dispute between the parties as to arrangements for the children, the district judge will examine Form M4 and check that the arrangements proposed are acceptable. When he has done this, he can certify that either:

(1) there are no children of the family to whom s 41 applies; or
(2) there are such children, but that the court need not exercise its powers under the Children Act 1989.

If, having considered Form M4, he is not satisfied that the arrangements are satisfactory, he can give one of the following directions:

(1) that the parties file further evidence as to the arrangements for the children (eg a medical report);
(2) that a welfare report be prepared;
(3) that either, or both, parties attend before him.

The evidence so obtained might satisfy him that in fact the arrangements are satisfactory, in which case he can issue a certificate that there is no need for the court to exercise its powers under the Children Act 1989.

If, on his initial consideration or, having made directions and further investigations the district judge considers that:

(1) the exercise of his powers is, or is likely to be, necessary but the court is not in a position to exercise them without further consideration; and
(2) there are exceptional circumstances which make it desirable in the interests of the child to do so, then he may direct that the decree nisi of divorce is not made absolute, until the court directs.

This power will be used very rarely and only if delaying the decree will actually be in the interests of the child. This might apply where both parents were happy to proceed with the divorce but had not attempted to make arrangements for the children; withholding the decree absolute could persuade them of the seriousness of their behaviour.

Where there are pending proceedings under the Children Act 1989

Where an application has already been made under the Children Act 1989, it is open to the district judge either to grant a certificate under s 41 of MCA 1973 enabling the divorce to go ahead, or, to delay the grant of the decree absolute by making a direction that there are exceptional circumstances making it desirable to delay the grant of the decree absolute.

3.9.13 Decree nisi

The decree nisi will be read out on the appointed day by the judge or district judge in open court. However, unless there is any dispute as to costs, neither party need attend. A copy of the decree nisi is sent to the parties. This decree does not dissolve the marriage.

3.9.14 Decree absolute

The final step in the undefended divorce procedure is to obtain the decree absolute which will end the marriage.

Petitioner's application

Once 6 weeks have elapsed since the grant of the decree nisi, the petitioner can apply for the decree absolute by lodging Form M8 together with the prescribed fee (FPR 1991, r 2.49(1) and Appendix 1). In extremely rare cases, the court does have the power to reduce this 6-week period (*Practice Direction* [1977] 2 All ER 714). However, when urgency is anticipated it is better to speed up the earlier part of the divorce proceedings rather than relying on this power.

If the petitioner is receiving advice under Legal Help, she will be exempt from the fee.

The district judge will grant the decree absolute provided that the matters set out in FPR 1991, r 2.49(2) are satisfied.

(1) That there is no appeal or re-hearing relating to the decree nisi.
(2) That the provisions enabling the respondent's financial position to be considered under MCA 1973, s 10(2)–(4) do not apply or have been complied with.
(3) That the court has complied with MCA 1973, s 41 and there is no direction to delay the decree absolute.
(4) That no intervention by the Queen's Proctor or any other person is pending.

The decree absolute certificate (Form M9) is sent to the petitioner and the respondent. The marriage is now dissolved.

It is important not to apply for the decree absolute automatically after the 6-week period as there could be good reasons to delay. For example, it might be important to preserve the petitioner's right of occupation under FLA 1996 (see **8.6**), or even at this late stage the petitioner might be considering a reconciliation.

If the petitioner delays applying for the decree absolute for more than 12 months after the decree nisi, the application must be accompanied by a written explanation for the delay. This is to ensure that there has not been an attempted reconciliation which may have prejudiced the grounds and that no child has been born who should be considered under MCA 1973, s 41.

Respondent's application

The petitioner may choose not to apply to make the decree absolute for the reasons mentioned above, or perhaps where the petitioner knows that the respondent is anxious to remarry and wishes to use the delay as a negotiating weapon in the financial proceedings. In this situation, the respondent can apply for the decree absolute once a period of some 4½ months has elapsed from the date of the decree nisi (ie 3 months after the earliest date (ie 6 weeks after decree nisi) on which the petitioner could have obtained the decree absolute) (MCA 1973, s 9(2)). The petitioner must be served with notice of the application (FPR 1991, r 2.50(2)). The court will then consider the respondent's application and any objections that the petitioner has made. The court can then decide to make the decree absolute, require further investigations or, if necessary, rescind the decree nisi.

3.10 DEFENDED DIVORCES

As defended divorces are so rare, the detail of defended procedure is outside the scope of this book and reference should be made to specialist textbooks. Certain points should, however, be borne in mind.

3.10.1 Legal Representation

It is extremely rare for Legal Representation to be granted for defending divorces.

If, however, Legal Representation is granted, detailed explanation and advice must be given to a client contemplating a defended divorce of the effects of the statutory charge (see **2.6**).

3.10.2 Notice of intention to defend

If the respondent intends to defend, he will normally return the Acknowledgement of Service stating that he intends to defend the petition. He must give this notice within 7 days from service of the petition (FPR 1991, r 10.8(2)(a)).

If he does not file this notice, he can still file an answer. If he does give notice, he is under no obligation to file an answer if he changes his mind.

3.10.3 Filing an answer

The answer is the defence to the petition and must be filed within 28 days of service of the petition (FPR 1991, r 2.12(2)). Problems are often encountered with this time-limit, sometimes because the respondent decides to defend only after it has expired; delay in obtaining Legal Representation can also mean that the time-limit is exceeded. In these circumstances, reference should be made to FPR 1991, r 2.14.

When the case becomes defended, the district judge can transfer the case to the High Court. He will do this only if he considers that, owing to its complexity, difficulty or gravity, it is more appropriate to deal with it in the High Court.

3.10.4 Subsequent procedure

Further statements of case can be filed. Directions for trial will be given. Eventually, usually after a long delay, there will be a hearing in open court.

3.11 COSTS

Applications are not made for costs in undefended divorces under Legal Help, but are sometimes made where the petitioner is paying privately and it is a fault-based divorce. If an application is made, the decision is always in the discretion of the court but the general principle is that an order for costs will be made in favour of the successful party.

3.12 CHAPTER SUMMARY

3.12.1 Divorce law

(1) No divorce proceedings can begin until one year after the marriage. Decrees of nullity and judicial separation can be brought at any time after the marriage.

(2) The English courts will have jurisdiction to hear a divorce only if either party is domiciled in England and Wales or was habitually resident here for at least one year before beginning the proceedings.

(3) The only ground for divorce is that the marriage has broken down irretrievably.

(4) One or more of 'the five facts' must be proved:

Fact A: Adultery and Intolerability
Fact B: Behaviour
Fact C: Desertion
Fact D: 2 years' Separation and Consent
Fact E: 5 years' Separation.

(5) Section 10(2) of MCA 1973 enables a respondent in a Fact D or Fact E divorce to ask the court to consider his financial position after the divorce.

(6) Section 5(1) of MCA 1973 is a defence to a Fact E divorce. The respondent must prove that the divorce would result in grave financial or other hardship and it would be wrong to dissolve the marriage.

(7) Section 41 of MCA 1973 imposes a duty in divorce proceedings to consider the welfare of any 'child of the family'.

(8) A decree of nullity can declare that a marriage either never existed at all (a void marriage) or that it did exist but, due to certain circumstances, it has been ended (a voidable marriage).

(9) A decree of judicial separation can be obtained by proving one of the five facts and is a legal separation.

3.12.2 Divorce procedure

Undefended divorce: special procedure checklist

PETITIONER

RESPONDENT

(1) Files at court:
  (a) Marriage certificate;
  (b) Petition + copy(ies);
  (c) Form M4 + copy (this should be
    sent to respondent for signature
    before filing);
  (d) Form M3 (reconciliation) (only if
    solicitor on court record);
  (e) Fee or application for exemption.

(2) Receives from court notification of
  cause number allocated.

(3) Receives from court:
  (a) Copy petition;
  (b) Copy Form M4;
  (c) Notice of Proceedings;
  (d) Acknowledgement of Service
    (Form M6).

(4) Returns completed Form M6 to court.

(5) Receives from court photocopy of
  completed Form M6.

(6) Files at court:
  (a) Request for Directions;
  (b) Affidavit of Evidence + exhibits.

(7) *Both* parties receive from court:
  a copy of the district judge's certificate,
  a copy of s 41 certificate and notice of
  the date fixed for pronouncement of
  decree nisi in open court by
  judge/district judge.

(8) Decree nisi pronounced – parties need
  not attend unless directed.

(9) *Both* parties would be notified of any
  directions made by court if district judge
  not satisfied with arrangements for
  children, eg further information or
  appointment at court.

(10) *Both* parties receive from court copy of
  decree nisi.

(11) Petitioner files notice of application for
  decree nisi to be made absolute (after 6
  weeks from grant of decree nisi).

(12) *Both* parties receive from court copy
  decree absolute.

3.13 FURTHER READING

Rayden and Jackson *Divorce and Family Matters* 17th edn (Butterworths, 1997) (plus service)
Butterworths Family Law Service (looseleaf)
The Family Court Practice (Family Law, 2000)
Black, Bridge and Bond *A Practical Approach to Family Law* 6th edn (Blackstone Press, 2000)

Chapter 4

ANCILLARY FINANCE: THE LAW

4.1 INTRODUCTION

This chapter deals with the law relating to financial provision on marriage breakdown. It covers the range of financial orders available to spouses under MCA 1973, and the principles applied by the court when making those orders. This chapter also deals with the wide range of orders available for children under MCA 1973. However, in the majority of cases, maintenance for children is now governed by the Child Support Act 1991 to the exclusion of MCA 1973. The Child Support Act will be considered in Chapter 7.

Nevertheless, a significant minority of maintenance applications for children will continue to be dealt with by the court and the court also retains sole jurisdiction to make lump sum and property adjustment orders in favour of children. It should also be borne in mind that, as financial provision between spouses is closely linked with provision for any children, it is important to appreciate the impact of the Child Support Act 1991 on orders made by the court under MCA 1973.

The current position is that, generally, financial arrangements are finalised after the divorce has gone through (indeed, the main financial orders cannot come into effect until after decree absolute). However, if Part II of FLA 1996 comes into force, a divorce order will not be made (apart from in exceptional cases) until the court is satisfied about the parties' arrangements for the future, including financial arrangements.

4.2 THE POWERS OF THE COURT

4.2.1 Orders available

The powers of the court to make financial orders are found in ss 22 to 24A of MCA 1973. The orders fall into two main categories: income orders and capital orders. The *income orders* are:

(1) maintenance pending suit;
(2) periodical payments;
(3) secured periodical payments.

The *capital orders* are more diverse and include:

(1) lump sum orders;
(2) property adjustment orders (for property to be transferred or held on trust);
(3) orders for sale.

4.2.2 When available

Spouses may apply for any of these orders or, indeed, all of them on or after the filing of the divorce petition. However, with the exception of maintenance pending suit (MPS), the application cannot be heard until decree nisi and no order will take effect until decree absolute. By contrast, most applications for provision for children may be made and heard at any time and such orders take immediate effect.

Petition	*Decree nisi*	*Decree absolute*
Application for financial provision can be made	Order for financial provision for spouse can be made	Order for financial provision can come into effect————————→
		(Periodical payments can be back-dated to the date of the application)
Order for MPS for spouse can be made and take effect	————————————→	MPS ends
Order for financial provision for child(ren) can be made and take effect	——————————————————————————→	

A party should take care to apply for financial provision before remarrying because after they have remarried they are no longer entitled to apply (see MCA 1973, s 28(3) and **9.4.2**).

4.3 INCOME ORDERS

4.3.1 Maintenance pending suit

An order for periodical payments for a spouse cannot take effect until decree absolute. However, the divorce client may be in urgent need of money before then. Such clients may wish to apply for MPS under MCA 1973, s 22. As the name suggests, MPS is an order for regular payments designed to tide a spouse over until the divorce is determined. At that time, an order for full periodical payments may take effect. In practice, however, the court will often not hear an ancillary relief application until some time after decree absolute is declared. If this would cause hardship to the applicant, an application for an interim periodical payments order could be made.

The application for MPS may be made, heard and take effect at any time after the petition has been filed. Any order will terminate on the grant or dismissal of the divorce. MPS is not available for a child, nor is it necessary, because periodical payments may be obtained for a child of the family (if appropriate) as soon as the petition is filed, or alternatively an application may be made to the Child Support Agency for a maintenance assessment.

MPS applications are not frequently pursued as potential applicants often prefer to rely on welfare benefits. There are a number of reasons for this.

(1) Most applicants will require Legal Representation in order to make an application. This inevitably causes delay, so that, in any event, the applicant has to resort to welfare benefits in the interim.

(2) Generally, the court orders only modest sums to be paid because the purpose of MPS is to provide adequate temporary provision during the proceedings.

(3) If the maintenance is so small that it has to be supplemented by income support or jobseeker's allowance, there is no advantage to the applicant as her benefit will be reduced by the maintenance pound for pound (see Chapter 6).

(4) There may be enforcement problems, especially in the early stages of the divorce, if a reluctant respondent or an aggrieved petitioner is still struggling to come to terms with the divorce or his responsibility to maintain the other party (or both).

(5) There may be a risk that an application for MPS might jeopardise the prospects of an uncontested divorce or negotiations over the final settlement.

Despite its drawbacks, MPS may be worth pursuing, particularly if a party with ample means leaves another with onerous responsibilities and no ability to meet them.

4.3.2 Periodical payments

Periodical payments usually take the form of weekly or monthly sums. Periodical payments may be paid to a spouse (MCA 1973, s 23(1)(a)) or, in exceptional cases to a child of the family (see the Child Support Act 1991, s 8(3) discussed at **7.3.3**), or to the spouse caring for the child on that child's behalf (MCA 1973, s 23(1)(d)). Periodical payments may be ordered for children even if the divorce petition is dismissed either at the time of dismissal or within a reasonable period after the dismissal.

All periodical payments to a party terminate on the death or remarriage of the payee. Unsecured periodical payments terminate on the death of the paying spouse (MCA 1973, s 28). A periodical payment order (PPO) is unaffected by the remarriage of the payer save that remarriage could prompt an application to discharge (or reduce) the order if the payer would then be supporting their new spouse.

The court may limit the term of the PPO to years or months if it considers that a party should be able to become independent after a period of adjustment, for example, to allow a wife to retrain and obtain employment. The court is under a duty to consider whether such a limitation on maintenance is feasible (see MCA 1973, s 25A(2) and **4.6**).

In the few cases where the court has jurisdiction to make a PPO in favour of a child, it will terminate on the child's 17th birthday unless it is in the child's interest for it to continue until he is 18 (MCA 1973, s 29). The usual reason for such an extension is that the child will be continuing with full-time education.

The maintenance may continue beyond a child's 18th birthday only if the circumstances in s 29(3) apply, ie:

(1) the child is (or intends to be) in further education, academic or vocational; or
(2) there are special circumstances, for example, the child is mentally handicapped.

4.3.3 Secured periodical payments (MCA 1973, s 23(1)(b) and (c))

A party may be ordered to secure periodical payments which are payable to the other party or a child of the family. This is a device to ensure that the payee will continue to receive the periodical payments even if the payer's income fluctuates or if problems of enforcement are anticipated. Secured PPOs work by charging an asset with a sum fixed by the court from which the periodical payments can be met. Typically, that asset will be income producing, for example, shares or rented property. The income yielded by the charged asset will be paid to the payee up to the amount specified in the PPO. Alternatively, a non-income producing asset such as a valuable painting could be secured. If the periodical payments were not made from other sources, the asset would be liable to be sold and the proceeds used to pay the sum secured.

Secured PPOs terminate in the same circumstances as unsecured PPOs, save for one exception: unlike ordinary PPOs, secured PPOs do not terminate on the death of the payer. However, his death would be taken into account on any application by his estate to vary or discharge the order.

4.4 CAPITAL ORDERS

The purpose of capital orders is to settle once and for all any disputes in respect of the couple's capital. For most couples the matrimonial home represents the main, if not the only, family capital. This is considered in detail in Chapter 8. Some couples will, of course, have considerable assets in addition to the home, including savings, securities, etc which may be the subject of a lump sum order, a property adjustment order or an order for sale.

4.4.1 Lump sum orders

Under MCA 1973, s 23(1)(c) and (e), the court can order a party to pay to the other, or to a child of the family, a cash lump sum. There are two main reasons for making such an order:

(1) to adjust the final division of the parties' assets. The order is frequently used in conjunction with an order dealing with the matrimonial home;
(2) to recompense the applicant for expenses incurred prior to the application as a result of inadequate support from the respondent for the applicant or a child of the family.

A spouse is entitled to apply for one lump sum order only (although, see **10.8.1** which deals with the court's new power to make a second lump sum or property adjustment order on an application for variation or discharge of a periodical payments or a secured periodical payments order). The lump sum order may specify payment by several instalments. In common with the other capital orders, a lump sum order cannot be varied. However, there is jurisdiction to deal with an application to vary, suspend and even to discharge instalments of a lump sum. Where the court orders payment of the lump sum to be by instalments or to be deferred, for example, to allow the payer time to raise the money, it may order interest to be paid at a specified rate. There is also power to secure payment of the instalments in the same way as for periodical payments.

It is sometimes the case that although there may be no funds immediately available for the payment of a lump sum, it is anticipated that money will be forthcoming. Examples include an expected dissolution of a partnership or maturity of an assurance policy releasing capital. In such a case, the court may adjourn an application, although it will do so only where there is a real likelihood of a change of circumstances within a relatively short period. The court has said that an application should not be adjourned for longer than about 5 years (see *Roberts v Roberts* [1986] 2 All ER 483). It has also refused applications for adjournment based on a party's hopes of inheritance on the grounds that it was too uncertain whether and when the inheritance would occur (see *Michael v Michael* [1986] 2 FLR 389, CA, and **4.5.1**).

Lump sum orders are also available for children. Whilst they are not common, they may be appropriate in high income families or if a child has a special need, for example he is disabled or has special educational needs. Unlike for spouses, more than one lump sum order can be made for a child, so several orders could be made over a period of time. The Child Support Agency has no jurisdiction to make capital awards for children.

4.4.2 Property adjustment orders

Under MCA 1973, s 24, the court has wide powers to redistribute family property between the parties and the children of the family. It may do so by ordering that property be transferred, for example, from one party to the other, or held on trust. Such orders are final. Consequently, no application may be made (not even for a child) for further property adjustment, nor is it possible to vary these orders (but, again, see **10.8.1** on the court's new powers to make a property adjustment order on a variation of a periodical payments order).

4.4.3 Orders for sale

The court has power under MCA 1973, s 24A to order a sale of any property in which either party is beneficially entitled. The court can only make this order once it has also made one of the following orders:

(1) a secured periodical payments order;
(2) a lump sum order;
(3) a property adjustment order.

The order for sale may be made at the same time as the above orders or later. The order cannot take effect until decree absolute. The court has power to order that the sale shall not take place until a specified event has taken place or period has expired. For example, it may order that the property in question is not to be sold until essential works on it have been completed. Alternatively, the court may defer the sale to enable a party wishing to avoid the sale and remain in the property (or keep the car/shares, etc) to raise a lump sum to 'buy out' the other party's interest.

Orders for sale may also be used as a method of enforcement by ordering the sale of an asset if the owner has defaulted on a lump sum order (see Chapter 10).

The order for sale may contain consequential and supplementary provisions, directing, for example, how the sale price is to be fixed or who should have the conduct of the sale.

If a party owns property jointly with another person, for example where a husband and his new partner are co-owners of a flat, the court must give the third party, here the partner, the opportunity to make representations on the matter before it decides whether to order the sale of the property. Alternatively, it may be, say, that the partner is living in a property, but has no interest in it. In such a case, the s 24A order may include a consequential direction that she is to be given first refusal on the property before it is placed on the open market.

Although ss 24 and 24A apply to all types of property, for most families the matrimonial home is the most significant asset and, therefore, the issue on which feelings often run high. There are various ways of resolving disputes over the home and these are considered in detail in Chapter 8.

4.5　DECIDING WHAT ORDERS TO MAKE

The court has a great deal of discretion and flexibility when deciding on the appropriate division of matrimonial assets on divorce.

When the court is considering provision, whether for the parties to the marriage or for a child of the family, it must begin by considering the statutory criteria laid down in MCA 1973, s 25.

Section 25(1) states:

> 'It shall be the duty of the court in deciding whether to exercise its powers under sections 23, 24 or 24A above and, if so, in what manner, to have regard to all the circumstances of the case, first consideration being given to the welfare while a minor of any child of the family who has not attained the age of eighteen.'

The section goes on to list factors applicable to provision for spouses (s 25(2)), children of the family (s 25(3)) and further factors for children of the family who are not natural children of both parties (s 25(4)). Those factors are examined below. Section 25 does not represent an exhaustive list of factors. Indeed, s 25(1) makes it plain that the court must take into account 'all the circumstances of the case'. Thus, the interests of third parties, for example a party's new partner and children, will also be taken into account. Another example of something that would be taken into account as part of 'all the circumstances' would be a separation agreement previously entered into by the parties (see *G v G (Financial Provision: Separation Agreement)* [2000] 2 FLR 18 and **11.3.4**).

4.5.1　Provision for a spouse

Section 25(2) of MCA 1973 lists the following eight factors to be considered by the court when dealing with ancillary relief for a spouse:

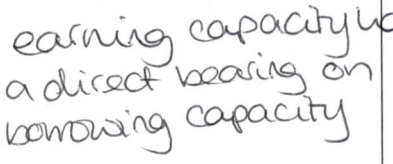
earning capacity has a direct bearing on borrowing capacity

'(a)　the income, earning capacity, property and other financial resources which each of the parties to the marriage has or is likely to have in the foreseeable future [but see s 25B and **4.7.3**], including in the case of earning capacity any increase in that capacity which it would be in the opinion of the court be reasonable to expect a party to the marriage to take steps to acquire;

(b)　the financial needs, obligations and responsibilities which each of the parties to the marriage has or is likely to have in the foreseeable future; *training, relatives*

(c)　the standard of living enjoyed by the family before the breakdown of the marriage; *— middle - high income families*

(d)　the age of each party to the marriage and the duration of the marriage; *— longer together the more important the factor.*

(e)　any physical or mental disability of either of the parties to the marriage;

(f)　the contributions which each of the parties has made or is likely in the foreseeable future to make to the welfare of the family, including any contribution by looking after the home or caring for the family; *— White v White*

✱ *very important — usually middle + high income*

(g) the conduct of each of the parties, if that conduct is such that it would in the opinion of the court be inequitable to disregard it; *—must be serious & relevant to facts* *no adultry — trying to kill etc*

(h) in the case of proceedings for divorce or nullity of marriage any benefit (for example, a pension) which, by reason of the dissolution or annulment of the marriage, that party will lose the chance of acquiring.' *— Get pension*

(a) Resources

Although the statute does not list the factors in any specific order of importance, it is clear that generally the determining factor will be the parties' resources, income and capital. This is as much the case for PPOs as for lump sums and property adjustment orders. Whilst it is convenient to consider the various orders for financial provision separately, in reality the orders interrelate. For example, a husband with a high income may be able to transfer the home to his wife because he is able to raise a mortgage to purchase a new home for himself, but this would be a sensible solution only if the wife has enough income to finance the costs of running her home.

The court will take into account the parties' income from all sources. Earnings are the starting point. Fringe benefits such as a company car, free petrol, paid telephone bills, etc will also be taken into account.

As well as looking at actual earnings, the court will also consider potential earnings. When assessing a party's earning capacity the court will take a realistic approach. If a wife has qualifications which are in demand and has recent work experience, the court will bear in mind her ability to earn a living. However, if she is at home with pre-school (or even older) children, the court will not expect her to leave them and take up a job. Before deciding on a party's earning capacity, the court will carefully consider the person's skills, age and time out of work, the possibility and cost of retraining and the job market. If the court is of the view that a party is perversely refusing to work in order to frustrate a financial application against him, it could make an order by attributing a notional earning capacity to him.

Earning capacity may be significant in determining the duration of periodical payments or a party's occupation of the matrimonial home. If the court considers that a party could reasonably be expected to take steps to increase his earning capacity by, say, undertaking further training, this could prompt the court to limit the period for which maintenance is payable (see **4.6**). It might also result in a reduction of a party's share on sale of the home if a return to work or significant promotion is anticipated with reasonable certainty.

As a general rule, means-tested welfare benefits will not be regarded as a resource since the supporting spouse cannot free himself of his responsibilities to maintain his family by casting that burden onto the taxpayer (*Barnes v Barnes* [1972] 3 All ER 872). However, there will frequently be cases where there are insufficient resources to maintain two households. In such cases, it would be an affront to common sense to ignore the availability of state benefits. The non-means tested child benefit will always be treated as a resource of the party caring for the child. If both parties are claiming benefit, it would be rare for the court to make any order because, as a general principle, the court would not make an order reducing the payer's income below subsistence level (see **7.2.3**).

The court will give a wide interpretation to 'property' and 'financial resources'. The court is not limited to considering assets acquired jointly or during the marriage or even existing assets. As with income, the court may take into account a party's future prospects, for example, a terminal gratuity or an interest under a settlement or inheritance (but generally only if the donor has already died). If it is uncertain whether or when a party might acquire the anticipated property or how much that property will be worth, it might be appropriate for the court to adjourn the application. In such a case, no final decision will be made, leaving the parties to wait and see whether (and to what extent) the anticipated property materialises during the period of the adjournment. In the case of *Michael v Michael* [1986] 2 FLR 389, Nourse LJ said it would be wrong to take into account the possibility of a wife's inheritance from her mother who was in her sixties and suffered from high blood pressure, saying the world was full of women in their eighties who had high blood pressure in their sixties.

Income from other members of the household such as 'board' paid by a working child or lodger, will be taken into account as a resource. More problematic is the extent to which the means of a party's new partner are taken into account. The court cannot redistribute a third party's assets and, therefore, it cannot, for example, order a new wife to pay maintenance to the former wife. However, if a second wife was earning and contributing to the household expenses, it would be wrong if the court was unable to take that fact into account. The practice which has emerged, therefore, is that the court will assess the extent to which contributions made by the new partner reduce the party's outgoings, thereby increasing the money available for maintenance payments (see *Slater v Slater and Another* (1982) 3 FLR 364, CA). The paying spouse would still be expected to share the living costs with his new partner and, therefore, even if that partner was very wealthy and meeting all the expenses, this would not result in the payer being liable to pay his entire income to his first family. If the applicant has a new partner the same principles apply: to the extent that he is supporting the applicant her needs will be reduced. Clearly, the court will have regard to the stability of that relationship and may decide to preserve the party's option to apply to vary an order should the relationship break down. If the payee remarries, she will lose her entitlement to maintenance altogether.

If a party has not remarried, the court will not speculate on that party's prospects of improving his financial circumstances by finding a partner. Nevertheless, if a party does have a firm intention to remarry or cohabit at the time an order for provision is being sought (including an order by consent), this will amount to a material fact which should be disclosed to the other party and to the court. This information may affect the outcome of proceedings or negotiations, for example, as periodical payments terminate on remarriage they may be more appropriate than a lump sum or property adjustment order if a party is soon to be amply supported and housed by his new spouse. If remarriage plans are not disclosed, then any order made is liable to be set aside (see *Livesey (formerly Jenkins) v Jenkins* [1985] AC 424 and **10.7**).

(b) Needs

Section 25(2)(b) of MCA 1973 directs the court to consider the parties' needs, obligations and responsibilities: for most couples the primary task will be to assess each party's essential needs. The most basic of these needs is the provision of accommodation for both parties and any children. Also important will be the expenses connected with the accommodation and the costs of food and clothing.

These costs will vary from case to case depending on the size of the home, the number of people living in it and the general cost of living in the particular locality. In addition to considering these basic needs, the court must also consider the parties' existing obligations, for example, hire-purchase, bank loans, school fees, insurance premiums and television rental, etc. The courts have tended to construe s 25(2)(b) as confining them to have regard only to such requirements as are reasonable – as Ward J stated in *Delaney v Delaney* [1990] 2 FLR 457, CA:

> 'In all life, for those who are divorced as well as for those who are not divorced, indulging one's whims or even one's reasonable desires must be held in check by the constraints imposed by limited resources and compelling obligations.'

However, there will usually be little to gain in increasing the legal costs burden by challenging a party's existing outgoings unless he is being excessively extravagant. If a party is already committed to make certain payments, the courts will be reluctant to disregard the impact of those liabilities on that party's disposable income.

One of the most controversial obligations is that of the respondent who has 'indulged' himself by forming a new relationship (and possibly by having further children). It was noted at *(a)* above that the resources of a party's new partner would be borne in mind when assessing that party's disposable income. It is, therefore, only reasonable that if the new partner is financially dependent upon the party, this fact will be taken into account. The court will consider the extent to which the financially dominant party can meet the needs of the other party and the children of the family bearing in mind his additional responsibilities towards his new partner (and family). The result may be that a substantially reduced order is made, in some cases leaving the applicant to look to the State to meet her needs. The point was made graphically in the case of *Delaney* (above):

> 'Whilst this court deprecates any notion that a former husband and extant father may slough off the tight skin of familial responsibility and may slither into and lose himself in the greener grass on the other side, nonetheless this court has proclaimed and will proclaim that it looks to the realities of the real world in which we live, and that among the realities of life is that there is a life after divorce. The respondent husband is entitled to order his life in such a way as will hold in reasonable balance the responsibilities to his existing family which he carries into his new life, as well as his proper aspirations for that new future.'

It follows from this that if a respondent has obligations to wives and children of former marriages, these will also be taken into account when considering the application of any subsequent spouse.

Where the parties are well off, the court will look beyond their basic needs to try to achieve an equitable distribution of the couple's resources. In doing so, the court will have regard to the parties' standard of living during the marriage and their contributions to the welfare of the family (see *Gojkovic v Gojkovic* [1990] 1 FLR 140, CA). Indeed, in cases such as *White v White* [1998] 2 FLR 310, CA, where parties had effectively worked in partnership, contributing together to the wealth built up during a long marriage, the courts appear to be moving towards a more-or-less equal sharing of their jointly acquired assets rather than focusing on the s 25 factor of 'needs'.

(c) Standard of living

In applying s 25(2)(c) the court will not attempt the impossible by seeking to preserve both parties' standard of living at its level prior to the breakdown of the marriage. On separation, there will be the increased costs of running two households usually without any increase in either party's income. Instead, the court will endeavour to ensure that the inevitable reduction in the parties' standard of living is borne by them evenly.

Where a couple have lived frugally and enjoyed only a modest standard of living, perhaps preferring to invest their resources in their business or to save for their retirement, the court will look at the wider picture. An applicant would not be penalised for having lived carefully during the marriage by an order for humble provision. On the contrary, the order should reflect the contributions made by the thrifty housekeeper towards the family's prosperity.

(d) Ages of the parties and the duration of the marriage

Taken in isolation, the importance of s 25(2)(d) is not immediately obvious. However, taken in conjunction with the other factors, its significance is more apparent: a young wife without children ending a short marriage is likely to have an earning and borrowing capacity and, therefore, a package of orders to enable a couple to achieve financial independence (known as a clean break) may be appropriate. On the other hand, an older spouse leaving a long marriage may have little or no earning capacity, but is likely to have made a greater contribution to the marriage and there are usually more family assets to distribute. A middle-aged or elderly couple may not necessarily have enjoyed a long marriage. However, if a mature couple have had only a short marriage the court will bear in mind the consequences of that marriage on the parties. In particular, it will have regard to any loss of prospects resulting from the marriage, for example, jobs or promotion sacrificed or tenancies surrendered on entering into the marriage (see *S v S* [1977] 1 All ER 56, CA). A similar principle applies to young couples ending a short marriage of say, 2 years, but who have children. The needs of the children will outweigh the fact that the marriage was short, not least because children are likely to diminish the earning capacity of the parent raising them (see *C v C (Financial Relief: Short Marriage)* [1997] 2 FLR 26, CA).

It is the cohabitation during the marriage which is relevant in s 25(2)(d): the Court of Appeal in *Krystman v Krystman* [1973] 3 All ER 247 refused to order financial provision where the couple lived together for only 2 weeks of their 26-year marriage. As for cohabitation prior to marriage, the court is not required to take this into account under s 25(2)(d), however, it may be taken into account when the court considers 'all the circumstances of the case' under s 25(1) (*Kokosinski v Kokosinski* [1980] Fam 72). In the more recent case of *Gojkovic* (above), the wife received a substantial award based on her contributions to the family fortune made largely during their pre-marital cohabitation.

(e) Disability

If a party suffers from a physical or mental disability this may affect that party's resources as he may have a reduced (or no) earning capacity. It will also affect the sufferer's needs if, for example, expensive care, treatment or equipment is required. The court will also bear in mind the effect of any future deterioration in the party's condition. It has been held that damages awarded to compensate a party for personal injury are rightly to be regarded as a resource for that party under s 25(2)(a) notwithstanding that they were assessed to compensate that party for their loss, pain and suffering.

(f) Contributions to the family

The court is required by s 25(2)(f) to consider the parties' past and anticipated future contributions to the welfare of the family, both materially and otherwise. Where the wife has contributed in non-financial terms to the marriage, it is not necessary for her to show the extensive contributions in kind of the sort required to establish a proprietary interest under a constructive trust (see Chapter 15). The court is not deciding the ownership of the family assets, but rather how each party's assets should be shared.

It has been recognised for some time that a wife who cares for the home and the family contributes as much to the family as the wife who goes out to work (see *Wachtel v Wachtel* [1973] 1 All ER 829). In the *Gojkovic* case (above), the judge at first instance found that the wife had made 'exceptional contributions to the wealth generated during their relationship and marriage' and that she 'was in at the beginning, committed (as he was) to contributing financially, physically and emotionally'. Upholding the judge's decision to award the wife a lump sum of £1m, Butler-Sloss LJ makes it clear: the 'share is not to be calculated exclusively in relation to her needs ... Equally important as financial needs is, however, the contribution made by each of the parties to the welfare of the family...'.

The party who has been primarily responsible for raising the children will have that contribution recognised. The court will bear in mind the impact of that role on the carer's career. It will also take into account the continuing contributions that the parent will make as the children grow up.

Conversely, the court may also take into account any negative contribution made by a party: in the case of *E v E (Financial Provision)* [1990] 2 FLR 233, FD, Mrs E, while having an adulterous affair, was said to have spent thousands of pounds on clothes and to have withdrawn from family life. The judge found that 'the wife's contribution to the welfare of the family was negative' and added: 'I do not find it necessary to consider conduct as a separate item. Such conduct as has been shown can properly be dealt with by considering the contribution the wife has made to the welfare of the family'. Whilst, then, it would be exceptional for adultery to be taken into account under s 25(2)(g) (see *(g)* below), if affairs have resulted in a party failing to contribute to the family, this may be taken into account.

(g) Conduct

Either party to the divorce may apply for financial provision: it is not a case of the 'guilty respondent' maintaining the 'innocent petitioner'. Whether, and to what extent, one party will be required to support the other will depend on all the factors appearing in s 25 of which conduct is but one.

Prior to 1984 the court took into account only such conduct as could be described as 'gross and obvious' (*Wachtel v Wachtel* above). Since s 25(2)(g) was introduced (by the Matrimonial and Family Proceedings Act 1984, s 3), the court is required to consider conduct which it would be inequitable to disregard. That must include, but is not confined to, gross and obvious conduct (*Kyte v Kyte* [1987] 3 All ER 1041, CA).

In practice, it will be rare for a party's misconduct to be raised; if substantial allegations are made the case may be transferred to the High Court (see Practice Direction [1992] 3 All ER 151). Conduct may be an issue, however, where it has a direct bearing on the parties' finances. Examples of cases where conduct was an issue include:

(1) *Martin v Martin* [1976] 3 All ER 625, CA: the husband frittered away joint assets in recklessly hopeless business ventures.

(2) *K v K (Conduct)* [1990] 2 FLR 225: the husband had a serious drink problem which contributed to his refusal to obtain employment and his neglect of the house which ultimately forced its sale. Although the husband succeeded in obtaining a lump sum his application for periodical payments was dismissed.

(3) *Jones v Jones* [1975] 2 All ER 12, CA: the court transferred the house into the wife's sole name having taken into account her husband's attack on her hand with a razor blade which put an end to her career as a nurse. In *H v H (Financial Provision: Conduct)* [1994] 2 FLR 801, the court again transferred the house into the wife's sole name as a result of a serious attack on the wife by the husband; this time because the husband's conduct and subsequent imprisonment and loss of his job meant that he had destroyed his ability to support the wife and children to the standard he had previously done so.

(4) *Evans v Evans* [1989] 1 FLR 351, CA: the court discharged a maintenance order made in favour of the wife after she was convicted (and imprisoned) for inciting others to murder the husband.

The fact that an applicant has committed adultery will not bar her from seeking financial provision. The adultery itself will not be relevant unless there are aggravating circumstances, as there were in *Bailey v Tolliday* (1983) 4 FLR 542 where the petitioner's father was the co-respondent.

Another possiblity is that a party's misconduct may relate to the proceedings themselves, such as failure to make full and frank disclosure of means. In *Clark v Clark* [1999] 2 FLR 498, CA, the court distinguished between marital misconduct, which may affect the quantification of orders made, as opposed to litigation misconduct, which generally should only be penalised in costs. Examples of cases involving litigation misconduct include the following.

(1) *T v T (Interception of Documents)* [1994] 2 FLR 1083: the wife intercepted the husband's mail and broke into his office in an attempt to ascertain his true financial position. The court's approach was that, whilst this misconduct would not be brought into the reckoning of the substantive award, it was relevant in respect of costs.

(2) *P v P (Financial Relief: Non-Disclosure)* [1994] 2 FLR 381: the court found the wife guilty of misconduct when she concealed a number of assets and the presence of a cohabitee. Again, although she was not penalised by a reduction in the overall provision, she was ordered to pay her own costs (estimated at £40,000).

In *Clark* (above), the wife had committed both marital and litigation misconduct. However, in that case, both types of misconduct were reflected by reducing the wife's award for a lump sum because the reality was that both the husband's costs (approximately £200,000) and the wife's costs (approximately £250,000) were effectively being funded from the husband's assets. This meant that there was no point in making any order for costs.

FLA 1996, assuming it comes into force, will change the wording of s 25(2)(g) to:

'The conduct of each of the parties whatever the nature of the conduct and whether it occurred during the marriage or after the separation of the parties or (as the case may be) dissolution or annulment of the marriage if the conduct is such that it would in the opinion of the court be inequitable to disregard it.'

This may appear to be placing a greater emphasis on the issue of conduct. Presumably though, it is just intended to restate the court's current approach of considering all possible types of conduct, whether arising during the marriage or during the court proceedings themselves, and exercising its discretion on a case-by-case basis. The Lord Chancellor has said:

> 'The role of conduct in ancillary relief proceedings has not changed and there is therefore no question, as has been suggested in some quarters, of conduct being introduced through the back door.'

(h) Potential financial loss

When dealing with applications ancillary to divorce or nullity (but not judicial separation), s 25(2)(h) requires the court to consider any potential benefits a party might lose as a result of the termination of the marriage. The loss of pension rights is an example. As a widow or widower the applicant would normally be entitled to the deceased spouse's pension: that right would be lost on the termination of the marriage. This can be a serious problem to, say, a financially dependent middle-aged wife of a long marriage. In such cases there may be an argument for giving that spouse a greater share of the other matrimonial assets to mitigate the problem and perhaps also for preserving the wife's claim under the Inheritance (Provision for Family and Dependants) Act 1975. Alternatively, the wife could apply under the provisions of the Pensions Act 1995 or the new Welfare Reform and Pensions Act 1999 (see **4.7**).

Other contingent benefits which a party might lose include a share in life policies which are yet to mature. The lost opportunity to share in the other party's prospective inheritance will only be taken into account if it is sufficiently certain in time and amount (see **4.4.1**).

It should be noted that some legislative provisions, including MCA 1973, s 25, cannot be interpreted in accordance with the European Convention on Human Rights. Article 5 of the Seventh Protocol states that 'spouses shall enjoy equality of rights and responsibilities of a private law character between them, and in their relations with their children, as to marriage, and in the event of dissolution'. Yet, under s 25, the starting point in an application for ancillary relief is not necessarily equality between the spouses. Because of the difficulty in interpretation of this and other provisions, this Article was specifically excluded from being incorporated into the Human Rights Act 1998.

4.5.2 Provision for children

The interests of the children of the family are borne in mind when any financial order is made under MCA 1973. Section 25(1) requires the court 'to give first consideration to the welfare while a minor of any child of the family' when considering making any financial order on divorce. Therefore, when considering its powers to provide for the parties, any order made will reflect not only the needs of those parties but also of the children.

The court has wide powers to make capital orders in favour of the children of the family. However, it is not usual for the court to make capital orders in favour of children: in *Lord Lilford v Glyn* [1979] 1 WLR 78, Orr LJ stated 'a father, even the richest father, ought not to be regarded as under financial obligations or responsibilities to provide funds for the purpose of such settlements that are envisaged in this case on children who are under no disability and whose maintenance and education are secure'. In contrast, provision will be required for children's maintenance. It has already been noted (at **4.1**) that applications for children's maintenance usually will be made under the Child Support Act 1991 to the Child Support Agency rather than to the court. This is considered in detail in Chapter 7. However, the court will continue to have limited jurisdiction to deal with maintenance orders for certain children and in such cases the factors in s 25 must be considered.

When considering what orders should be made for children, the court is guided by s 25(3) in all cases. Section 25(4) lists further factors to be taken into account where the payer is not the natural parent of the child.

Children of the family

Section 25(3) directs the court to consider the following factors when making orders for children of the family:

> '(a)   the financial needs of the child;
>
> (b)   the income, earning capacity (if any), property and other financial resources of the child;
>
> (c)   any physical or mental disability of the child;
>
> (d)   the manner in which he was being and in which the parties to the marriage expected him to be educated or trained;
>
> (e)   the considerations mentioned in relation to the parties to the marriage in s 25(2)(a), (b), (c) and (e).'

The factors are generally self-explanatory but one or two points are worth noting. Clearly, the needs of the child will increase with age: the section does not refer to the child's future needs as these needs are best dealt with by further applications for increased maintenance as and when required.

Most young children do not have any income or earning capacity. However, maintenance may be sought for children who are receiving wages, grants or scholarships whilst in education or training and such sums would be taken into account. In wealthier families, children may have trust income to be borne in mind.

The court will wish to ensure that adequate provision is made for children with a disability. It might, in particular, consider making secure PPOs to provide for a stable income. It might also be appropriate to make lump sum orders to meet capital expenditure on, for example, special equipment adapted for the child's handicap. The disability may also affect the duration of the order as special circumstances could lead to the provision continuing well into adulthood.

Section 25(3)(e) requires the court to look at the parties' resources, needs, standard of living and any disability. This is because the parties' ability to provide for their children is directly related to and dependent upon their own circumstances.

Step-children

Section 25(4) requires the following additional factors to be considered where the child in question, although a child of the family, is not the natural child of the party against whom an order is being sought:

> '(a)   whether that party assumed any responsibility for the child's maintenance, and, if so, to the extent to which, and the basis upon which, that party assumed such responsibility and to the length of time for which that party discharged such responsibility;
>
> (b)   whether in assuming and discharging such responsibility that party did so knowing that the child was not his or her own;
>
> (c)   the liability of any other person to maintain the child.'

The section recognises that a child may be a child of more than one family and, as a consequence, several people may be liable to maintain that child. For example, a husband may have treated his wife's child from a previous relationship as his own: in such a case both the husband and the father could be looked to for support. Clearly, the factors in s 25(4) will be highly relevant in determining the extent of this support. If the child's father is meeting the child's maintenance requirement under the Child Support Act 1991 (see Chapter 7), this may relieve the step-father from paying maintenance.

4.6 THE CLEAN BREAK

4.6.1 The principle

The object of the clean break is to settle once and for all the parties' financial responsibility towards each other and to end their financial inter-dependence to enable them to leave their past behind them and begin anew. The advantages of such an approach have long been recognised but with the enactment of the Matrimonial and Family Proceedings Act 1984 which introduced s 25A into MCA 1973, the concept of the clean break was given statutory backing. Since the 1984 Act the court has a duty to consider whether a clean break should be achieved.

Section 25A(1) states:

> 'Where on or after the grant of a decree of divorce or nullity of marriage the court decides to exercise its powers under s 23(1)(a), (b) or (c), 24 or 24A above in favour of a party to the marriage, it shall be the duty of the court to consider whether it would be appropriate so to exercise those powers that the financial obligations of each party towards the other will be terminated as soon after the grant of the decree as the court considers just and reasonable.'

Although the court has a duty to consider the appropriateness of a clean break, it has been made clear (see *Barrett v Barrett* [1988] 2 FLR 516, CA) that s 25A does not oblige the court to make a clean break wherever possible. Rather, the court must weigh all the statutory factors in deciding whether a clean break is appropriate on the facts of the particular case. It will never be appropriate to have a clean break between a parent and child, as a party can never sever his responsibility towards a child of the family. It is possible, however, to have a clean break between the parties even where there are children involved. In cases where the court has jurisdiction to make orders for children, it might award less than it would otherwise do because the parent with whom the children are residing has agreed a clean break settlement. For example, the father might be using a significant amount of his income to pay for a loan which was raised in order to make a generous lump sum payment for the mother who is caring for the children. The father would clearly have less income available to support the children directly but they will be benefiting indirectly from the lump sum payment. However, should the mother subsequently apply for a maintenance assessment under the Child Support Act 1991 the father might then find himself being required to pay substantially more maintenance than he had bargained for. This is because when calculating the absent parent's liability to pay maintenance under the 1991 Act, generally no account is taken of any clean break made on divorce. However, if the clean break settlement was made before April 1993 (ie before the Child Support Act 1991 came into force) then some allowance can be made (see **7.3.7**).

4.6.2 The practice

Income orders

So far as periodical payments are concerned, the most extreme form of clean break is an order dismissing the application coupled with a bar against the making of any further applications. Section 25A(3) empowers the court to make such an order:

> 'Where on or after the grant of a decree of divorce or nullity of marriage an application is made by a party to the marriage for a periodical payments order in his or her favour, then, if the court considers that no continuing obligation should be imposed on either party to make or secure periodical payments in favour of the other, the court may dismiss the application with a direction that the applicant shall not be entitled to make any further application in relation to the marriage for an order under s 23(1)(a) or (b) above.'

The court may even take such a step without the consent of the applicant but would generally only do so where compelling reasons exist. Less extreme than this immediate clean break is an order for 'term maintenance'. Such an order allows a party to receive maintenance for a limited period only in order to tide him over while he adapts to becoming financially self-sufficient. The clean break will be deferred to a future date. The term of the maintenance will vary from case to case: it may be for 6 months to enable the party to find a job, or for 2 or 3 years to allow for retraining. If there are children, it may be for a longer period until they are less dependent on the applicant. If the children are very young, the court is unlikely to consider term maintenance to be appropriate (see *Suter v Suter and Jones* [1987] 2 All ER 336, CA).

It is also not usually considered appropriate to provide for the termination of periodical payments for a spouse in her late forties or fifties, unless she has substantial capital of her own and significant earning capacity (see *Flavell v Flavell* [1997] 1 FLR 353, CA). The courts, particularly in recent years, are much more likely to favour at least a nominal periodical payments order (eg 5p per year), thereby keeping the spouse's periodical payments claim 'alive' so that it can be varied, if necessary, in the future (see *SRJ v DWJ (Financial Provision)* [1999] 2 FLR 176, CA).

The benefits of term maintenance have been given statutory support by s 25A(2) which states:

> 'Where the court decides in such a case to make a periodical payments or secured periodical payments order in favour of a party to the marriage, the court shall in particular consider whether it would be appropriate to require those payments to be

made or secured only for such term as would in the opinion of the court be sufficient to enable the party in whose favour the order is made to adjust without undue hardship to the termination of his or her financial dependence on the other party.'

The question arises as to what happens if events do not work out according to plan and the applicant fails to achieve the anticipated financial independence? The answer is that most applicants could apply under MCA 1973, s 31 to extend the maintenance for a further period. It is essential that any such application is made before the expiry of the term as the order itself ceases at that point. In deciding whether to grant such a request, however, the court would enquire into the reason for the applicant's failure to become self-sufficient. If, for example, the availability of work decreases and the court is satisfied that the applicant has made genuine efforts to seek employment, it is likely to deal with the application sympathetically.

The court is empowered under s 28(1A) to direct that the applicant will not be entitled to make any application to extend the term regardless of any change of circumstances. Whilst this has the advantage for the payer of certainty in that he will eventually be rid of the obligation to maintain his ex-spouse, the inflexibility can lead to hardship to the payee and consequently such directions are rare (see *Waterman v Waterman* [1989] 1 FLR 380, CA).

An alternative approach, mentioned above, is to order substantive maintenance for a fixed period after which it will drop to a nominal sum of, say, 5p per year, so keeping alive the payee's option of applying for an increase. Such an order is not a clean break at all as it affords no certainty to the payer. However, substantive maintenance would only be revived beyond the original term if the circumstances justified it.

Capital orders

A clean break is commonly achieved by means of a lump sum payment in return for a dismissal of all other claims. A party may be so anxious to achieve an immediate clean break that he is prepared to borrow in order to raise capital. The party may prefer to pay a relatively substantial lump sum rather than have the burden of even modest maintenance hanging over him for an indefinite period. Lump sums are discussed further at **8.7**. It may be that there is no clean break initially between the parties, but that one occurs later on; see **10.8.1**, which deals with the court's power to impose a clean break at a later stage, by making lump sum adjustment orders, on an application for variation or discharge of an existing periodical payment or secured periodical payments order.

There are only two ways of dealing with the matrimonial home to achieve an immediate clean break: by immediate sale, or a transfer into one party's sole name. These and other orders for the matrimonial home are considered in detail in Chapter 8.

As part of a clean break package a provision is often included under s 15 of the Inheritance (Provision for Family and Dependants) Act 1975. This enables the court to direct that neither party may apply under s 2 of the Act for financial provision out of the other's estate.

4.7 PENSIONS ON DIVORCE

A pension is often a person's most valuable asset, or it will be when it comes to being paid, so it is not surprising that dividing it should be a major consideration in settling the financial aspects of divorce, particularly for older couples. Until recently, the courts have been reluctant to interfere in the operation of the pension scheme itself in order to redress the balance for one party to a marriage who has had a lesser earning capacity than the other. The Pensions Act 1995 and the Welfare Reform and Pensions Act 1999, have made significant reforms in this area.

There are now three possible ways of dealing with pension rights on divorce. These are:

(1) follow the traditional approach by adjusting the other matrimonial assets to take account of pension rights (often described as 'off-setting');

(2) apply the Pensions Act 1995 which allows for all or part of any pension or lump sum arising at retirement to be 'earmarked' for the other spouse;

(3) apply for the pension to be split so that the pension benefits are physically subdivided at the time of the divorce; the parties will then have two entirely separate pensions which they can contribute to in the future in the normal way. This 'pension-sharing' is provided for in the Welfare Reform and Pensions Act 1999, which is in force from 1 December 2000.

4.7.1 The traditional approach – 'off-setting'

MCA 1973 refers, in a limited way, to pension rights. Section 25(2)(a) says that when the courts consider the 'financial resources' of the parties this can include those which will be available 'in the foreseeable future'. However, this phrase is not defined and the courts have sometimes interpreted it as meaning not more than ten years away (*Milne v Milne* [1981] 2 FLR 286 and *Hedges v Hedges* [1991] 1 FLR 196). This used to mean that pension rights which are payable after that time were often ignored completely, despite their potential value.

Although s 25(2)(h) says the court must have regard to the value of any benefit which a party will lose the chance of acquiring as a result of the divorce, such as pension rights, the courts, in the past, did not have any powers to make orders specifically dealing with the parties' pension arrangements. So, what, if anything, could the courts do to take account of valuable pension rights? Until recently, the best that the courts have been able to do in making appropriate settlements on divorce is to allocate to one spouse (normally the wife) a proportion of the matrimonial assets equivalent to the approximate value of the pension benefits lost. This means that a trade-off is being made between the pension rights and other matrimonial assets. However, this is not always an entirely appropriate solution: there are problems of valuation, and there is the fact that the trade-off must be made immediately at the time of the divorce yet the pension benefits themselves will be in the future and are contingent on certain events (eg retirement, death) and possibly may never materialise. In past years there was also the problem that the value of the matrimonial home (most couples' other main asset) might have fallen. This meant that there may not have been sufficient other matrimonial assets to trade-off against pension benefits.

4.7.2 The Pensions Act 1995 – 'earmarking'

Section 166 of the Pensions Act 1995 brought about important changes in relation to provision for pensions on divorce. Three new sections were inserted into MCA 1973 – ss 25B, 25C and 25D. These sections allow the court to 'earmark' certain payments under a pension to be paid not to the member of the pension scheme but to his former spouse.

Section 25B

This section says that, in relation to benefits under a pension scheme, the words 'in the foreseeable future' in s 25(2)(a) shall not apply. This means that the court can take into account any future pension benefits.

The section also gives the court the power, when making a financial provision order, to direct the trustees or managers of a pension scheme to pay some (or even all) of the pension to the spouse without the pension rights. If the pension is not yet payable (ie the member-spouse has not yet retired) the court may make a deferred order. Such orders will effectively be like deferred maintenance orders.

Section 25C

Most pension schemes include a lump sum benefit payable on retirement or on the death of the member before retirement. This section gives the court the power to make a lump sum order which directs the trustees or managers of the pension scheme to pay the whole or part of that lump sum, when it becomes due, to the other spouse.

Section 25D

This section deals with supplementary provisions, such as valuations and what happens if the member-spouse transfers from one pension scheme to another.

The court can only apply its 'earmarking' powers under these sections in relation to an application for financial provisions arising where the petition was filed with the court on or after 1 July 1996. Orders could be made from 1 July 1996, although orders earmarking pension payments (as opposed to lump sums) could only be in relation to benefits falling due on or after 6 April 1997.

It seems that applicants may not be making as much use of these new powers as was perhaps anticipated. There have only been two reported cases – *T v T (Financial Relief: Pensions)* [1998] 1 FLR 1072, and *Burrows v Burrows* [1999] 1 FLR 508. In both cases, the courts held that the earmarking provisions allowed under ss 25B–D did not create a statutory right to a share in a spouse's pension fund. The court, in determining whether to make an earmarking award and the amount, if any, should exercise its discretion under the established s 25 criteria.

4.7.3 The Welfare Reform and Pensions Act 1999 – 'pension sharing'

The Pensions Act 1995 gave the courts more possibilities for redressing the harsh effects of loss of pension rights on divorce. Nevertheless, there were still problems. Earmarking of orders will usually be deferred until the member-spouse retires or dies. This means that the other spouse has no control over the money until that time and, for example, the member-spouse could decide to retire early or late. Also, such orders are contrary to the clean break principle. As a result of these, and other problems, it seems that, as mentioned above, very few pension earmarking orders are being made in practice.

The Pensions Act 1995 stopped short of the proposals set out in the report 'Pensions on Divorce' produced in 1993 by an independent working group appointed by the Pensions Management Institute in agreement with The Law Society. This report proposed that the courts should be able to split pension rights at the time of divorce. This could be done by directing that a transfer payment equal in value to a proportion of the member-spouse's pension rights should be made to a pension arrangement which could then provide retirement benefits for the other spouse. In this way, both parties would have immediate control over their own pension provisions.

Although the government of the day resisted pension sharing in the Pensions Act 1995, it was defeated on this issue when FLA 1996 was debated in the House of Lords. As a result, s 16 of FLA 1996 provided, in principle, for pension sharing by the courts and has been followed by the Welfare Reform and Pensions Act 1999 (WRPA 1999), in force from 1 December 2000.

When a pension sharing order can be made

Schedule 3 to WRPA 1999 inserts a new s 24B into MCA 1973, which states:

> '(1) On granting a decree of divorce or a decree of nullity of marriage or at any time thereafter (whether before or after the decree is made absolute) the court may, on an application made under this section, make one or more pension sharing orders in relation to the marriage.'

This pension sharing provision will only apply to petitions filed after 1 December 2000 as the legislation is not retrospective. Also, pension sharing will be available on divorce (or nullity) but not on judicial separation.

Any pension sharing order made will not take effect until the divorce decree has been made absolute.

Types of pension which can be shared

A party will be able to apply for a pension sharing order if their spouse is a member of an occupational pension scheme or personal pension scheme. Pension sharing will also apply to most public service pensions and the State Earnings Related Pension Schemes (SERPS) but not to the basic state retirement pension.

The pension sharing order

WRPA 1999 inserts a new s 21A into MCA 1973:

> '(1) for the purposes of this Act, a pension sharing order is an order which—
>
> > (a)   provides that one party's—
> >
> > > (i)   shareable rights under a specified pension arrangement, or
> > >
> > > (ii) shareable State scheme rights
> > >
> > > be subject to pension sharing for the benefit of the other party, and
> >
> > (b)   specifies the percentage value to be transferred.'

The types of pension covered by this section has already been mentioned above.

On the making of a pension sharing order, the transferor loses the percentage required to be transferred which reduces the value of his fund – 'the pension debit'.

The transferee acquires the right to be credited with that amount – 'the pension credit'. The transferee thus gains an amount which will fund a quite separate pension of his or her own which is not in any way contingent on the transferor taking his own pension.

Depending on the type of pension scheme involved, the transferee may have a choice as to whether to become a member of the transferor's pension scheme, but in their own right (known as an 'internal transfer') or to transfer to a different pension scheme (an 'external transfer').

Pension rights will be valued using the method already in use for valuing the rights of 'early leavers' from occupational pension schemes or members of personal pension schemes who wish to transfer their accrued rights to another pension scheme. This is known as the Cash Equivalent Transfer Value.

The amount to be transferred must be expressed as a percentage of this value rather than in cash terms (WRPA 1999, s 249(2)). It is important to remember that an order may be made stipulating any percentage the court considers appropriate, not necessarily 50:50.

Any solicitor advising a client about pension sharing must be careful not to infringe the provisions of the Financial Services Act 1986. For advice on, for example, whether to opt for an internal or external transfer, the client needs to be referred to an Independent Financial Adviser.

Pension sharing and the other options

The Government has estimated that there will be 50,000 pension sharing orders per year. However, there will still be many cases where pensions are not an issue or, if they are, pension sharing may not necessarily be the most appropriate course of action. There is no obligation on the court to make a pension sharing order and 'off-setting' or earmarking remain an alternative. The court must, as always in ancillary relief matters, consider each case on its facts by applying the principles and factors set out in MCA 1973, s 25.

One restriction on the options available to the court is that it is not possible to make both a pension sharing order and a pension earmarking order in relation to the same pension arrangement. Therefore, the court could not, for example, earmark the lump sum death benefit and share the member's other rights. Also a pension sharing order may not be made in relation to a pension arrangement which is already the subject of a pension sharing order in relation to the marriage (MCA 1973, s 24B(3) and (4)).

4.8 ANCILLARY RELIEF IN THE FUTURE

FLA 1996, Part II, if it comes into force, will not substantially change the law relating to ancillary relief. The law will continue as set out in MCA 1973 but with some modifications as a result of Schs 2 and 8 to the 1996 Act.

The most significant change will be in the timing of financial orders. As explained at **1.6**, under FLA 1996, a divorce will not be granted until financial arrangements have been made and the 9- or 15-month period for consideration and reflection has passed. However, financial orders will not actually take effect until the divorce is granted (apart from exceptional cases). This means that divorce will take longer and a party will often have to wait longer for a financial order than is currently the case.

In order to mitigate the cases of hardship that this is bound to cause, the courts will have the power to make interim periodical payment orders and interim lump sum orders (instead of maintenance pending suit). The power to make interim lump sum orders will be an important development as this is something which the courts, at present, are not able to do (see *Wicks v Wicks* [1998] 1 FLR 470, CA).

Whether or not Part II of FLA 1996 comes into force, further reform is possible. The Lord Chancellor has asked the Ancillary Relief Advisory Group to consider whether the current ancillary relief provisions contained in MCA 1973 should be amended. He has asked the Advisory Group to consider, in particular, a system similar to that in Scotland so that, in the absence of a pre- (or post-) nuptial agreement, property would be split 50/50 between the parties unless, for example, such a split would do substantial injustice to one of the parties or to a child of the marriage, or there is some other substantial reason why such a split should not be enforced. Such a system would be a radical departure from the current law and practice.

4.9 FINANCIAL PROVISION DURING MARRIAGE

It may be that a spouse is in need of financial provision during a marriage and yet is not ready to make a decision regarding divorce or judicial separation. In such circumstances, a spouse may bring proceedings under MCA 1973, s 27 in a divorce county court or under the Domestic Proceedings and Magistrates' Courts Act 1978 (DPMCA 1978) in the family proceedings court.

4.9.1 Matrimonial Causes Act 1973, s 27

MCA 1973, s 27 allows either party to a marriage to apply for financial provision on the ground that the respondent has failed to provide reasonable maintenance for the applicant or has failed to provide or make a proper contribution towards the reasonable maintenance for any child of the family. The court can make orders for periodical payments (including secured provision) and lump sums. In contrast to DPMCA 1978, there is no ceiling on the amount of any lump sum, although as with the 1978 Act there is no power to make property adjustment orders. In determining whether to make provision, the court will have regard to all the circumstances of the case including many of the factors set out in s 25 (see **4.5.1**).

The duration of periodical payments orders made under s 27 are precisely the same as those for ordinary periodical payments made on divorce (see **4.3.2**). The court also has power to make interim orders and orders for periodical payments may be varied under MCA 1973, s 31 in the usual way (see **10.8**).

Application under MCA 1973, s 27 has never been common. The need for such applications is now diminished since, where a married couple are separated and have natural children, the appropriate application for maintenance for the children will be to the Child Support Agency rather than under MCA 1973, s 27.

4.9.2 Financial provision in the family proceedings court

The Domestic Proceedings and Magistrates' Courts Act 1978 enables a party to a marriage to seek financial provision in the family proceedings court during the subsistence of the marriage. The court may make orders for periodical payments for a spouse as well as for a child of the family and it may make lump sum orders. There are two main types of application under DPMCA 1978: contested applications under s 2, and applications by consent under s 6.

Contested applications

In order to bring an application under DPMCA 1978, s 2, the applicant must establish one of the grounds in s 1, ie that the respondent has not sufficiently provided for the applicant or a child of the family, or the respondent's behaviour has been unreasonable, or the respondent has deserted the applicant. The court will have regard to the factors listed in s 3 which are broadly similar to MCA 1973, s 25.

Any lump sum order made on a contested application is limited to £1,000 although, unlike MCA 1973, s 23, there is no bar against making further applications.

Agreed applications

If the parties agree financial provision, either may apply for an order under DPMCA 1978, s 6 to endorse their agreement.

The court is also able to approve agreements to pay a lump sum of any amount.

Duration of periodical payments

Whether the order is made pursuant to ss 2 or 6 it may be backdated to the date of application. The order will cease on the death of either party or on the remarriage of the payee. It is unaffected by the termination of the marriage although it will usually be discharged and replaced by any order made under MCA 1973, s 23 by the divorce county court. Periodical payments to a spouse for herself or for the benefit of a child will cease if the parties resume cohabitation for a continuous period of more than 6 months (s 25(1)). Payments ordered to be payable direct to a child will be unaffected by cohabitation. The child's maintenance will terminate in the same circumstances as under MCA 1973, s 29(3) (see **4.3.2**).

Use of DPMCA 1978 is less common following the enactment of the Child Support Act 1991 (considered in detail in Chapter 7 below). If a couple separate, the parent with care may seek provision through the Child Support Agency unless the child does not qualify (eg a step-child). If a maintenance assessment could be made under the Child Support Act 1991, it must be pursued through the Agency rather than the family proceedings court. However, DPMCA 1978 may be invoked by children who are in higher education (and therefore no longer liable to be maintained under the Child Support Act 1991) and for lump sum orders.

4.10 CHAPTER SUMMARY

(1) On divorce, a divorce county court (or the High Court) can make one or more of the following financial orders in favour of a spouse:

maintenance pending suit;

periodical payments;

secured periodical payments;

lump sum order;

property adjustment order;

order for sale;

pension earmarking order;

pension sharing order.

(2) The court can also make any of these orders (except for maintenance pending suit) in favour of a child. However, in most cases, periodical payments for a child are now dealt with by the Child Support Agency and it is unusual to obtain the other types of order, such as a lump sum order, for a child.

(3) Whenever the court considers making a financial order on divorce, it must consider:

(a) the general principle in s 25(1)	– all the circumstances of the case with first consideration given to the welfare of any child of the family under 18 years; and
(b) the factors in s 25(2)	– income, earning capacity and other resources;
	– needs and responsibilities; standard of living;
	– age of the parties and duration of the marriage;
	– disability; contributions to the family;
	– conduct;
	– potential financial loss.

There are other factors for the court to refer to when considering making financial orders for a child or stepchild (s 25(3) and (4)).

(4) Under s 25A, the court always has a duty to consider whether a clean break should be achieved.

(5) It is important to be aware of the significance of pensions on divorce and the ways in which the court can try to adjust the financial position of the parties on retirement.

(6) A spouse who is not divorcing can still apply to the court for financial provision, either:

(a) to the divorce county court, under s 27 of MCA 1973, for periodical payments and/or a lump sum order; or

(b) to the family proceedings court, under the DPMCA 1978, for periodical payments and/or a maximum £1,000 lump sum order.

4.11 FURTHER READING

Rakusen, Hunt and Bridge *Distribution of Matrimonial Assets on Divorce* 3rd edn (Butterworths, 1989); 1992 supplement (Butterworths, 1992)

Black *A Practical Approach to Family Law* 6th edn (Blackstone Press, 2000)

Jackson *Matrimonial Finance and Taxation* 6th edn (Butterworths, 1996); 2000 supplement (Butterworths, 2000)

Bird *Pension Sharing – The New Law: Welfare Reform and Pensions Act 1999* (Family Law, 1999)

Salter *Pensions and Insurance on Family Breakdown* 2nd edn (Family Law, 1999)

Duckworth *Matrimonial Property and Finance* (Jordans, 2000)

Family Law Bar Association *At A Glance 2000–2001: Essential Court Tables for Ancillary Relief* 9th edn (FLBA, 2000)

Chapter 5

TAX ON MARRIAGE BREAKDOWN

5.1 INTRODUCTION

This chapter deals with the effect of marriage breakdown on the tax position of the couple.

5.2 TAX ON MARRIAGE BREAKDOWN

Where the assets owned by the divorcing couple are numerous and complicated, it may be wise to enlist the help of an accountant when considering tax planning. None the less, the solicitor should be aware of the major tax effects of marriage breakdown and some basic tax planning points. For a reminder of the basic principles of income tax, capital gains tax and inheritance tax, see LPC Resource Book *Pervasive and Core Topics* (Jordans).

5.2.1 Income tax

Changes to the income tax regime which came into effect in April 2000 effectively removed scope for tax planning.

There is now:

– no tax relief on maintenance payments, whether for a spouse or a child (maintenance is tax free in the hands of the recipient);
– no married couple's or single parent allowance;
– no tax relief on mortgage interest payments.

Consequently, how maintenance payments are arranged will no longer be influenced by fiscal considerations.

There are four ways that maintenance may be paid:

(1) purely voluntary payment;
(2) under a written agreement;
(3) by court order (whether made by consent or after a contested hearing);
(4) in compliance with a maintenance assessment by the Child Support Agency.

Voluntary payments are normally only a short-term arrangement. As between a written agreement and a court order, it is a question of balancing the potential advantages of speed, lower costs and flexibility of an agreement against the better provisions for disclosure and enforcement with a court order (see **11.3.3** and **11.3.4** for a more detailed comparison).

The only aspect of income tax which is specifically relevant to the family unit now is the new children's tax credit, to be introduced from 5 April 2001. This will be given in the form of a tax allowance (of an amount similar to the old married couple's allowance) for which relief will be given at 10 per cent. Only one allowance is available to any one taxpayer, regardless of the number of children living with him or her. Also, only one allowance is available per couple (whether married or living together as husband and wife). Where a child lives, for example, with each parent for part of the year, the one allowance is apportioned between them as they may agree, or, if they cannot agree, on the basis of the length of time the child has lived with each of them during the tax year.

5.2.2 Capital gains tax

Capital gains tax is charged on the chargeable gains made by a person on the disposal of chargeable assets. On marriage breakdown, capital assets commonly have to be sold or divided between the spouses and this may give rise to a chargeable gain. A number of exemptions may be available however, to reduce or eliminate that gain.

Capital gains tax and the home

The home is often the largest capital asset and any transfer of it, or of a share in it, could potentially give rise to capital gains tax. However, liability may be avoided due to two important exemptions:

(1) The private residence exemption: to qualify for full exemption, an individual must have occupied the home as his only or main residence throughout the period of his ownership. If he has occupied during part only of his ownership then the relief will be proportionately reduced, except that he is deemed to have occupied during the last 3 years of ownership whether or not this is in fact so (further details of this exemption can be found in the LPC Resource Book *Conveyancing* (Jordans)).

(2) Extra-statutory concession D6: this will apply where:

   (a) a husband and wife separate or divorce and one of them moves out of the home whilst the other continues to live there;

   (b) under the subsequent financial settlement the non-occupying spouse transfers the home or an interest in it to the occupying spouse; and

   (c) the non-occupying spouse has not elected to treat another property as his only or main residence.

If these conditions are fulfilled, the non-occupying spouse will be treated as having continued to occupy so that his gain will be exempt.

How do these exemptions work in practice?

SALE OF THE HOME TO A THIRD PARTY

If the sale is within 3 years of the separation, any gain is exempt, being covered by the private residence exemption. If the sale is later, the proportion of the non-occupying spouse's gain not covered by the exemption may be taxable. When calculating the gain, an indexation allowance applies up to April 1998. For 1998/99 onwards, the gain is reduced by taper relief according to the length of ownership. The annual exemption, if available, can then be applied to reduce the gain. (The spouse who has continued to occupy, will, of course, be covered by the private residence exemption.)

TRANSFER OF THE HOME BETWEEN SPOUSES

This will be necessary where the court orders an outright transfer, or deferred trust of land or deferred charge where this requires a transfer, ie disposal of some interest in the home. The transferor's gain may be exempted under the following rules:

(1) where the transfer takes place in the tax year of separation, the rule relating to disposals between spouses (donor spouse is deemed to have disposed at a consideration which gives rise to neither a gain nor a loss); or

(2) where the transfer takes place within 3 years of separation, the deemed occupation rule; or

(3) extra-statutory concession D6 if later.

Where none of the above applies, probably because the transferor has made an election in respect of another home and the separation exceeds 3 years, the gain will be calculated in the same way as above. A proportion of the gain will thus be exempt due to the private residence exemption. Indexation and/or taper relief, together with the annual exemption may help reduce the remainder.

FUTURE SALE OF HOME SUBJECT TO A DEFERRED TRUST OF LAND OR DEFERRED CHARGE

When the deferred trust of land or deferred charge is set up, one spouse may be required to transfer some, or all of their interest in the home to the other. The CGT consequences of this have been dealt with above. However, when the house eventually comes to be sold, possibly many years into the future, a further CGT liability may arise.

The occupying spouse's gain will be exempt under the private residence exemption. The position of the non-occupying spouse will depend on whether the home was subject to a deferred trust of land or a deferred charge.

Deferred trust of land

As the court order created a settlement, it would appear that the non occupying spouse will avoid capital gains tax liability completely because of rules exempting gains on property occupied by a beneficiary entitled to do so under a settlement (Taxation of Chargeable Gains Act 1992, s 225).

Deferred charge

Where the charge is expressed as a proportion of the proceeds, for example, one-third, the value of that share may have increased by the time the property is sold. In this situation, the non-occupier is likely to be liable to capital gains tax, the redemption moneys being a capital sum derived from an asset, ie the charge (Taxation of Chargeable Gains Act 1992, s 21). Indexation and/or taper relief, together with the annual exemption may help to reduce the bill. However, if the deferred charge is for a fixed sum (rather than a proportion of the proceeds), there is no charge to capital gains tax when the debt is paid (Taxation of Chargeable Gains Act 1992, s 251).

Other assets

Disposals giving rise to liability to capital gains tax are most likely to arise either:

(1) on sale of an asset, for example, a valuable painting, to raise a lump sum; or

(2) on the transfer of property, for example, shares, between the parties.

Example
A husband and wife bought a painting jointly 7 years ago for £10,000. They separated 2 years ago. The ancillary relief order is made today, when the painting is worth £16,000. Under the order the husband must transfer his share in the painting to his wife. The husband has made a gain of £3,000 (£16,000 – £10,000 = £6,000, husband's gain is half of this).

The gain on many disposals of matrimonial property may, however, be eliminated or reduced by an exemption or relief. The following should be considered:

(1)   wasting assets, for example, the family car or electrical items;
(2)   tangible moveable property disposed of for a consideration of less than £6,000;
(3)   the indexation allowance and/or taper relief;
(4)   the annual exemption.

Where the capital assets are distributed in the year of separation, the transferor spouse can avoid liability altogether due to the spouse rule. This will be unusual, however. In other cases, the impact of capital gains tax cannot be ignored as it may alter the effect of any negotiated settlement or court order. Thus, for example, if the wife has shares worth £50,000, these will not be sufficient on their own to fund a lump sum of £50,000 if capital gains tax is payable on their sale.

5.2.3 Inheritance tax

Inheritance tax is charged on the value transferred by a chargeable transfer. As a general rule, there will not be any liability to inheritance tax on transfers resulting from marriage breakdown. This is due to the following exemptions and reliefs.

The spouse exemption (Inheritance Tax Act 1984, s 18)

The spouse exemption exempts transfers between the parties before decree absolute, even if separated. However, this exemption will rarely apply since lump sum and property adjustment orders are not effective until decree absolute (see **4.4.1** and **4.4.2**).

Dispositions for family maintenance (Inheritance Tax Act 1984, s 11)

This relief provides that a disposition is not a transfer of value if made by one spouse for the maintenance of the other spouse or of a child of either spouse and applies both before and after divorce. The term 'maintenance' is not defined in the Act but clearly covers periodical payments. There is, however, doubt as to whether it is wide enough to cover capital provision such as lump sum or property adjustment orders. However, capital orders should be covered by the following relief.

Dispositions without donative intent (Inheritance Tax Act 1984, s 10)

This provides that a disposition is not a transfer of value if it was not intended to confer a gratuitous benefit and that either:

(1)   it was made in a transaction at arm's length between unconnected persons; or
(2)   it was such as might be expected to be made in such a transaction.

To avoid any doubt about the application of this exemption to transfers on marriage breakdown, the Senior Registrar of the Family Division has, with the agreement of the Inland Revenue, issued the following statement:

'Transfers of money or property pursuant to an order of the court in consequence of a decree of divorce or nullity will, in general, be regarded as exempt from [inheritance tax] as transactions at arm's length which are not intended to confer any gratuitous benefit' ((1975) 119 SJ 596).

5.2.4 Stamp duty

Where property is transferred under a separation agreement or court order on divorce, the instrument effecting the conveyance is exempt from stamp duty (Finance Act 1985, s 83 and Stamp Duty (Exempt Instruments) Regulations 1987, SI 1987/516).

5.3 CHAPTER SUMMARY

(1) The payment of maintenance, whether to a spouse or child, does not give rise to any income tax consequences.

(2) Capital gains tax may have to be paid when the matrimonial assets are divided on divorce.

(3) Where the asset is the home and it is transferred from one spouse to the other, CGT will not usually be payable. However, if the home is sold to a third party some CGT may have to be paid by the non-occupying spouse.

5.4 FURTHER READING

LPC Resource Book *Pervasive and Core Topics* (Jordans)
Whitehouse *Revenue Law: Principles and Practice* 17th edn (Butterworths, 1999)

Chapter 6

WELFARE AND LOCAL AUTHORITY HOUSING

6.1 INTRODUCTION

When a married couple separate and the main earner leaves the home, the other spouse may be left with little or no money. Although this may be only a temporary situation and it is possible to apply for maintenance (see **4.3.1** and **4.9**), it may be preferable for that spouse to apply for welfare benefits (for reasons explained at **4.3.1**). In addition, since it is more expensive to run two households than one, many people, particularly if they are lone parents, find themselves reliant on welfare benefits on a more permanent basis after marriage breakdown. The matrimonial solicitor thus needs to have a working knowledge of the main benefits available and how they may be affected by any financial settlement which the couple later reach.

The following is an outline of the most important benefits for the family client. Further detail on these and other benefits can be found in specialist publications such as those mentioned at the end of the chapter.

Where examples are given, for the sake of simplicity, notional figures are used for the amount of benefit payable.

6.2 CHILD BENEFIT

Child benefit is payable irrespective of the claimant's income (ie it is not means-tested), and is non-taxable. It is a weekly sum payable in respect of each child to the person responsible for maintaining that child. A 'child' is defined as being someone under 16, or under 19 if still in full-time secondary education. A higher amount of benefit is paid for the eldest child.

6.3 INCOME SUPPORT

Income support has now largely been replaced by the jobseeker's allowance. However, income support is still available for lone parents who are looking after a child or children under 16 and so will continue to be important where a marriage has broken down.

6.3.1 Eligibility

The claimant must:

(1) be present in Great Britain;
(2) be at least 16;

(3)   not be in full-time work or full-time non-advanced education (most students will also be ineligible to claim). 'Full-time work' means working for at least 16 hours per week;

(4)   not have income which exceeds his family's 'applicable amount' (see below);

(5)   not have capital exceeding £8,000. Any capital owned by a dependent child will be ignored but, if he owns capital of more than £3,000, no income support can be claimed for him. Some capital will be ignored: for example, the value of the home.

6.3.2 Applicable amount

The maximum amount of benefit payable is called the applicable amount. The applicable amount will be made up of the following.

(1)   Personal allowance: the amount of this will depend upon the age of the claimant.

(2)   Allowance for children: the amount will depend on the number of dependent children and their ages.

(3)   Family premium: this is available for all families with a dependent child or children.

(4)   Various other premiums, for example, for pensioners and those with disabilities.

(5)   Mortgage interest (rent is covered by housing benefit, see **6.6**): interest at a standard rate will be paid on mortgages of up to £100,000 direct to the lender. Mortgage interest only is paid and not other housing costs, for example, repayments of capital, insurance premiums payable on an endowment policy or payments for the insurance of the building or contents.

Borrowers who take out a new mortgage after 1 October 1995 and subsequently claim income support will not have their mortgage payments included in their applicable amount for 39 weeks. Existing borrowers who start claiming income support will not be able to include their mortgage interest payments for 8 weeks and will only be able to include half of their mortgage interest payments in their applicable amount for the following 18 weeks. A claimant who is a 'new borrower' may be treated as an 'existing borrower' where that claimant is a lone parent and claiming income support because her partner has deserted her.

6.3.3 Income

Any income the claimant may have will reduce the amount of benefit payable pound for pound. The claimant's income will include:

(1)   any earnings of the claimant net of tax, national insurance contributions and half of pension contributions. It is possible for a claimant to work for less than 16 hours per week and still claim income support. Earnings of dependent children, for example, from a paper round, will not be included. There is an earnings disregard of £15. Thus, for example, if Sally is a lone parent who earns £50 per week net from a part-time cleaning job, only £35 will count as income for income support purposes;

(2)   any maintenance payments paid to the claimant, whether for his/her own benefit or the benefit of a dependent child, for example, under a CSA maintenance assessment;

(3)   child benefit;

(4) income from capital. If the claimant has capital of more than £8,000, she will be ineligible for income support (see above). Any interest actually earned on capital of less than that amount will be ignored. However, capital of over £3,000 will be deemed to produce income at the rate of £1 per week for every £250 of capital over the £3,000 limit. So, for example, capital of £5,000 will be deemed to produce income of £8 per week (£5,000 - £3,000 = £2,000/250 = £8).

Any income will be deducted from the applicable amount to determine the amount of income support payable.

6.3.4 Passport benefits

Income support is a 'passport' to certain other benefits, ie where the claimant is claiming income support he will automatically be entitled to these other benefits as well. These passport benefits include:

(1) free school meals;
(2) exemption from NHS charges for prescriptions, dental treatment and eye-tests and vouchers to help with the cost of glasses;
(3) free milk and vitamins for expectant and nursing mothers and pre-school children;
(4) full housing and council tax benefits;
(5) the opportunity to apply for interest-free loans from the social fund (see **6.8**).

In addition, a claimant who is in receipt of maintenance may be able to make use of the diversion procedure (see **6.9.1**).

These passport benefits can be quite valuable. Thus it may be worth making a claim for income support even where the amount of income support paid will be small in order to take advantage of them. It is also important to consider the passport benefits when negotiating maintenance payments. It is often unwise to accept an offer of maintenance which is just sufficient to take the client off income support, as the value of these benefits will be lost (see **7.2.3**).

6.4 JOBSEEKER'S ALLOWANCE

The jobseeker's allowance was introduced on 7 October 1996 to replace unemployment benefit and, for many people, income support. It will be the appropriate benefit for the client to claim if he is not in full-time work and either has no children living with him or lives with a new partner who is also not in full-time work.

6.4.1 Eligibility

Eligibility is similar to that for income support but there is also a requirement that the claimant signs on as available for and actively seeking work.

In addition, the claimant's partner (if any) must not work for more than 24 hours per week.

Any capital of a partner will be added to the claimant's own when assessing eligibility.

6.4.2 Applicable amount

This is the same as for income support. However, the personal allowance will be higher where the claimant is part of a couple.

6.4.3 Income

This is similar to income support. The income of any partner must be included. The earnings disregard is £5 if the claimant is single or £10 if part of a couple.

6.4.4 Passport benefits

These are the same as for income support.

6.5 WORKING FAMILIES TAX CREDIT

Working families tax credit is a benefit for those in full-time work on low wages with a dependent child or children. It is administered by the Inland Revenue and paid either directly by them, or credited or paid through the wage packet.

6.5.1 Eligibility

The claimant must:

(1) be present in Great Britain;
(2) be working full-time (and/or her partner must be working full time). As for income support, full time means at least 16 hours per week. Thus, where a claimant's partner works for at least 16 hours but no more than 24 hours each week, the claimant will have a choice between working families tax credit and jobseeker's allowance. Calculations will need to be done to see which benefit should be claimed (eg if the couple have a mortgage, jobseeker's allowance may pay a higher amount);
(3) have at least one dependent child;
(4) not have capital exceeding £8,000. The rules relating to capital are the same as for jobseeker's allowance.

Working families tax credit may be claimed by either the man or the woman in a couple, according to their choice. Once the claim is made, it will be paid, or credited, at the same level for 26 weeks when it will be reassessed. Thus, if the claimant has her hours of work reduced, the amount will not be increased during this time (unless the hours are reduced below 16, when working families tax credit will cease immediately and income support or jobseeker's allowance may be claimed).

6.5.2 Amount

The maximum amount of working families tax credit payable will depend on the number and ages of the children. There is a fixed amount payable for the adult(s) in the family (the amount is the same for both couples and lone parents). To this basic tax credit is added an amount for each child (which increases with their age). Anyone entitled to working families tax credit who has or takes a job of more than 30 hours per week will receive an extra premium of £11.05 per week. Finally, there is added a childcare tax credit of up to 70 per cent of childcare costs of up to £100 for one child or £150 for two or more children. This gives the maximum amount of working families tax credit.

The maximum credit will be paid, or credited, where the claimant's income does not exceed a threshold (currently £90) which is increased annually.

Where the claimant's income exceeds this threshold, the maximum credit will be reduced by 55 pence for every pound of income the claimant has above the fixed sum.

Example
Tariq, a lone parent, earns £100 per week. The maximum credit for himself and his two children is £60 per week. The threshold is £90 per week. Tariq will receive:

£60 – [55% × (£100 – £90)]

ie £60 – (55% × £10) = £54.50 working families tax credit.

Income is calculated in much the same way as for income support, but there are some differences. For example, there are no earnings disregards, but there is a total disregard of any maintenance received. Child benefit is not included as income. The rules relating to income from capital are the same.

6.6 HOUSING BENEFIT

6.6.1 Eligibility

The claimant:

(1) must be liable to make payments of rent in respect of his home. Where a spouse is not technically liable to make such payments, but is liable in practice, housing benefit will be available. For example, if the husband, who is the tenant of a council flat which is used as the family home, leaves home, then the wife will be able to claim housing benefit;

(2) need not be in receipt of income support, jobseeker's allowance or working families tax credit;

(3) must not have capital exceeding £16,000. Other rules relating to capital are the same as for jobseeker's allowance.

6.6.2 Amount

(1) On 1 January 1996 the method of assessing the amount of housing benefit to be paid was changed and is now quite complex. Factors to be taken into account include whether the amount of rent being paid is too high, whether the accommodation is considered too large and the average rents in the area. Where the claimant is on income support or jobseeker's allowance, the benefit will be a maximum of 100 per cent of the rent payable, but may be less.

(2) Housing benefit will be reduced by approximately 65 pence for each pound by which the claimant's income exceeds the income support level.

(3) Income is calculated in much the same way as for income support. However, there are some disregards, for example for maintenance received, child care bills and earnings.

(4)   The amount of benefit will be reduced if one or more non-dependants (who are not on income support or jobseeker's allowance) share the property.

Where the claimant is a council tenant, housing benefit will reduce the amount of rent payable so that no money will pass through his hands. Where the claimant is a private tenant, he will receive an allowance which should be paid to the landlord.

6.7 COUNCIL TAX BENEFIT

6.7.1 Eligibility

The claimant:

(1)   must be liable to pay council tax. Couples (whether married or cohabiting) will be jointly responsible for their council tax bill. Each of them can claim council tax benefit;
(2)   need not be in receipt of any other benefits;
(3)   must not have capital exceeding £16,000. Other rules relating to capital are the same as for jobseeker's allowance.

6.7.2 Amount

(1)   For claimants on income support (or whose income does not exceed the income support level), the amount is usually 100 per cent of the council tax payable.
(2)   Council tax benefit will be reduced by approximately 20 pence for each pound by which the claimant's income exceeds the income support level.
(3)   Income is calculated in much the same way as for housing benefit.
(4)   Council tax benefit may also be reduced where there are one or more non-dependants (who are not on income support) living with the claimant.

Council tax benefit is given by a reduction in the council tax bill.

6.8 THE SOCIAL FUND

The social fund is a fund operated by the Benefits Agency out of which loans and grants may be paid to those in need. The first part of the fund, which is known as the 'regulated social fund', makes payments which are mandatory where the claimant meets all the qualifying conditions. The second part of the fund is known as the 'discretionary social fund'.

6.8.1 The regulated social fund

There are three types of payment which are made from the regulated social fund.

(1)   Maternity grants to those on income support, jobseeker's allowance or working families tax credit (or disability working allowance). If the claimant has savings of £500 or more, the grant will be reduced by the amount of the excess. The maternity grant is paid at a flat rate.
(2)   Funeral grants paid to those in receipt of means-tested benefits who were the partner or close relative of the deceased and are therefore responsible for making arrangements for the funeral. There is a ceiling on the amount which can be claimed. If the claimant has savings of £500 or more the grant will be

reduced by the amount of the excess. Wherever possible, the Benefits Agency will recover these costs from the deceased person's estate.

(3) Cold weather payments to those on income support or jobseeker's allowance where this includes one of the pensioner or disability premiums or the family includes a child under 5 years of age. Payments will be made automatically whenever the average temperature for 7 days in a row is, or is forecast to be, freezing point or below.

6.8.2 The discretionary social fund

Payments from the discretionary social fund may be by way of grant or loan. There are three types of payment which may be made.

(1) Community care grants to those on income support or jobseeker's allowance (or who expect to receive income support or jobseeker's allowance in the near future). Such grants can be made in a number of situations, for example, to help elderly or disabled people to lead independent lives in the community when they leave hospital or residential care. Community care grants may also be made, for example, to ease exceptional pressures on families and are subject to a wide discretion on the part of officers administering the fund. There is no maximum amount laid down for a community care grant, but claimants will have to use any savings they have in excess of £500 before a grant is payable.

(2) Crisis loans to meet expenses which arise as the result of some disaster such as flood or fire. A crisis loan could, for example, cover living expenses for a short period (usually 14 days), or such items as essential household equipment. The loan is interest-free. The rate and period of repayment are based on the claimant's income and circumstances. To be eligible for a crisis loan, the claimant does not have to be in receipt of any other welfare benefit, but he must be without sufficient resources to meet the immediate short-term needs of himself and/or his family. The maximum amount of a crisis loan is £1,000.

(3) Budgeting loans to those who have been on income support or jobseeker's allowance for at least 26 weeks to meet large, one-off expenses, for example, a replacement cooker or furniture. Again, claimants will be expected to use any savings they have in excess of £500 before a loan will be made. The social fund officer has a wide discretion as to the amount and purpose of these loans. However, there is an overall maximum of £1,000. The loans are interest-free and repaid by deductions from benefit, the amount of the deduction depending on the claimant's individual circumstances.

6.9 WELFARE BENEFITS AND MARRIAGE BREAKDOWN

6.9.1 Maintenance and income support/jobseeker's allowance

Any maintenance paid to the claimant (whether under a court order for herself or as child maintenance assessed by the Child Support Agency) will count as income and will reduce income support or jobseeker's allowance paid pound for pound. Thus, where the maintenance is not sufficient to take the claimant above the income support/jobseeker's allowance level, she will receive her income partly from maintenance payments and partly from income support/jobseeker's allowance. If the payer is erratic in his payments, the claimant will be forced to apply for further income support/jobseeker's allowance to top up her income whenever payments are not made.

To avoid this problem and to ensure that the claimant receives a regular income, she can ask for her child support maintenance to be paid to the Child Support Agency. She will then receive the child support maintenance as part of her income support/jobseeker's allowance.

It may also be possible to assign the benefit of any maintenance order in her favour to the Benefits Agency. The Benefits Agency will then collect payments due under the order and pay the claimant her full benefit entitlement. The Benefits Agency will also be responsible for enforcing any arrears. Before the Benefits Agency accept an assignment under this 'diversion procedure', any county court maintenance order must be registered in the family proceedings court. In addition, they will usually allow the diversion procedure to be used only where the payer has defaulted on past payments (practice differs from area to area, but usually the payer must have missed at least two monthly payments out of the last 12 payments).

If the maintenance eliminates the income support/jobseeker's allowance claim altogether, the claimant will also lose her passport benefits (see **6.3.4**).

6.9.2 Maintenance and working families tax credit

Any maintenance paid will not affect the amount of working families tax credit received.

6.9.3 Maintenance and housing benefit/council tax benefit

Unless the claimant is on income support, any maintenance can reduce her entitlement to housing benefit and council tax benefit or even eliminate it.

6.9.4 Lump sum payments

Where a lump sum payment brings the claimant's capital above the relevant capital limits, entitlement to the appropriate benefit will be eliminated.

Where a lump sum payment brings the claimant's capital to over £3,000 but under the relevant capital limits, the capital will be deemed to produce income (see **6.3.3**).

Special rules apply to lump sum payments where the claimant is on income support or jobseeker's allowance. These rules are meant to ensure that the claimant cannot avoid losing income support or jobseeker's allowance by accepting a lump sum payment rather than maintenance. Thus, when a lump sum payment is intended as a form of maintenance, it will be treated as income and may debar the claimant from income support or jobseeker's allowance for a period of time while the lump sum is used up. The formula applied when decapitalising lump sums is:

$$\frac{\text{Lump sum}}{\text{Weekly income support} + 2} = \begin{array}{l}\text{Number of weeks income support or}\\\text{jobseeker's allowance is eliminated}\end{array}$$

Example
Willa receives £48 income support per week. She receives no maintenance from Den, her ex-husband, but one day Den offers her a lump sum of £500, which she accepts. Willa will be denied income support for:

$$\frac{500}{48 + 2} \quad = \quad 10 \text{ weeks}$$

During this time, Willa must live off the lump sum at the rate of £50 per week.

None of the above rules will apply where the lump sum payment represents the claimant's share in the home and it is used to buy another home within 6 months, when the payment will be ignored.

6.9.5 Property adjustment

The value of the claimant's home is generally ignored in assessing benefits.

6.10 LOCAL AUTHORITY HOUSING

The family solicitor must be able to give immediate advice to a client who finds herself in a situation where she is, or might be, without a roof over her head. The two most common situations where this might occur are where the client has been subjected to domestic violence (see Chapter 14) or when she cannot stay in the former matrimonial home for financial reasons (eg because there are large mortgage arrears and the home must be sold).

Local authorities are under certain duties to provide help (including, in some cases, accommodation) to people who are homeless or threatened with homelessness. These duties are set out in the Housing Act 1996. The duty owed will depend upon whether the person applying is homeless or threatened with homelessness, whether that homelessness is intentional and whether the applicant has a priority need.

6.10.1 Homelessness

A person is homeless if:

(1) there is no reasonable accommodation which he and his family are entitled to occupy; or

(2) he has such accommodation but he cannot secure entry or occupation is likely to lead to violence or threats of violence from someone else living there. This latter ground is likely to be of particular relevance in cases of domestic violence (see Chapter 14).

A person may also be entitled to local authority help if he is 'threatened' with homelessness, which means that he is likely to become homeless in the next 28 days.

6.10.2 Intentional homelessness

A person is intentionally homeless if he deliberately does or fails to do anything in consequence of which he ceases to occupy accommodation which was available for occupation by him and his family and which it would have been reasonable for him to continue to occupy.

6.10.3 Priority need

The applicant will be treated as having a priority need if:

(1) he has dependent children who are living with him or might reasonably be expected to live with him; or

(2) his homelessness resulted from flood or fire or other disaster; or

(3) he (or a member of his household) is vulnerable through old age, mental illness or handicap, physical disability or other special reasons; or

(4) she (or a member of the household) is pregnant.

6.10.4 Local authority duties

The duties set out below are all subject to the overriding duty set out in s 197. This states that, where other suitable accommodation is available, ie accommodation other than local authority housing, the local authority is under a duty to give advice and assistance to the applicant to enable the applicant to secure that accommodation. Where such accommodation is not available, the local authority has the following duties:

(1) to rehouse a homeless person with a priority need who did not become homeless intentionally. This duty obliges the local authority to provide accommodation for a minimum period of 2 years, provided that the applicant continues to have a priority need. The authority may continue to provide accommodation after the 2-year period but is not obliged to do so. If it does continue to provide accommodation, this provision must be reviewed at least every 2 years;

(2) to provide temporary housing for a homeless person with a priority need who did become homeless intentionally. This accommodation must be provided for such period as the authority considers will give the homeless person a reasonable opportunity of finding his own accommodation. The authority is under a further duty to give advice and assistance to help him find such accommodation;

(3) to advise and assist a homeless person without a priority need to help him find his own accommodation.

6.10.5 Local connection provisions

Generally, the local authority to which the applicant applies will be the one under the duty mentioned above. However, that local authority may not be under such a duty if the applicant has no local connection with its area. This is so that local authorities in, for example, seaside areas do not become overwhelmed with applications. In this case, the local authority can refer the applicant to a local authority with which he does have a local connection (provided that the applicant is not at risk of domestic violence in that authority's area).

The applicant will have a local connection with the area in which he is normally resident, or where he is employed, or where he has family associations.

6.10.6 Local authority tenancies

A local authority tenancy is classed as a secure tenancy under the Housing Act 1985. This means that a council tenant has a great deal of security of tenure. In particular, he cannot be evicted without an order for possession from the court and such an order is only available on specified grounds, for example, non-payment of rent. This security depends partly on the tenant (or one of them where the property is on a joint tenancy) remaining in occupation.

On divorce, the court can order the tenant spouse to transfer the tenancy to the other spouse, and when this is done security of tenure is not lost (see further, **8.5**).

6.11 CHAPTER SUMMARY

(1) On marriage breakdown one or both of the parties may need to claim welfare benefits. The following may be available:
- child benefit.
- income support or jobseeker's allowance or working families tax credit.
- housing benefit.
- council tax benefit.
- loans or grants from the social fund.

(2) Local authorities have duties towards homeless people. Where a person is homeless unintentionally and has a priority need (eg if she has a child with her) the local authority must generally rehouse her for at least 2 years.

6.12 FURTHER READING

George et al *Welfare Benefits Handbook 2000/2001* 2nd edn (Child Poverty Action Group, 2000)

Encyclopedia of Housing Law and Practice (Sweet & Maxwell, looseleaf)

Chapter 7

CALCULATING MAINTENANCE

7.1 INTRODUCTION

The powers of the court and the principles on which it exercises those powers were considered in Chapter 4. This chapter will examine the methods used by the court to arrive at final figures for maintenance. In addition to considering the court's powers under MCA 1973, the chapter covers the Child Support Act 1991 (CSA 1991) which deals with maintenance for most children. In response to some of the criticisms raised against the Child Support Agency, CSA 1991 has been amended by the Child Support Act 1995. Throughout this book, any reference to CSA 1991 includes the 1995 Act.

For the sake of simplicity, only notional figures have been used in the examples in this chapter.

7.2 MAINTENANCE FOR A SPOUSE

The amount of maintenance to be paid by one spouse to the other will depend on numerous variables and a case-by-case approach will be taken by the solicitor and the court. Figures cited in reported decisions are of little assistance as there are rarely two cases with identical facts. However, one variable will always be significant and that is the presence or otherwise of dependent children. If there are children to provide for, this will have a significant impact on each party's needs and resources. The maintenance being paid and received for children must be taken into account when calculating maintenance for a spouse. In many instances, there will be insufficient resources remaining for maintenance to be paid to a spouse after paying maintenance for children. Increasingly, this is likely to be the case given that assessments under CSA 1991 result in greater sums being paid for children. It is especially so in low income families. In middle and higher income families, spouses may wish to pursue claims for their own provision in addition to maintenance for their children.

7.2.1 High income families

In high income families, the courts will be less concerned about meeting an applicant's basic needs as ensuring a fair apportionment of the family's wealth. In doing so, it will bear in mind the standard of living enjoyed prior to the breakdown of the marriage as well as all the other relevant factors in MCA 1973, s 25. Commonly, where significant capital is available, it will not be appropriate for there to be any maintenance payable between spouses. In such cases, a clean break will be favoured instead (see **4.6**). In determining how much the capital order should be, elaborate calculations may be made (by specialist accountants) to assess how much income a lump sum is anticipated to yield over the expected lifetime of the payee. These are known as *Duxbury* calculations (see **8.7**).

A clean break will not always be appropriate in wealthy families as there may be insufficient liquid capital. Assets may be tied up in land or in a business. It will frequently be counter-productive to realise such assets as their loss could have a disproportionately adverse effect on the income generated by the assets as a whole. In such cases, it would be more sensible and profitable for the assets to be retained and for a maintenance order to be made instead.

There is no generally accepted formula for calculating how much maintenance a payee spouse should receive over and above her basic living expenses. Argument will centre on MCA 1973, s 25 factors in such cases and weight will be placed on any positive (or negative) contribution the payee has made towards the family's prosperity.

7.2.2 Middle income families

The approach taken by the courts to the large group of people who are neither wealthy nor on or near subsistence level has varied over the years.

The one-third approach

The traditional approach taken by the court was to award the payee spouse sufficient maintenance to bring her income up to one-third of the parties' joint net income (*Wachtel v Wachtel* [1973] Fam 72). This formula has been used to assist the court to arrive at a starting point upon which it can consider MCA 1973, s 25 factors. It is a rough guide only and the courts have frequently warned against using it too rigidly. The final figure decided on by the court may be significantly above or below the one-third starting point but the method has nevertheless been called 'a very useful guide to an order for periodical payments for a wife' (*Page v Page* (1981) 2 FLR 198). On the other hand, the Court of Appeal has recently suggested that a useful rule of thumb was to halve the payer spouse's income – half for him and half for the payee spouse and children (*Scheeres v Scheeres* [1999] 1 FLR 241, CA). Such starting points may continue to be used, particularly in cases where no maintenance is payable under CSA 1991. However, in cases where a maintenance assessment has or is to be made by the Child Support Agency the court is more likely to calculate whether the absent parent can afford to make any additional periodical payment to the parent with care of the children, using the net effect approach.

The net effect approach

Before deciding on a figure for maintenance the court and practitioners should pause to consider the impact of the proposed maintenance on the payee and payer. It is important to consider the reality behind a particular figure to ensure that the payer can afford to make the proposed payment and that the payee can manage to live off her income (which will of course include the proposed maintenance). It is important to compare the size of their respective households and the extent of their liabilities. If maintenance is also being paid for children, this must also be borne in mind as it represents an additional obligation for the payer and an additional resource for the parent to whom it is being paid.

The solicitor should calculate the parties' net income, taking into account any income tax, national insurance and pension contributions. The parties' unavoidable expenditure such as rent, mortgage, council tax and water rates, etc, should be deducted from their net incomes. The figure for the proposed maintenance must be added to the payee's income and correspondingly deducted as an expense from the payer's income. The resulting balance for each party should be compared. With the remaining money the parties must feed and clothe themselves and any dependants. If this exercise shows that one party's standard of living will fall disproportionately in comparison with the other's as a result of the order, the proposed figure for maintenance must be readjusted and the calculation repeated.

Given that the payments for children under CSA 1991 will generally be larger than were commonly ordered in the past, the carer will often receive little or no additional maintenance for herself. To establish whether a claim for maintenance for the parent with care is appropriate, the net effect calculation described above should be carried out. Initially, the solicitor should calculate the disposable income of each party based on the payment of the assessed maintenance for the children. If the exercise reveals that the payer has a large disposable income relative to his needs, then it will be worthwhile making a claim for maintenance on behalf of the parent with care. In many instances, however, this exercise will confirm that the payer will have insufficient disposable income after meeting his obligations under CSA 1991 to make additional payments to the spouse caring for the children.

Example

This example uses *notional figures* to establish whether maintenance should be paid to a wife in addition to child support.

Fergus and Rose have two children, aged 8 and 10. Fergus earns £25,000 annually (gross) and Rose earns £7,000 annually (gross). Fergus has been assessed to pay £120.00 per week by the Child Support Agency. Rose has remained in the family home with the children and Fergus is in rented accommodation.

Stage 1: Calculate each spouse's net income:

	Fergus	Rose
	£	£
Earnings	480.00	135.00
Less tax	96.00	14.00
National Insurance	36.00	12.00
	348.00	109.00
	–	24.00
Child benefit	348.00	133.00

Stage 2: Take child maintenance of £120.00 into account:

	Fergus		Rose
	£		£
Net income	348.00	Net income	133.00
less	120.00	plus	120.00
	228.00		235.00

Stage 3: Deduct each spouse's unavoidable expenses:

	Fergus			Rose
	£	£	£	£
Net income		228.00		235.00
Less expenses:				
Fuel	10.00		15.00	
Council tax	4.00		8.00	
Mortgage	–		135.00	
Rent	50.00		–	
Insurance	10.00		15.00	
Car tax and petrol	22.00		–	
TV licence	2.00		2.00	
Pension	30.00		5.00	
Bus fares	–		5.00	
Childcare	–	128.00	20.00	205.00
Balance available		100.00		48.00

The final task is to compare the money left for other living expenses, such as food, clothes, etc, bearing in mind the parties' respective households. Here, Fergus has significantly more than Rose after meeting his own expenses. Rose, on the other hand, has to maintain a household of three and clearly this will be difficult unless she is given additional maintenance.

7.2.3 Low income families

In the case of low income families the one-third approach will rarely be appropriate. If the payer has low earnings and the payee none, the payer could not afford to lose one-third of his income and the payee could not survive on it. In such cases, alternative means of calculating maintenance are used.

If there are clearly insufficient resources for both parties to be independent of welfare benefits, the court and practitioners take a pragmatic approach. Although generally a spouse cannot cast his or her responsibility to maintain the other and their children onto the State, common sense dictates that in low income cases the availability of welfare benefits must be taken into account. The calculation of maintenance in such cases will often be a relatively straightforward process, as it will be a matter of identifying how much the payee needs to live on and how much the payer can spare. The court will never order a party to pay a sum which would place him below a notional subsistence level. This means the payer would be allowed to keep sufficient money to pay his housing costs as well as the sum he would be entitled to were he to claim income support or jobseeker's allowance. The reason for this is plain: there would be little incentive for such a person to earn a living or to pay the maintenance if he would be worse off than if he were unemployed.

The court is even reluctant to make an order which would reduce the payer to this subsistence level. In the past, it was more common for the payer to be able to retain a percentage (say 15 per cent) of his net earnings above his subsistence level. Since CSA 1991, the court may consider allowing the respondent to retain a more generous notional 'protected income', calculated along the lines of CSA 1991 (see **7.3.6(*4*)**).

If the payee is receiving income support or jobseeker's allowance and will continue to do so when maintenance is paid, she will not be any better off as a result. This is because any maintenance she receives forms part of her income when calculating her benefit entitlement and reduces her entitlement pound for pound. Her income will, therefore, remain at the level of her applicable amount.

Example

For example, Lucy is 45, unemployed and has no dependent children. Her applicable amount for jobseeker's allowance is £45. She has no income of her own and, therefore, receives £45 jobseeker's allowance. Her husband Bill is ordered to pay her £10 per week maintenance. Thereafter, she will receive only £35 jobseeker's allowance but when this is added to her maintenance her income remains at £45 per week.

In such circumstances, clients may be unenthusiastic about claiming maintenance. However, if the client has any prospects of finding employment, even modest maintenance when combined with wages may, in time, assist her to become independent of State benefits altogether.

Careful calculation must be made in the case of low income families to ensure that the payee is not worse off with maintenance than without it. This can arise if the maintenance raises the payee's income to, or only slightly above, her applicable amount. If this occurs, she will lose her right to income support (or jobseeker's allowance), but more particularly to the passport benefits to which a claimant is automatically entitled. She will lose the right to free prescriptions and school meals for her children and as a result would be worse off. She would also lose the right to full housing benefit and full council tax benefit although she would be able to make a means-tested claim. It will often be appropriate to accept a reduced sum of maintenance to ensure that the payee is still eligible for income support (or jobseeker's allowance), thereby enabling her to continue to qualify for these other benefits. This is discussed further in Chapter 6.

Where both parties are in receipt of income support or jobseeker's allowance, it will not usually be appropriate to apply for maintenance for a spouse. If a spouse is earning and receiving the working families tax credit, it may be possible (although uncommon) for very modest maintenance to be paid to the other spouse. The position is different, however, with children's maintenance. Even parents on income support or jobseeker's allowance may be expected to pay maintenance for their children under CSA 1991 (see below). In low income families in particular, if maintenance is payable for children, it is likely that the absent parent will have insufficient resources to pay maintenance for the parent with care as well. If, after paying the child maintenance, the payer's income is close to his subsistence level, no spouse maintenance will be paid.

7.3 MAINTENANCE FOR CHILDREN: THE CHILD SUPPORT ACT 1991 (INCLUDING THE CHILD SUPPORT ACT 1995)

Chapter 4 dealt with the statutory criteria used by the court when considering applications for child maintenance under MCA 1973 on marriage breakdown. These factors are of a general nature and do not assist the court in arriving at specific figures for maintenance. Accordingly, the orders for children's maintenance could vary enormously from one court to another.

However, the intention is that most applications for child maintenance are now made under CSA 1991 where the approach is entirely different; this legislation introduced a precise method of assessing maintenance using a detailed formula. The universal formula produces predictable and consistent results. Under CSA 1991, there is very little discretion involved in calculating children's maintenance. On the whole, there is no opportunity for any argument over the weighting of factors and interests.

One feature of the legislation is that much of the detail regarding the law appears not in CSA 1991 itself but in the many Regulations. Application for child maintenance must usually be made to the Child Support Agency although in certain cases (see **7.3.3**) application may be made to the court. The Agency operates under the authority of the Secretary of State for Social Security. This Agency has, in theory at least, ousted the jurisdiction of the courts in the vast majority of cases. The Child Support Agency, through its child support officers is responsible for making maintenance assessments, carrying out reviews every 2 years and, where necessary, collecting and enforcing the maintenance. It will also provide information and advice. Fees were charged (to both parents) for the Agency's services (although, broadly, those on benefit were exempt from paying those fees). However, due to problems with the service that the Agency is providing, fees are currently suspended.

7.3.1 Co-operation with the Agency

The driving force which led to the introduction of CSA 1991 was the desire to reduce the huge sums of income support paid to lone parents. Very many lone parents received only modest or no maintenance at all from the absent parent and consequently were forced to claim state benefits. In an effort to reduce this burden on the tax payer, s 6 requires all lone parents with care claiming certain welfare benefits (including income support and jobseeker's allowance, but not the new working families tax credit) to authorise the Secretary of State to pursue the absent parent for maintenance. The child support officers carry out this function on behalf of the Secretary of State. Section 6 requires such a claimant to complete a maintenance application form and to provide information to assist the officers to recover maintenance from the absent parent.

The most important (and controversial) information is the naming of the absent parent. Many mothers might not wish to look to the absent father to maintain a child who may have had no relationship with him. Indeed, the absent parent may not even be aware that he has fathered the child. Despite such reluctance, the mother will be obliged to co-operate with the Agency or face the consequences. Unless a parent can show a legitimate reason for failing to co-operate, she will be penalised by reduction of her benefit. For 3 years, her benefit will be reduced by 40 per cent of the adult personal allowance. If at any time during that period she decides to co-operate, her benefit will cease to be reduced and will recommence at the normal rate.

It will be legitimate to refuse to co-operate if there would be a risk of the parent with care or any child living with her suffering harm or undue distress as a result. Thus, if a parent is genuinely and reasonably afraid that co-operation might provoke a violent response from the absent parent this would constitute good cause and her benefit would not be reduced. There is no requirement to substantiate that belief with hard evidence although she would be required to be interviewed about her concern by a child support officer. If satisfied that the assertion is not implausible, the officer should waive the requirements to co-operate and allow the parent to continue to receive her full benefit entitlement.

7.3.2 When does CSA 1991 apply?

Section 11 of CSA 1991 provides:

> 'For the purposes of this Act, each parent of a qualifying child is responsible for maintaining him.'

This calls for a number of definitions to be considered.

Section 55(1) defines 'a child' as a person under 16 or an unmarried person under 19 receiving full-time education which is not advanced education.

Section 3(1) defines the 'qualifying child' as such if:

> '(a)   one of his parents is in relation to him an absent parent; or
> (b)   both of his parents are, in relation to him, absent parents.'

As the name suggests, an absent parent is one who is not living in the same household as the child (s 3(2)). The term 'parent' takes its usual meaning of being a person who is in law the mother or father of the child, ie the natural parent or adoptive parent of the child. It does not extend to a step-parent. Clearly, this includes unmarried as well as married parents and it is immaterial whether or not the absent parent knows the child is his. In the case of disputes over parentage, the child support officer may not make a maintenance assessment until the court has determined parentage.

CSA 1991 also refers to the person with care. Section 3(3) defines this person as one with whom the child lives and who usually provides the child's day-to-day care (this may not necessarily be the child's parent). It will generally be the person with care who will apply for the maintenance assessment although the absent parent may choose to apply for an assessment against himself.

The child support officer only has jurisdiction to make a maintenance assessment if the qualifying child, the person with care and the absent parent are all habitually resident in the UK.

7.3.3 The jurisdiction of the court

By virtue of CSA 1991, s 8, the Agency, in theory, has almost exclusive jurisdiction to deal with child maintenance.

Section 8(3) states:

> 'In any case where subsection (1) applies, no court shall exercise any power which it would otherwise have to make, vary or revise any maintenance order in relation to the child and absent parent concerned.'

The cases covered by s 8(1) are those where a child support officer would have jurisdiction to make a maintenance assessment with respect to a qualifying child and his absent parent. In other words, if an application could be dealt with by the Agency it must be pursued there. However, the court retains jurisdiction to deal with those cases in which the Agency has no jurisdiction. The court, therefore, continues to deal with maintenance for step-children who are children of the family, and for those natural children who are too old to be qualifying children, for example, those aged 19 or over who are in education or training. If either the child, absent parent or person with care is not habitually resident in the UK the Agency will have no jurisdiction, but the court would have jurisdiction. The court also retains jurisdiction to make capital orders on behalf of children, ie a lump sum or property adjustment order. The court has power to revoke existing maintenance orders in all cases.

In the limited cases where the court retains jurisdiction, it will have the widest discretion to determine the amount of a child's periodical payments. It will consider the factors listed in MCA 1973, s 25(3) and (4) giving first consideration to the child's welfare as directed in s 25(1) (discussed in Chapter 4). Prior to CSA 1991, the courts would often be guided in part by the income support child rates or by the National Foster Care Association allowances for foster-children. Both rates increase with the age of the child. CSA 1991 has resulted on average in higher maintenance payments for children which may influence the court's attitude towards applications before it. It might be persuaded by an argument that, although a child may not qualify for an assessment by the Agency, it nevertheless needs provision at a level similar to a 'qualifying child's' maintenance (see *E v C (Child Maintenance)* [1996] 1 FLR 472). It will, therefore, be worthwhile calculating what a parent would be ordered to pay for a child were an application to the Agency possible. If the child is a step-child, regard must be had to the liability of the child's natural parents to maintain the child. Consequently, the step-parent may be ordered to pay an amount significantly less than a natural parent would be required to pay under CSA 1991 formula, particularly if the parent with care could claim against the natural parent through the Agency.

In cases where a maintenance assessment has been (or is about to be) made, this must be taken into account in proceedings by the carer for maintenance for herself as it will have a direct bearing on both parties' means (see **7.2.2**).

As well as dealing with those cases which cannot be dealt with by the Agency the court retains jurisdiction to make maintenance orders for children in the three circumstances specified in s 8.

Supplementary maintenance

Section 8(6) specifies the first of these. The court will have jurisdiction if it is of the view that maintenance should be paid in addition to that assessed by the Agency. This will only apply to relatively wealthy families as it is a prerequisite that the Agency has already made an assessment up to the maximum level.

There are unlikely to be many applications under this subsection as the courts will rarely be persuaded that further sums should be paid. The circumstances when a child might require further assistance, for example, because he needs school fees or because of a disability, are in any event separately provided for in s 8(7) and (8).

Educational expenses

Section 8(7) provides that the court may continue to exercise its jurisdiction if the child is in education and provision is required to meet some or all of the expenses connected with it.

Typically, applications under this section will be made to cover the cost of school fees which are not fully met from the maintenance assessment. They may also be made to cover the payment of school uniforms, sports equipment, books, etc.

Children with a disability

If a child has a disability, this is not taken into account by the Agency when making the maintenance assessment. Such children, however, will frequently have additional expenses to meet their needs. Section 8(8) enables the court to make an order to supplement the maintenance assessment to meet expenses attributable to that disability.

Section 8(9) defines a child as disabled if he is blind, deaf or dumb or is substantially and permanently handicapped by illness, injury, mental disorder or congenital deformity or such other disability as may be prescribed.

7.3.4 Maintenance agreements and consent orders

Section 8(3) restricts the jurisdiction of the court to determine maintenance for children. However, it is still open to parents who are not claiming the main welfare benefits to arrange maintenance for children without going to the Agency, and it seems that, in practice, many couples are making an effort to avoid the involvement of the Agency in the following ways.

Separation agreements

Separation agreements represent an alternative method of finalising family finances on the breakdown of the relationship. They are frequently used by those who are unable or do not wish to obtain a court order and who have agreed their own arrangements and wish to put their agreements in writing. A separation agreement is not a court order but is enforceable in the same way as any other binding contract (see **11.3.1**).

Following CSA 1991, parents may still make separation agreements and s 9(2) specifically preserves this right for non-benefit cases. However, just as in the past such agreements could not oust the jurisdiction of the court to determine maintenance, neither can the jurisdiction of the Child Support Agency be ousted. Section 9(3) and (4) rule out any attempts to undermine the Agency's jurisdiction by prohibiting applications to it. As a result, any carer who enters into a separation agreement (even one which expressly purports to restrict the parties' rights to make any further claims) will, nevertheless, be able to apply to the Agency for a maintenance assessment. Indeed, as s 6 compels a parent with care who is receiving benefit to authorise the Secretary of State to take action under the Act, a party to an agreement may find himself reluctantly obliged to renege on the agreement and co-operate with the Agency.

Consent orders

Some couples may want to do more than just put their agreement in writing; they may want their agreement embodied in a court order. If so, they can apply for a consent order.

Consent orders (ie court orders in terms agreed by the parties) have for some time been of widespread use and will continue to be important. Prior to CSA 1991, couples were encouraged to consider the family finances as a package deal. A consent order would embody an overall agreement covering the home, maintenance of the parties and children. Frequently, a clean break would be agreed whereby a parent would forgo maintenance entirely or accept only nominal maintenance for herself and the children in return for a capital settlement. On the whole, the opportunity for such a package deal approach is now closed because maintenance is determined without negotiation by the Agency. Clearly, it will be necessary for the solicitors to anticipate what the Agency's maintenance assessment will be as it will inevitably have an influence on the issues remaining to be dealt with by the consent order.

In spite of the clear wording of s 8(3) which prohibits the court from making (varying or reviving) maintenance orders where the child support officer would have jurisdiction, s 8(5) preserves the power of the court to make an order if:

(1) a written agreement (whether or not enforceable) provides for the making or securing by an absent parent of the child of periodical payments to or for the benefit of the child; and

(2) the maintenance order which the court makes is, in all material respects, in the same terms as that agreement.

This provision was implemented by the Child Maintenance (Written Agreements) Order 1993, SI 1993/620. Therefore, a separation agreement may be converted into a court order in the same terms. All that is required is for there to be a written agreement (a draft consent order signed by the parties is sufficient documentation). As a result of s 8(5) and the Regulations, parents may continue to side-step the Agency and embody a clean break agreement in a consent order. However, respondents must be advised that, as with separation agreements, such an order will not prevent the carer from choosing to make an application to the Agency under s 4 (or being required to do so under s 6). Any such assessment will have the effect of automatically revoking any prior periodical payments order in favour of a qualifying child. However, during the transitional period (see **7.3.5** below) no application can be made to the Agency under s 4 unless the court order is first revoked. Consequently, an application for the written agreement to be reflected in a court order effectively bars an application to the Child Support Agency during the transitional period, although not beyond it.

7.3.5 Transitional arrangements

The Agency began operating on 5 April 1993. Since it first opened for business, it has been dealing with all new maintenance applications irrespective of whether the applicants were claiming welfare benefits. Existing claimants of welfare benefits are gradually being taken on by the Agency.

It was the government's original intention that the Agency would begin from April 1996 to take on non-benefit cases where there is either a written maintenance agreement which was made before April 1993 or an existing court order. However, due to the enormous backlog of cases the Government has decided to defer, for an indefinite period, the Agency taking on these cases. Until such time as they are taken on by the Agency, these cases will remain within the jurisdiction of the courts. However, if the order or agreement is revoked an application may be made to the Agency immediately. The decision whether or not to revoke an existing order rests with the court. It may not be prepared to revoke its original order which would in effect block an early application to the Agency. In the case of *B v M (Child Support: Revocation of Order)* [1994] Fam Law 370, an order was made for the maintenance of three children in 1986. The mother wanted to apply under CSA 1991 for an assessment in respect of the two younger children and applied for the original maintenance order to be revoked to enable her to do so. The father successfully appealed against the district judge's revocation. The court stated that the proper course would be to vary the original order and that it was inappropriate to exercise its discretion to revoke the order purely because the mother wished to apply to the Agency. However, the court made it clear that each case must be considered on its merits.

Until the Agency has jurisdiction to make an assessment the court will retain its power to vary the order. However, once the Agency has acquired jurisdiction to deal with a particular case, the court will not be able to make any further orders in that case (other than for discharging previous court orders). If an order was made prior to the 1991 Act coming into force, should neither party choose to approach the Agency (neither being required to do so under s 6) the court order will simply continue.

The court will retain the power to make consent orders under s 8(5) even when the Agency is fully effective.

7.3.6 The formula

When an application is made to the Child Support Agency, a formula is applied in order to calculate the maintenance payable in respect of a child by the absent parent. It is applied to those required to make the application (by virtue of s 6) and those who choose to pursue a claim (under s 4) in the same way. The key elements of the formula are set out in Sch 1 to the Act, and in the Child Support (Maintenance Assessments and Special Cases) Regulations 1992, SI 1992/1815. The formula, of necessity, is very complicated as it is applied universally to widely varying cases. This book deals with the key elements of the formula but does not examine its many intricacies. In practice, specialist books should be referred to and solicitors may use one of several computer software packages designed to perform the calculations speedily and efficiently.

The formula is based on the annually revised income support rates and has the following five key elements.

(1) The maintenance requirement

The maintenance requirement (MR) is the notional amount needed to cover the day-to-day expenses of maintaining a child. This is arrived at by adding the following income support allowances and premiums:

(a) child's personal allowance (which varies according to his or her age);
(b) family premium;
(c) a portion of the adult personal allowance where the child is under 16.

Child benefit is deducted from the total.

The adult personal allowance included will be whichever income support allowance is appropriate to the particular individual (eg lone parent over 18). By including the allowance for the carer, the Act recognises that the provision of child care is costly, whether it is undertaken by a parent or a professional carer and the absent parent is required to contribute towards that cost. It is not a means of requiring spousal or inter-parental maintenance.

The portion of the adult personal allowance to be taken into account varies according to the age of the youngest child as follows:

– where the youngest child is under 11 years of age, the full adult allowance is included;
– where the youngest child is 11 years or older, it is reduced by one-quarter; and
– where the youngest child reaches 14 years of age, it is reduced by a further one-quarter.

Example 1 (using notional figures)

Salim and Yasmin are separated. Yasmin is caring for Samina, aged 5 and Nadim aged 12.

The MR is calculated as follows:

		£	£	£	£
(a)	personal allowances for the children				
	Samina	15.00			
	Nadim	20.00	35.00		
(b)	family premium		15.00		
(c)	adult allowance (full)		45.00	95.00	
	less child benefit			18.00	
	total MR =				77.00

Example 2 (using notional figures)

Patrick and Carol are divorced. Patrick is caring for their twin boys, Rupert and Giles aged 13.

The MR is calculated as follows:

		£	£	£	£
(a)	personal allowances for the children				
	Rupert	20.00			
	Giles	20.00	40.00		
(b)	family premium		15.00		
(c)	adult allowance (less 25%)				
	45.00 – 11.25		33.75	88.75	
	less child benefit			18.00	
	total MR =				77.75

(2) Assessable income

The next step is to calculate the assessable income (AI) available to each parent.

Net income

less exempt income

= assessable income

First, calculate each party's net income (ie after deducting tax, national insurance and half of pension contributions) from all sources. The income of any partner living with the parent will not be included. There are Regulations concerning the inclusion of children's income.

Each parent's exempt income is then deducted from their net income. Exempt income represents the amount each parent may reserve for his or her own notional expenses. Essentially, it consists of the amount which each parent would be able to claim in income support plus their actual housing costs (provided they are not unreasonable) including, in the case of the absent parent, those arising from the needs of his new partner or family. Housing costs will include rent and mortgage interest together with linked sums for the repayment of the mortgage, ie the policy premium on an endowment mortgage.

Exempt income also includes a flat rate allowance to take into account the cost of travel to work. However, this allowance applies only to those who travel more than 150 miles per week and is not available to the self-employed.

In certain circumstances, a notional weekly allowance will be made when calculating exempt income. This is to take into account any capital transfer made by the absent parent to the parent with care under a clean break settlement made before CSA 1991 came into force (see **7.3.7**).

Although both parents are liable to maintain their children, if the parent with care is receiving income support (jobseeker's allowance or working families tax credit), it will not be necessary to calculate that parent's assessable income.

(3) The deduction rate

THE BASIC ELEMENT

A basic deduction rate (BDR) of 50 per cent is then applied to the combined assessable income of both parents until the MR is met. Both parents are responsible for the maintenance but the parent with care will not actually make any payment. Neither parent will be obliged to pay more than half of their individual AI even if this fails to meet the MR.

> *Example*
> David and Jane are separated with two children who live with Jane. The MR is £75 and David's AI is £120 per week. Jane has no income of her own. The 50% BDR applied to David's AI of £120 requires him to pay £60 per week. He will not be able to meet the full MR of £75 and will not be obliged to do so as he cannot be required to pay more than half of his AI.
>
> If Jane takes a part-time job giving her an AI of £20 per week their combined AI rises to £140 per week. Half of the total AI is £70 which is still less than the MR of £75. As a result, David is required to pay only 50% of his assessable income, ie £60 as before.

It may be seen, therefore, that where half of the combined AI is not greater than the maintenance requirement the absent parent's liability is confined to half of his AI. However, where the application of the BDR produces a figure in excess of the MR, it is necessary to make further calculations to consider whether any additional maintenance is payable.

THE ADDITIONAL ELEMENT

If the basic element calculation establishes that 50 per cent of the combined AI exceeds the MR, the amount of maintenance has to be recalculated.

A further calculation is done to work out the additional element to be paid over and above the MR. However, there is a ceiling on the amount an absent parent can be required to pay beyond the MR and this is calculated by reference to income support allowances. The income support personal allowance and family premium for each child is multiplied by one-and-a-half to give a figure for the maximum additional element that can be added to the MR.

(4) Protected income

This protects the basic income of an absent parent by ensuring an assessment will not take his and his household's disposable income below the minimum standard applicable to his circumstances. It recognises that the absent parent may have obligations which are not fully taken into account when calculating his exempt income, for example, responsibilities assumed towards his step-children.

When calculating protected income, a broader approach to the household's needs is taken than when calculating exempt income where only the payer's essential needs are taken into account. This means that, in certain circumstances, for example where the payer has a new family, the notional household needs allowed when calculating protected income may be more than was allowed for as exempt income in the original maintenance assessment.

In addition to the notional household's needs, the payer is entitled to retain a standard margin of £30 plus 15 per cent of the balance of his net income beyond this.

> *Example*
> Paul lives with Petra and their child, James. Paul has initially been assessed to pay £24 to another child.
>
> His net income is £170 and the household's notional needs are £120.
>
> The protected income is calculated as follows:

		£	£	£
(a)	Notional household needs	120.00		
(b)	Plus, standard margin	30.00		
(c)	Plus 15% × remaining net income			
	= 15% × [170 – [120+30]]			
	= 15% × 20 =	3.00		
	Total protected income	153.00		
	Net income		170.00	
	Less protected income		153.00	
	Balance available for child support			17.00

Paul cannot afford to pay the initial assessment of £24, consequently it will be reduced to £17 per week.

(5) 30 per cent maximum ceiling

Since April 1995, no absent parent will be assessed to pay more than 30 per cent of his normal net income in child maintenance. This represents a significant departure from the original formula where the absent parent could be ordered to pay substantially above that proportion provided it did not exceed the maximum additional element and provided he retained his minimum protected income.

Example
Bill has three children for whom the maintenance requirement is £115.

	£	£
Net income	300.00	
Less exempt income	80.00	
Assessable income =		220.00

When the basic deduction rate of 50% is applied to his AI this produces a figure of £110. As this is just short of the MR he would, under this preliminary calculation, be assessed to pay £110. However, his protected income and 30% maximum levels must be checked.

Protected income calculation:

	£	£	£
Notional household needs	140.00		
Plus standard margin	30.00		
Plus 15% × remaining net income			
= 15% × [300–170]			
= 15% × 130 =	19.50		
Total protected income	189.50		
Net income		300.00	
Less protected income		189.00	
Balance available for child support			110.50

According to this calculation, Bill has sufficient protected income to pay the maintenance of £110 calculated above. However, the 30% maximum provision must also be checked.

30% maximum calculation:

	£
Maximum child support	
= 30% × net income	
= 30% × 300.00 =	90.00

This is less than the original assessment of £110. Bill, therefore, makes a saving of £20 as a result of this 30% maximum cap on the amount of maintenance payable.

Minimum payment

Certain persons are exempt from paying any maintenance, for example, those eligible for disability benefits or who are in receipt of income support or jobseeker's allowance *and* have a family premium included in their applicable amount (ie have a child in their household).

Unless a person falls into an exempt category, every absent parent will be required to pay a minimum amount of maintenance even if that places their disposable income below their protected income.

The minimum payment is currently about £5.00 per week. Absent parents on income support (but with no child in their household) will have their minimum payment deducted from their benefit at source.

Special cases

So far it has been assumed that one parent has had the exclusive care of the children whilst the other has been the sole absent parent. Clearly, this will not always be the case as families organise themselves in a variety of ways. The formula must be adjusted to take these variations into account. Regulation 19 of the Child Support (Maintenance Assessments and Special Cases) Regulations 1992 deals with the situation where both parents are absent with the child being cared for by a third party, perhaps a friend or another relative. In this case the formula will operate in the normal way, the only difference being that both parents will actually make the payment to the person with care.

Regulation 20 deals with the reverse situation where both parents share the care of the child. Provided the absent parent cares for the child for at least 104 nights each year (howsoever spread), the formula will be adjusted pro rata to reflect this contribution. There are, therefore, tactical advantages to the absent parent of ensuring contact is maintained with the child.

Regulation 22 deals with cases where an absent parent may have several persons with care raising his children in different households. In such a case, maintenance will be assessed for the children with each carer and reduced proportionately if payment of the maintenance would reduce the payer below his protected income.

Regulation 23 deals with applications by a person who is caring for children who do not share the same parents. The formula is adjusted to ensure that all the absent parents share responsibility for the care provided by the person with care.

Child maintenance bonus

If the parent with care is on income support or jobseeker's allowance, any child maintenance received reduces her benefit pound for pound. However, the Child Support Act 1995 has introduced a provision whereby, from April 1997, the parent with care on income support or jobseeker's allowance builds up a credit of £5 per week for each week in which child support maintenance has been paid. If the parent then leaves income support or jobseeker's allowance to take up work of 16 hours or more per week, she receives that money as a bonus lump sum (up to a maximum of £1,000).

7.3.7 Pre-CSA 1991 clean break settlements

One of the main criticisms of the original formula was that it failed to take into account any capital transfers made by the absent parent to the parent with care. For example, one parent may have transferred the matrimonial home to the other parent, in return for which that parent agreed to forgo maintenance (entirely or in part) for herself and the children. An absent parent who, having entered into such a clean break agreement prior to CSA 1991, subsequently faces a maintenance assessment, is likely to feel very aggrieved as this strikes at the very basis of the original settlement.

In response to these criticisms, the formula was revised in April 1995 to take such disposals broadly into account. However, this applies only to capital transfers made before CSA 1991 came into force (ie before April 1993). A notional weekly allowance is made when calculating exempt income based on the value of the transfer.

Where a transfer has taken place, it is assumed that the ex-partners were each entitled to half of the total value of the asset (irrespective of whether this was actually the case). Only to the extent that the absent parent transferred property or capital to the parent with care will it count as a contribution to child maintenance.

Example

If a property worth £50,000 with a mortgage of £30,000 was transferred to the parent with care then the absent parent would be assumed to have given up only £10,000 of the £20,000 equity, the other £10,000 being deemed to belong to the parent with care in any event.

The formula will take into account only transfers above £5,000 and transfers greater than this will be divided into broad bands.

Value of capital transferred:	Exempt income allowance (per week):
£5,000–£9,999	£20
£10,000–£25,000	£40
£25,000 +	£60

This broad-brush approach will entitle the absent parent to claim the appropriate notional figure as exempt income thereby reducing his assessable income and consequently reducing the child support maintenance payable.

The absent parent may also seek to have the original order set aside in the light of the unanticipated maintenance assessment. However, in the case of *Crozier v Crozier* [1994] 1 FLR 126, the High Court resisted just such an application stating that the factors justifying re-opening the original order set out in *Barder v Barder* (see **10.7**) were not satisfied. One effect of the new broad-brush allowance in the formula is likely to be that the court will now be even more reluctant to set aside any prior clean break order. This is because any potential injustice to an absent parent who has transferred substantial capital to the parent with care can be partially mitigated by this allowance. The hardship may be mitigated further by invoking the departure system (see **7.3.8** below).

7.3.8 The departure system

The Child Support Act 1995 introduced a radical change to the 1991 Act by providing for a departure from the standard formula and the introduction of discretion to determine certain cases individually.

Under the departure system, once the maintenance payable under the formula has been assessed, either parent can apply for a departure from the assessment. This departure will be allowed only in certain tightly defined circumstances.

In the first instance, this discretion will be exercised by the Child Support Agency. If either parent is unhappy with the Agency's decision, they can apply to the Child Support Appeal Tribunal (CSAT). The CSAT will exercise independent discretion with the power to substitute its decision for that of the Agency. Appeal on that will be to a Child Support Commissioner and subsequently the courts.

The Government's intention is that the standard formula assessment should continue to be the norm and that to qualify for a departure an absent parent will have to meet the following conditions:

(a) that because of the special circumstances of the case he faces special additional expenses not taken into account in the formula; and

(b) that he would face hardship if he were to pay maintenance at the level determined by the formula.

Examples of exceptional expenses might include the high costs of travel to maintain contact with the child, certain debts of the former relationship between the parents and exceptionally high cost of travel to work beyond those allowed in the formula. The departure system will also cover cases where capital was transferred under an agreement made before April 1993, in recognition of which, child maintenance was set lower than it would otherwise have been. If a parent can show that the broad-brush capital allowance under the formula (see **7.3.7** above) is inappropriate in the particular circumstances, then the formula will be departed from.

Instead of the absent parent applying, the parent with care may wish to apply for a departure. For example, if the absent parent's lifestyle is inconsistent with his declared income or the absent parent is being credited, under the formula, with 100 per cent of housing costs when in fact these are being met, wholly or in part, by his new partner.

7.3.9 Proposals for reform

CSA 1991 represented a major change in the way maintenance for children is determined. The main weakness inherent in the former practice of resolving children's maintenance through the courts was the variation in the level of maintenance from court to court and case to case. Such unpredictability is not conducive to achieving negotiated settlements.

In contrast, CSA 1991 formula for calculating child maintenance is of universal application and produces predictable results. However, hand-in-hand with the strength of this non-discriminatory formula came the weakness of inflexibility which could lead to harsh results in certain cases. In response to some of the criticisms raised against CSA 1991 the Government has introduced a number of changes to the original formula. Significantly, it has also introduced the possibility, in limited circumstances, for departure from the formula. Most of these changes are primarily in favour of the absent parent.

The Government has continued to monitor closely the effect of the child support system, and has now produced further proposals for reform in the new Child Support, Pensions and Social Security Act 2000.

The Act proposes radical reforms, in particular, replacing the current complicated formula with an extremely simple one. It provides that the non-resident parent should pay a proportion of his net income as follows:

Number of children	Proportion of net income
one	15%
two	20%
three or more	25%

If the non-resident parent has children living with him, the amount will be reduced. Staying contact will affect the payment due to be made too. The proposal is that child support payments would be reduced by one-seventh for every night of the week the child spends with the non-resident parent. There will also be reductions in liability for low earners and a minimum payment, as now, of around £5 per week.

The Act also introduces various measures to try to deal with parents who either fail to provide, or misrepresent, information to the Agency or who do not pay or persistently pay late. Such behaviour might, for the first time ever, constitute a criminal offence and a parent could face a fine (of up to £1,000). The Act also looks at alternative methods for enforcing co-operation, such as confiscating driving licences.

Another important proposal in the Act is that if the parent with care is on income support, they will be allowed to keep up to £10 a week of the maintenance paid for the child(ren). The Government has suggested that over 250,000 children will benefit from this change.

In order to try to avoid the problems which occurred when the present child support system was introduced too quickly, the Government only plans to start introducing the new reformed system from, probably, 2002 onwards.

Some commentators and practitioners have expressed concern about the new, simple formula in particular. One criticism is that it is possible that the amount of maintenance due under the reformed system would, in most cases, be less than that due under the existing formula, so children (and, indirectly, the taxpayer) will not benefit. Another point is that, under the new system, the income of the parent with care is ignored. It would make no difference to what the non-resident parent pays whether the parent with care earns nothing or £100,000 (for example). Also, unlike the existing system, the Act does not propose any maximum level of assessment, so there is no 'cut off' point for a non-resident parent on a large income.

Finally, another significant proposed change is that, although the court will still be able to make an order for child maintenance if there is consent, either party will be able to opt out of the commitment and 'in' to the Child Support Agency once the court order has been running for a year.

7.4 CHAPTER SUMMARY

(1) In practice, it is not possible to isolate issues of maintenance from the other issues of where the children are going to live and what is going to happen to the matrimonial home and other property.

(2) Maintenance for a spouse is dealt with by the courts under MCA 1973. The court will consider what the CSA assessment will be for any relevant children and then decide whether any payment in addition for the spouse can be afforded

and is appropriate, bearing in mind the s 25 factors. The court will consider the net effect of any proposed order.

(3) The CSA will deal with maintenance for a child where the child is:
- under 16;
- under 19 and in full-time non-advanced education.

(4) The courts will deal with maintenance for a child in the following circumstances:
- where the child is a stepchild;
- where the child is 16 or over and in advanced education;
- where either parent or the child is not habitually resident in the UK;
- to provide top-up maintenance;
- to cover education expenses;
- to cover disability expenses; or
- by making a consent order, if the parent with care is not on welfare benefits.

(5) A complicated formula is applied to calculate maintenance for a child under CSA 1991. The five key stages of calculation are:

   (a) calculate the maintenance requirement;
   (b) calculate each parent's assessable income;
   (c) apply the deduction rate;
   (d) check the protected income level; and
   (e) check the 30 per cent of net income maximum.

(6) Various changes to CSA 1991 have been made in recent years, in particular, the introduction of the departure system. The Child Support, Pensions and Social Security Act 2000 proposes a radical change in the future, replacing the current formula with a simple system based on a flat-rate percentage of the absent parent's net income.

7.5 FURTHER READING

Roger Bird *Child Maintenance* 4th edn (Family Law, 2001)
Child's Pay (computer software published by Class Publishing (Freepost) London W6 7VR)

Chapter 8

THE MATRIMONIAL HOME AND LUMP SUMS

8.1 INTRODUCTION

The matrimonial home is generally the most important property owned by the family. As well as providing a home for the parties and their children, it is an important capital asset. The court must decide whether it is appropriate to retain the property so that it will continue to provide a home or whether to sell it and thereby realise the capital. The home also represents a liability as it must be maintained and in most cases it will be subject to a mortgage. In deciding what should be done with the home, the court is required to have regard to the factors in MCA 1973, s 25 considered in Chapter 4. These factors assist the court in deciding which type of order to make and what size each party's respective share in the home should be. Although the court will take into account the financial contributions made by the parties to the purchase of the home, it is not fettered by proprietary interests and such contributions will frequently be outweighed by other factors. The court has a wide discretion to determine how the property should be held and in what shares. It will take into account the parties' past and future non-financial contributions as well as the other factors referred to in s 25.

In a recent case, the House of Lords has stressed, once again, the importance of the s 25 factors and the fact that they are not ranked in any kind of hierarchy. Which of them carries the most weight will depend on the facts of a particular case. Also, the House of Lords made it clear that, when making a property adjustment order, there was no presumption that both spouses invariably had a right to be able to buy a new home from the assets available to the family. Instead, the court will exercise its discretion in each and every case, in the light of the relevant s 25 factors as applied to that case (*Piglowska v Piglowski* [1999] 2 FLR 763, HL).

Although this chapter is confined to considering the matrimonial home and lump sum orders, it is important to bear in mind that the court will not look at the home in isolation. It will decide upon a package of complementary orders dealing with income and capital. Any agreement concerning the home will require careful drafting. In Chapter 9, consideration is given to drafting the various orders examined in this chapter.

The following orders may be made and are considered below.

(1) Immediate sale.
(2) Outright transfer.
(3) Deferred trust of land.
(4) Deferred charge.

8.2 SELLING THE HOME

There is a variety of reasons why the court might exercise its powers under MCA 1973, s 24A to order the immediate sale of the matrimonial home and the division of the proceeds between the parties. Typically, an immediate sale of the house will be appropriate where the court is effecting an immediate clean break. Each party will be able to use their share of the equity towards purchasing separate homes. They will first redeem the existing mortgage from the proceeds of sale which benefits the parties by releasing them from a significant debt which bound them together. For the sake of clarity, any order for sale should deal with the liabilities to be met out of the proceeds of sale such as the existing mortgage, estate agent's commission and solicitor's conveyancing fees. When calculating the value of the equity the costs of purchase and removal should also be borne in mind. For a publicly funded client the statutory charge will also be paid out of the proceeds of sale. However, it may be possible for the payment of the charge to be postponed by registering it against the assisted party's new home (see **2.6**).

Section 24A(2) provides that the order may contain such consequential or supplementary provisions as the court thinks fit. This, therefore, gives the court the widest discretion to make directions about the sale, for example, which party's solicitors should have the conduct of the sale, how the price is to be determined and what payments should be made out of the proceeds, etc.

There will not usually be sufficient equity for both parties to be able to purchase alternative homes outright. However, if the couple are both earning, they may be able to do so with the aid of a new mortgage. If one party has only low earnings (or low earning capacity), that party may receive a greater proportion of the equity to enable him to re-accommodate himself. A party may be willing to forgo some of his share of the equity in order to achieve a clean break. This may be regarded as the lesser of two evils if the only other viable alternative is for the other party to remain in the property for many years. If the parties are relatively young and without children, the house is likely to be sold even if the equity is very small as there is a strong presumption in favour of a clean break in these circumstances. If there are young children the court will not readily order the sale of their home. The court must give first consideration to the welfare of minor children when determining what should happen to the matrimonial home and will wish to be satisfied that they will be suitably accommodated. The court will also have regard to the disruption which a move might cause to the children and to the adverse effect this could have on their stability and security. If a move to a cheaper area would involve a change in the children's schooling, the court would be most hesitant to order this. However, children frequently adapt well to change and if the home (or the school) has been unhappy, a move might benefit them. If the house is larger than needed and has a substantial equity, it may be unduly harsh on the absent parent to deny him the opportunity to realise some of his capital. In such a case, the court may order sale and perhaps give a weighted share of the equity to the parent caring for the children as she will require a larger property than the absent parent and will frequently have a smaller income.

An immediate sale may be ordered out of necessity if there are insufficient resources to retain and maintain the house. If the couple's finances were already stretched before the marriage breakdown, then plainly it would not be possible for one party to remain in the home and for the other party to accommodate himself as well. It may be that both parties will have to rent properties. Typically, the couple may have purchased the property relatively recently with the aid of a large mortgage and consequently there may be little or (in times of falling house values) no equity.

If one party wishes to sell the home while the other wishes to remain in it, the former could transfer his interest in the home to the latter in return for a lump sum. Whether or not such a 'buy out' can be achieved depends upon whether the spouse who wishes to stay has the means to make the lump sum payment. He may have savings or sufficient income to raise the sum by borrowing. Provided the equity is sufficient, the sum may be raised by increasing the mortgage. The spouse who wishes to sell may agree to a smaller lump sum rather than have the delay and inconvenience of sale on the open market.

8.3 RETAINING THE HOME

The matrimonial home may be retained for the occupation of one party and the children of the family. This occupation may be permanent in the case of an outright transfer, or in the medium to long term in the case of a deferred trust of land or deferred charge.

8.3.1 Outright transfer

Outright transfer is another method of achieving a clean break between the parties as it determines immediately and finally the ownership of the home. The court is unlikely to order an immediate outright transfer unless the transferee spouse has the means to pay the outgoings on the house, including the mortgage. It will also wish to ensure that the transferor spouse has suitable alternative accommodation. He need not necessarily own this accommodation: he may, for example, be provided with accommodation through his employment or he may be living in his new partner's home.

If the transferor is giving up a significant amount of capital, the court will seek to compensate him for this loss. An order for the transfer of a property may be coupled with a lump sum payment from the transferee to the transferor (see the example of Shah at **9.11.12**). The extent to which the transferor spouse will be compensated depends on the value of the equity and on MCA 1973, s 25 factors in general. If the equity is small, the transferor may not receive anything in return. In a sluggish market, a party may be glad to be relieved of responsibility for the property.

Another means of compensating a transferor is by releasing him from paying maintenance to the transferee. However, a spouse cannot be compensated by being released from his obligations to pay maintenance for his children. This is because, in many cases, the transferor will be bound to pay maintenance for the children under CSA 1991. When assessing the amount payable the Child Support Agency will not generally take into account any disposals of capital made by the absent parent on divorce (see **7.3.7**). Similarly, any agreement by the transferee to forgo any claim under CSA 1991 will be unenforceable (see **7.3.4**). Indeed, should the transferee find herself in need of welfare benefits, she will be obliged under CSA 1991, s 6 to pursue her ex-spouse for maintenance for the children. In the less common cases, where the court, rather than the Agency, has jurisdiction to make periodical payment orders for children, it will take into account all the circumstances of the case including a sacrifice by the transferor of his interest in the matrimonial home. As a result, the court may take the view that the transferor should pay only modest maintenance for the children.

Faced with the prospect of forgoing capital in the matrimonial home and paying substantial income in the form of CSA maintenance, it may be that outright transfers of the matrimonial home will be used less frequently than in the past. If the transferee spouse is unable to pay a lump sum to the transferor by way of compensation, the transferor may prefer to preserve his interest in the matrimonial home by means of a deferred charge or trust of land.

8.3.2 Deferred trust of land

The deferred trust of land is a compromise solution to the problem of the matrimonial home. Where the court is of the view that an immediate sale is inappropriate and an outright transfer too harsh on the transferring spouse, it can order the house to be held in the parties' joint names on trust of land. It will specify which spouse is to occupy the home pending sale. The sale of the property is postponed until the first of a number of specified triggering events occur. The order will also settle how the net proceeds of land are to be shared between the parties. The main advantage of the trust of land is that it allows a party and the children to remain in the home after the divorce and it enables the non-occupying spouse to retain an interest in the home which may be realised at a later date.

There are several variations on the trust of land, the differences lie in the events which trigger sale. The main variations are known as the '*Mesher*' order (see *Mesher v Mesher and Hall* [1980] 1 All ER 126, CA), the '*Martin*' order (see *Martin v Martin* [1978] Fam 12) and the '*Harvey*' order (see *Harvey v Harvey* (1982) FLR 141) named after the cases in which they were considered.

Mesher order

TRIGGERING EVENTS

Typically, the events which will trigger the sale in a *Mesher* order will be the first of the following to occur:

(a) the occupying spouse dies, remarries or voluntarily leaves the property; or
(b) the youngest child reaches a specified age (usually 17 or 18 years) or ceases full-time education (if this happens earlier/later).

For an example of a *Mesher* order, see Levy at **9.11.12**.

The advantage of this order is that it provides a secure home for the children of the family and offers medium-term security to the occupying spouse. In addition, each party will know fairly clearly when the sale will take place and can plan accordingly. The non-occupying spouse can be confident that the day will come when he will realise his capital and be released from making any contributions towards the outgoings on the former matrimonial home.

The court's attitude towards the sale of the home on the occupying spouse's remarriage varies. Given that the court's primary consideration is the welfare of the minor children, there is some force to the argument that the children's home should not be jeopardised by the remarriage of their parent. Their step-parent may have little or no resources of his own. On the other hand, the non-occupying spouse will feel aggrieved to watch another person living in his property with his ex-spouse and children. Consequently, most judges are prepared to order that the sale is triggered by the occupying spouse's remarriage. A more controversial trigger for sale is cohabitation by the occupying spouse with a new partner. Such orders require careful drafting, as cohabitation is by no means as clearly definable as marriage. Further, a cohabitee would be under no obligation to maintain his partner or her family. It is also arguable that such a trigger would be unduly restrictive on the occupying spouse's personal freedom and will rarely find favour with the court.

If the occupying spouse gives up occupation of the home, this would trigger sale. The order may, however, provide for the occupying spouse to move to an alternative property without having to settle the absent party's share. Care must be taken when drafting such a clause; the non-occupying spouse will wish to ensure that the substitute property will adequately protect his interest by being marketable and of sound construction, etc. The substitute property may also be cheaper or more expensive than the original property which requires further consideration.

Reference to the youngest child may be drafted so that the sale is triggered on the child reaching the specified age whether or not they remain in education. Alternatively, it may be worded so that the sale is postponed while the child is in full-time secondary (or even higher) education on the basis that the adult child will still require a home.

USE

As we have seen, the *Mesher* order is a compromise solution; it does not resolve all the difficulties with the matrimonial home. Its main shortcoming is that it is only a medium-term solution. The widespread use of *Mesher* orders has been criticised for simply postponing the 'evil day' so as to avoid facing the harsh reality of the present (*Harvey v Harvey* (1982) 3 FLR 141). Sooner or later the occupying spouse will have to leave the home and then start from scratch to find new accommodation. A wife may have to take that step at a vulnerable time in her life when she has a diminishing earning capacity. The court cannot predict with any accuracy how much time the occupying spouse will need to re-accommodate herself or what the housing and job market will be many years ahead. The court has no discretion to postpone the sale beyond the triggering events and it may not interfere with the appointment once it has been settled in the original order. On the other hand, the very fact that the sale is postponed will enable the wife to look to the future and make efforts to become financially independent. Her position may be eased to a certain extent by giving her a greater share of the net proceeds of sale on the assumption that the absent parent will have been able to establish himself and secure accommodation in the years which have elapsed since divorce.

Given that the absent parent may be required to pay a greater proportion of his income in maintenance to the children than in the past, he may be increasingly reluctant to forgo his interest in the matrimonial home entirely. It is possible, therefore, that *Mesher* orders may be used more frequently now for this reason. The absent parent may wish to retain an interest in the former matrimonial home in the hope of recouping some of the money he has been required to pay in maintenance for his children.

Martin order

The *Martin* order operates in a similar way to the *Mesher* order save that the triggers for sale make no reference to the children of the family. The result is that the house need be sold only if the occupying spouse so chooses by leaving or remarrying, or, ultimately, when she dies. Thus, she has the right to remain in the home for life. The *Martin* order will be most appropriate where one spouse is in a significantly weaker financial position than the other. For example, a middle-aged wife may not have worked for many years having cared for the home and family whereas the husband may be living with a new partner and have reasonable earnings. In such a case, the capital realised by the sale would be a bonus to the husband whereas the wife would have to apply her money towards a new property. The court is likely to order that the house should be retained to be used as a home for the wife for life. However, it would not make such an order if the matrimonial home were manifestly surplus to her needs. In such a case, an order for sale and division of the proceeds would be more appropriate.

The obvious advantage of this variation on the trust of land is that it avoids the 'evil day' encountered with the *Mesher* order. Provided the occupying spouse remains in the home and unmarried, she will not be faced with the prospect of a forced sale. The disadvantages of this type of order are equally apparent: the non-occupying spouse has an indefinite wait to realise his capital. Indeed, he may predecease his wife in which case only his estate would benefit. As the occupying spouse has a secure home for life with this type of order, she will not have the same need for capital when the house is sold. The non-occupying spouse may therefore acquire a greater share of the equity than is usually the case with a *Mesher* order. This may go some way to compensate him for the indefinite wait to realise his capital. The court would be unlikely to make a *Martin* order if the occupying spouse could not afford to pay the outgoings on the property, as this would be unduly harsh on the non-occupying spouse. If, exceptionally, the non-occupying spouse, is required to pay maintenance to the occupying spouse he could expect that fact to be reflected by an order giving him an even larger share of the equity upon sale.

Harvey order

In *Harvey v Harvey* (1982) 3 FLR 141, the court sought to mitigate the hardship which a *Martin* order causes to the non-occupying spouse. A *Harvey* order has triggers similar to the *Martin* order but in addition it provides for the payment of an 'occupation rent' by the occupying spouse. The obligation to pay the 'rent' is itself triggered by the children growing up or the mortgage being paid off, whichever first occurs. Although the order attempts to do justice between the parties, it is not without its difficulties and is not commonly made. Consideration would have to be made as to how the 'rent' is to be assessed and paid. The rent is taxable in the hands of the recipient spouse.

8.3.3 Deferred charge

A deferred charge is a further method of retaining a home for a spouse and the children. Although similar to the trust of land, the property remains (or is transferred) into the sole name of the occupying spouse. The non-occupying spouse's interest in the home is represented by a charge over the property. This charge cannot be enforced until one of the triggering events discussed above occurs (*Mesher* or *Martin* triggers). If the occupying spouse cannot pay the charge, at this point the property must be sold. The charge will usually be expressed as a proportion of the net proceeds of sale thereby allowing the charge holder to benefit from any increase in the value of the property (as in the Brown example at **9.11.12**). Less commonly, the charge may be expressed as a fixed sum but this has the obvious disadvantage of its value being eroded by the effects of inflation. The charge will be registered against the title and will take priority over any subsequent liabilities incurred by the owner.

In practical terms, there is very little difference between the deferred charge and the trust of land although the former is less advantageous from a capital gains tax point of view (see **5.2.2**). If the property is already in the parties' joint names, a trust of land will be the preferred method as it avoids interfering with the legal estate. On the other hand, if the property is already in the name of the occupying spouse, the deferred charge would be the preferred method.

8.4 THE INTERESTS OF THIRD PARTIES

8.4.1 Co-owners

If a party owns property with a third party the court may make an order only with respect to the spouse's share of the asset. It cannot interfere with the third party's interest. A third party who is not a legal owner but claims to be beneficially entitled to a property may intervene in proceedings for sale and make representations. So, for example, a parent of one of the parties who has been living in the matrimonial home, having contributed towards the deposit or mortgage, may apply to have the extent of his beneficial interest determined by the court. If the court decided that the property should be sold in such a case, it would probably direct that the parent should be offered the right of first refusal.

8.4.2 Lenders

Where both husband and wife are parties to a mortgage, they will both be bound by the mortgage. This is true unless one of them can argue that the mortgage should not be enforced against them because their consent to the mortgage was obtained by undue influence. For example, a wife may argue that the mortgage should be set aside as against the husband because she was induced to enter into the mortgage as a result either of his actual undue influence (ie he actually put unfair pressure on her or made misrepresentations) or as a result of his presumed undue influence.

Presumed undue influence arises where the wife shows that her relationship with her husband is one of trust and confidence in such matters, making it likely that some unacceptable influence may have been exerted. In a case of presumed undue influence, the wife would also have to show that the mortgage was manifestly disadvantageous to her.

The wife's right to have the mortgage set aside can also be exerted against the lender (ie the lender will not be able to enforce the mortgage against her) if the lender had actual or constructive notice of the risk of undue influence. The lender will be fixed with constructive notice in situations where the transaction is, on its face, not to the wife's advantage, for example where the loan is to guarantee the husband's debts or is for his business, rather than a normal loan for their joint benefit, and consequently there is a greater risk that undue influence may be applied (see *Barclays Bank plc v O'Brien* [1994] 1 FLR 1, HL, and *CIBC Mortgages plc v Pitt* [1993] 4 All ER 433,

HL). To avoid being fixed with constructive notice in these kinds of circumstances, the lender must prove that it took reasonable steps to warn the wife of the risks and advise her to have independent legal advice (see *O'Brien* (above), *Banco Exterior International v Mann* [1995] 1 FLR 602, CA, and *Dunbar Bank plc v Nadeem and Another* [1997] 1 FLR 318, ChD and *Royal Bank of Scotland v Etridge* [1997] 3 All ER 628, CA). If the lender fails to do this, it may well not be able to enforce the mortgage against the wife.

Leaving aside the cases of possible undue influence and returning to more usual circumstances, what is the position of a lender when a court is considering making a property adjustment order with respect to a matrimonial home on divorce?

If a property is ordered to be sold immediately, there will be no problem with the lender: on completion the mortgage (including any arrears which may have built up) must be paid. It may be necessary to obtain the lender's agreement to postpone any possession proceedings to allow a private sale if substantial arrears have built up. The lender may agree to extend the mortgage term or perhaps accept only capital payments in the short term. Only mortgage interest at a standard rate may be paid through income support (and full mortgage interest will not be immediately included in a claim, see Chapter 6).

If the property is to continue in the parties' joint names under a trust of land, this should not cause any difficulties with the lender. The parties may agree between themselves how the mortgage is to be paid. The occupying spouse may undertake to indemnify the non-occupying spouse for his liability under the mortgage. However, as joint owners and joint borrowers, the lenders have the right to look to both spouses to make the repayments. The lender's rights are unaffected by the terms of the trust. However, if the court alters the legal estate by transferring the property into a party's sole name, the lender is entitled to object. Invariably, the lender will be asked to release the transferor spouse from his liability under the mortgage and thereby relinquish the right to pursue the transferor for payment of the debt. Before agreeing to do so, the court will need to be satisfied that the transferee spouse will be able to meet the payments. If the lender is not confident that this will be the case, it may refuse to release the transferor. This condition may defeat the object of the transaction, ie of achieving a clean break. Full disclosure of the payee's resources should be made to the lender in advance of any hearing or agreement to avoid such an objection.

8.5 THE RENTED HOME

If the former matrimonial home is a rented property, the court will have to consider whether the tenancy can and should be transferred into the sole name of one party. Section 24 of MCA 1973, allows the court to transfer 'property': most tenancies will be regarded as 'property' for this purpose. If the tenancy contains a prohibition against assignment, the court cannot order the transfer under this provision unless the landlord consents. As with lenders, the landlord should be contacted at an early stage in the proceedings.

Statutory tenancies which arose under the Rent Act 1977 on the termination of a protected tenancy do not amount to 'property' for the purposes of MCA 1973, s 24 and cannot therefore be transferred under this section. However, under FLA 1996, Sch 7 (previously the Matrimonial Homes Act 1983, s 7 and Sch 1) a statutory tenancy can be vested in the name of one spouse. Strictly speaking this is not a transfer of the tenancy and so may be ordered notwithstanding a prohibition in the tenancy against assignment. However, the landlord would be entitled to make representations before the court and if his objections were reasonable they would be unlikely to be overridden. Protected, assured and secured tenancies may be transferred under MCA 1973, s 24. Protected, assured and secured tenancies may also be transferred under FLA 1996. There will, therefore, be a choice (in most cases) of whether to deal with the tenancy under MCA 1973, or FLA 1996. Legal Representation for ancillary relief will normally specify that orders may only be made under MCA 1973, and as proceedings will already have been brought under that Act, it will normally be convenient to use this jurisdiction.

8.6 PROTECTING THE MATRIMONIAL HOME

The matrimonial home is almost invariably the most important (and valuable) family asset. It is also true to say that the issue of what to do with the home is among the most contentious on marriage breakdown. It is a subject on which emotions frequently run high. One fear which a party may have is that the other party will seek to avoid his responsibilities by disposing of the property. Such a suspicion may be well founded. There are a variety of measures available to prevent a party from disposing of (or charging) the matrimonial home, or other property, and to reverse any attempt by a party to do so.

Whether or not any action need be taken will depend upon how the property is held.

8.6.1 Property in joint names

If the parties hold the property in joint names, neither party can deal with it unilaterally. Any sale or mortgage will require the consent and signature of both parties; therefore, no steps need be taken to guard against this other than advising the client not to sign anything without legal advice (see also **8.4.2** and the possible problem of undue influence).

However, consideration should be given to the question of the parties' beneficial interests in the property. If the parties hold the property jointly in law and equity then their interests will automatically pass to their survivor on death. Given the breakdown of the relationship, the parties are likely to want their share in the property to form part of their own estate. If this is the case, the joint tenancy must be severed to allow the parties to become beneficial tenants in common. This may be achieved by giving written notice of severance to the other party. The severance should be recorded on the title of the property, by a restriction on the proprietorship register (if the property is registered) or memorandum of severance on the conveyance to the parties (if the title is unregistered).

Even if this step is taken, if a party dies intestate prior to decree absolute, the spouse is liable to inherit by default through the rules on intestacy. Clearly, the client should be advised to make a will or any existing will may need to be reviewed.

8.6.2 Property in a party's sole name

Matrimonial home rights

If a spouse is not a legal owner of the property, she may feel in a vulnerable position. In such a case, the spouse should be advised of her matrimonial home rights with respect to the matrimonial home by virtue of FLA 1996, s 30 (previously the Matrimonial Homes Act 1983, s 1). These rights protect a non-owning spouse (husband or wife) against eviction from the matrimonial home without the leave of the court. A spouse will be non-owning for these purposes even if she owns an equitable interest. The rights only exist in respect of one property at a time and it must have been the matrimonial home at some stage.

The rights under FLA 1996, s 30 terminate on the death of the owning spouse or on the grant of a decree absolute, although the court has power under FLA 1996, s 33(5) to direct that the rights should continue beyond these events.

The matrimonial home rights should be registered so that they bind any subsequent buyers and lenders. As always, the rights will not take priority over any pre-existing interests, such as a prior mortgage.

In order to ascertain where the registration should be made, it may be necessary to carry out an Index Map Search at HM Land Registry. This will indicate whether or not the property is registered and, if it is, its title number. If it is registered, a notice should be placed on the register. If the title is unregistered, a Class F Land Charge should be registered against the name of the owning spouse. If a spouse fails to register the rights, she will be unable to assert her rights against any third party.

A non-owning spouse may also have concerns about the payment of the original mortgage. Whether or not a spouse has registered her rights, FLA 1996, s 30(3) obliges a lender to accept payments from a non-owning spouse. (A similar principle applies to payments of rent by a non-tenant spouse.) If possession proceedings are brought, the non-owning spouse must be notified (if she has registered her rights) and she may apply to be made a party to the proceedings. If the court is persuaded that the non-owning spouse is able to pay the mortgage and the arrears within a reasonable time, it will usually refuse an order for possession.

A non-owning spouse may also feel vulnerable if the owning spouse faces bankruptcy because bankruptcy vests the owning spouse's property in his trustee in bankruptcy. Even if not registered, the matrimonial home rights are binding on the trustee and on the creditors. However, the trustee may apply to the court to terminate the rights. If the application to terminate is made more than a year after the bankruptcy, the court is bound to grant it unless the circumstances are exceptional. The client should be advised of this and warned that having no alternative accommodation for herself and her children will not amount to exceptional circumstances.

Pending land action

The limitations of the matrimonial home rights may leave a spouse with inadequate protection. For this reason the registration of a pending land action should be considered. This can be done once proceedings have commenced in relation to property. A request for a property adjustment order in the prayer of the petition or Form A suffices. This prevents any dealing with the property. The registration is not confined to the matrimonial home and it is effective beyond the termination of the marriage. If the property in question is registered land, a caution should be lodged in the proprietorship register. If the land is unregistered, registration is by way of a pending action against the name of the owning spouse.

Injunctions: MCA 1973, s 37

(1) PREVENTING DISPOSALS

If the property has not had any registration made against it, or if the property is not land or the land is situated abroad, an injunction may be sought to prevent a party from disposing of it. An injunction may be granted under MCA 1973, s 37(2)(a) where the court is satisfied that a party is about to make a disposition of property with the intention of defeating the claim for financial relief or impeding its enforcement. The court has power to make whatever order it thinks fit to restrain the party from making the disposition. The applicant must have placed evidence before the court that the disposition is likely and the application is not simply being taken as a precautionary measure. There is a (rebuttable) presumption that the respondent to the injunction application intends to make the disposition in order to jeopardise the applicant's claim if it would have that consequence.

> *Example*
> Mrs Edwards learns that her husband is about to transfer the funds in his savings account to his girlfriend's account. Mrs Edwards can apply for an injunction to freeze the savings account. A copy of the injunction should be served on the bank.

(2) SETTING ASIDE

If the spouse does not learn of the disposition until after it has taken place, all is not lost. Section 37(2)(b) empowers the court to grant an injunction setting aside a reviewable disposition made with the intention of defeating a claim for ancillary relief.

A disposition will be reviewable unless it was made to a bona fide purchaser without notice of the respondent's intention. If the disposition took place less than 3 years before the application, the malevolent intention will be presumed.

> *Example*
> Mr Philips gave his valuable yacht to his brother 18 months ago. Regardless of whether the brother was aware of Mr Philips' purpose the disposition may be set aside as it was not made for valuable consideration.

(3) AVOIDING ENFORCEMENT

If a reviewable disposition is made after financial proceedings have been determined, with the object of avoiding enforcement of an order for financial relief, it may be set aside under MCA 1973, s 37(2)(c).

> *Example*
> Mr Clark is ordered to pay a lump sum of £10,000 to his wife. In order to frustrate this, he transfers his entire investments to his mother. Mrs Clark can seek an injunction to reverse this disposition and enforce the lump sum by means of an order for sale against the investments.

8.7 LUMP SUMS

8.7.1 Lump sums generally

The power of the court to make lump sum orders is discussed at **4.4.1**. Lump sums have also been examined throughout this chapter in the context of a division of the net sale proceeds of the matrimonial home. The assessment of the amount of a lump sum remains to be considered here.

Generally, no lump sum would be awarded where the family assets are modest, otherwise than in relation to a division of the net proceeds of the matrimonial home. However, if following the breakdown of the marriage, the applicant spouse has incurred debts due to the failure of the respondent to maintain her, the court may remedy the problem by ordering a lump sum. Careful thought should be given to the impact of any lump sum on the payee's eligibility for welfare benefits (see Chapter 6).

The impact of the statutory charge could also seriously erode the net value of any lump sum awarded (see **2.6**).

8.7.2 Lump sums in big money cases – Duxbury calculations

If the family assets are substantial, the court will usually consider making a lump sum order in addition to making an order regarding the matrimonial home. The reason for this can be traced to MCA 1973, s 25A which requires the court to facilitate a clean break wherever appropriate. If the family assets are substantial, there will be ample opportunity to achieve a clean break by making a lump sum order and dismissing any claim for spousal periodical payments.

In determining how much the lump sum should be, the court will have regard to the s 25 factors examined in detail in Chapter 4. Any contributions made by a spouse towards the family prosperity will be particularly influential.

In cases where a lump sum is to be preferred over maintenance, the courts have in the past based awards on actual assessments of the capital sum required to produce a given income for the remainder of the wife's life (see *Duxbury v Duxbury* [1987] 1 FLR 7, CA). Computer programs have been devised by accountants and lawyers which can calculate the lump sum which, if invested, will produce enough to meet the payee's needs for the rest of her life. The calculations are based on certain assumptions, such as to life expectancy and rates of inflation, etc. This complicated method is designed to produce an index-linked net income where both the capital and income are used with the result that the fund would be exhausted in the main, on the payee's death. This method cannot, however, protect a spouse against unforeseen future adversity: it may be appropriate to increase the lump sum to provide additional resources to cushion a spouse against such unfortunate eventualities. However, such awards of additional capital should not be automatic. In *O'Neill v O'Neill* [1993] 2 FCR 297, CA, the court reduced a wife's lump sum by £50,000 to £200,000 and made it clear that any award of capital must be justified and should not be made just because 'it is very nice to have, and reasonable that a person in her position should have, some not vast but nevertheless adequate capital resource'. Whichever method of assessment is used, such calculations can only ever be a guide to the court. The court will keep sight of its wide discretion and its obligation to consider all relevant factors in s 25. In various recent cases, the court has stressed that '*Duxbury* is a tool and not a rule' (as observed by Thorpe LJ in *White v White* [1998] 2 FLR 310). The court may depart from the figure produced by the *Duxbury* calculation because, for example, as Singer J pointed out in *A v A (Elderly Applicant: Lump Sum)* [1999] 2 FLR 969, 'each individual has an appreciable chance of doing better than the life tables and that at advanced age this renders particularly hazardous too close a regard' to *Duxbury* calculations. Also, in *G v G (Financial Provision: Separation Agreement)* [2000] 2 FLR 18, the judge considered that the sum for the wife produced by a *Duxbury* calculation would fail to take into account the significant financial contribution already made by the husband; and in *W v W (Ancillary Relief: Practice)* [2000] Fam Law 473, the judge regarded the concept of life long provision under the *Duxbury* approach as inapt bearing in mind the wife's age of 37 years.

8.7.3 Pensions and lump sums

The new powers of the court under MCA 1973, s 25C introduced by the Pensions Act 1995 (see **4.7.2**) extend the court's powers to make a lump sum order on divorce (MCA 1973, s 23) to include any lump sum payable under a spouse's pension scheme.

When the court considers whether to earmark any pension for the benefit of a spouse it will also look at any capital payments payable if the spouse with the pension dies before retirement age. This is an important power as any death in service payment can be used to compensate the surviving spouse for the loss of her share of the pension which, due to the death of the other spouse, will not now be payable. To enable the court order to be effective, MCA 1973, s 25C gives the court power to override the normal discretion of the pension scheme trustees and any nominations made by the other party. This will ensure that the trustees will pay the required amount to the surviving party.

8.8 CHAPTER SUMMARY

(1) Under ss 24 and 24A of MCA 1973, the court may make the following orders with respect to the matrimonial home:

- immediate sale (and division of the proceeds, if any);
- outright transfer to one spouse;
- home retained under a deferred trust of land (eg a *Mesher* order) or subject to a deferred charge.

When deciding what order to make, the court will consider the factors in MCA 1973, s 25. It must also take into account the interests of any third party, such as a lender.

(2) If the matrimonial home is rented, the court has powers under MCA 1973 and FLA 1996 to order the transfer of the tenancy to one spouse.

(3) Several measures are available (eg an injunction under MCA 1973, s 37) to protect against one party disposing of property in order to thwart the other party's financial claim. In particular, a non-owning spouse's matrimonial home rights, under FLA 1996, s 30 should be registered to prevent the owning spouse selling the matrimonial home.

(4) Lump sums are most commonly ordered either in the context of a division of the net sale proceeds of the home (or other property) or as a form of capitalised maintenance, particularly in cases of substantial assets (using a *Duxbury* calculation).

8.9 FURTHER READING

Hartley *Matrimonial Conveyancing* 6th edn (Longmans, 1997)
Rakusen, Hunt and Bridge *Distribution of Matrimonial Assets on Divorce* 3rd edn (Butterworths, 1989); 1992 supplement (Butterworths, 1992)
Duckworth *Matrimonial Property and Finance* (Jordans, looseleaf, 2000)
Family Law Bar Association *At a glance 2000–2001: Essential Court Tables for Ancillary Relief* 9th edn (FLBA, 2000)

Chapter 9

ANCILLARY FINANCE PROCEDURE

9.1 INTRODUCTION

This chapter deals with how to obtain a court order in divorce proceedings providing for the distribution of the matrimonial assets. The order may follow a court hearing or agreement between the parties. Throughout this chapter, the spouse who is applying for the order is called the applicant and the other spouse is called the respondent (regardless of who was the petitioner and respondent in the divorce itself). A pilot scheme was introduced in certain courts from 1 October 1996. The scheme was intended to improve the procedure and reduce costs by introducing far stricter court control together with court-led mediation. This scheme has now been extended to all courts from June 2000.

The drafting of an order to record any agreement between the parties or order of the court will then be considered. Finally, the chapter then briefly considers the procedure to be followed to obtain a maintenance assessment under CSA 1991.

9.2 PUBLIC FUNDING

Before funding is applied for, unless the client is exempt, the solicitor will first need to make a referral appointment for mediation (see FLA 1996, s 29 and **2.5.1**). If it transpires that mediation is unsuitable, then the solicitor can apply for funding in the usual way. At this stage, the appropriate application is likely to be for General Family Help, although if it is clear that there is no reasonable prospect of settlement then the solicitor should apply for Legal Representation.

9.3 OVERVIEW OF THE PROCEDURE

The main aims of the procedure (which is set out in rr 2.51A–2.70 of FPR 1991 (as amended)) are to identify the important issues for the parties and encourage them to reach agreement; to reduce unnecessary cost and delay by imposing a strict timetable; restricting disclosure of financial information and ensuring the parties are aware, at each stage, exactly what costs are being incurred in proceeding with the case. The Rules introduce an 'overriding objective' into the proceedings (FPR 1991, r 2.51B). This is similar to that contained in Part 1 of CPR 1998 and provides that cases should be dealt with proportionately and this will be achieved partly through active case management by the court.

The procedure falls into three phases, each of which ends with a court hearing:

Phase 1: Filing of the application until the end of the First Appointment

Phase 2:   End of the First Appointment until the end of the Financial
                  Dispute Resolution hearing (FDR)

Phase 3:   End of FDR until the Final hearing

In many cases, only the two phases will be needed to achieve a final consent order.

9.4 PRE-APPLICATION PROTOCOL

In line with civil proceedings generally, pre-application protocols are being
developed for family proceedings. The pre-application protocol for ancillary relief
applications (annexed to *Practice Direction (Ancillary Relief: Procedure) (25 May
2000)* [2000] Fam Law 509) came into effect at the same time as the new procedure.
It outlines the steps the parties should take to seek and provide information both
from and to each other prior to the commencement of any ancillary relief application.
It states that pre-application disclosure is usually only appropriate where both parties
agree to it and disclosure is not likely to be an issue. In other cases, it is better to
commence proceedings to take advantage of the court timetable and court managed
process.

9.5 THE APPLICATION

9.5.1 Making the application for ancillary relief

The method of application will depend upon whether the applicant is the petitioner or
the respondent in the divorce.

The petitioner-applicant makes the formal application in the prayer to the petition.
Therefore, the applicant can simply leave unamended the prayers relating to financial
relief which appear in the petition.

The petitioner-applicant must follow up the formal application in the petition by
filing a notice of intention to proceed in Form A. A respondent-applicant merely has
to file Form A.

Form A is a straightforward form in tick box format. However, further information
will need to be given if the application is in relation to land, for example, for a
property adjustment order. In these cases, FPR 1991 state that the Form A should:

(1)   identify the land;
(2)   state whether the title is registered or not and, if registered, its title number; and
(3)   give particulars of any mortgage or interest in the land (FPR 1991, r 2.59).

Where the applicant is seeking an order for earmarking or (after 1 December 2000)
sharing of a pension (see **4.7**), notice must be given in Form A.

It is good practice to apply for all available types of financial order (see Chapter 4).
This not only prevents the client falling into the remarriage trap (see **9.5.2**), but also
allows for a change in circumstances or for a clean break to be effected (see **4.6**).

9.5.2 Potential danger areas

Generally, the application should be made at an early stage. There are several reasons for this.

(1) If the petitioner-applicant omits to apply in the petition, then he may apply later using Form A but only if either the respondent has agreed to the terms of the proposed order or the petitioner obtains the leave of the court. Although leave will usually be given where the applicant has a seriously arguable case and a reasonable prospect of obtaining the relief sought, it will not be given if there has been an unjustifiable delay. Clearly, it is not worth taking the risk of leave being refused and so the application should be submitted as soon as possible.

(2) The remarriage trap: this is caused by MCA 1973, s 28(3) which states 'If after the grant of a decree … either party remarries … that party shall not be entitled to apply … for a financial provision order in his or her favour, or for a property adjustment order …'.

Example

Henry has petitioned for divorce. His wife Eileen is very pleased since she wishes to marry her new partner. The decree absolute is granted and Eileen remarries. Only at this stage does she consult her solicitor about obtaining a lump sum order. It is too late – she has fallen into the remarriage trap.

Note that, if Eileen had applied for a lump sum order at any time before remarrying, that application could be heard after her remarriage, as MCA 1973, s 28(3) only prevents the *making* of an application after remarriage.

(3) A lengthy delay in making or proceeding with the application may result in a less advantageous order being made if, for example, the delay has prejudiced the respondent.

(4) The court has power to backdate a periodical payments order to the date of the application (provided it believes the respondent has the means to pay). Therefore, the earlier the application, the further it can be backdated.

It is particularly important to remember to apply where the applicant is the respondent in the divorce as the solicitor must file the Form A without the benefit of any reminders. In contrast, the petitioner's solicitor is reminded by the petition itself.

Although the application should be made as soon as possible, the court has no power to make the order before decree nisi (and if it purports to do so, any order it makes is void). Also, most orders will not take effect until decree absolute (see **4.2**).

9.6 FILING AND SERVICE

9.6.1 Filing

The applicant needs to file at court:

(1) Form A in duplicate;
(2) General Family Help/Legal Representation certificate and notice of issue (if relevant);
(3) application fee;

(4)   notice of acting where the client received Legal Help in the divorce and now has General Family Help/Legal Representation. This is because the client will have been acting in person in the divorce. Now a solicitor is acting, he will need to ensure that his firm appears on the court file.

Upon filing the Form A, the court will at once (on Form C) fix the date for the First Appointment between 12 and 16 weeks ahead. The timing of this First Appointment cannot be altered without leave from the court. Within this period, much, if not most, of the important financial information-gathering and appraisal of the case will take place.

9.6.2 Service

The court must serve on the respondent a copy of Forms A and C within 4 days of filing (FPR 1991, r 2.61A(4)).

The applicant must serve on the respondent:

(1)   notice of issue of General Family Help/Legal Representation (if relevant);
(2)   copy of notice of acting (Legal Help divorce case only).

The Form A must also be served on any lender or person responsible for a pension arrangement mentioned in the application (FPR 1991, rr 2.59(4) and 2.70(6)). Although the applicant is required to confirm to the court prior to the First Appointment (see **9.8.1**) that this step has been taken, if it is overlooked and the lender or person responsible for a pension arrangement is not served with a copy of the application the hearing may have to be adjourned while the mistake is rectified, with a consequent costs penalty.

9.7 OBTAINING THE EVIDENCE

9.7.1 Duty of disclosure

Each party is under a duty of full and frank disclosure. This duty is underlined in the Pre-Application Protocol. Should they not give full disclosure, this may result in a reduced order (if they are the applicant), or a penalty in costs (see, eg *P v P (Financial Relief: Non-disclosure)* [1994] 2 FLR 381), or the final order being set aside at a later date (see *Jenkins v Livesey (formerly Jenkins)* [1984] FLR 452 and **10.7**). The bulk of the information needed should be contained in the parties' Form Es (see **9.7.2**).

9.7.2 The evidence

Both parties must complete and swear a statement of property and income (Form E). This form is quite lengthy and gives details of the parties and any children; means (including pension); capital and income needs; standard of living; contributions made to the family; conduct (in exceptional cases only); and any other relevant circumstances. Thus, all the essential information required by s 25 of the MCA 1973 should be included in Form E. Each party should also set out any order sought in Form E. Certain essential documents must be filed and served with the Form E:

(1)   last 3 payslips and last P60;
(2)   bank/building society statements for the last 12 months for all accounts;

(3)   any property valuation obtained during the last 6 months;

(4)   most recent mortgage statement(s);

(5)   the last 2 years' accounts for any business and/or partnership and any documentation relating to a valuation of these;

(6)   valuation of any pension; and

(7)   surrender value quotations for any life insurance policies.

Any necessary explanatory documents must also be annexed. Various computer packages have been developed to help the solicitor complete the Form E, for example *Quantum Slip* (Class Publishing). Thus there are no affidavits (although in complex cases affidavits may be ordered). Both Form Es should be filed and simultaneously exchanged at least 35 days before the first appointment.

Both parties should then draft the following documents.

(1)   A concise statement of the issues. This will require the parties to focus on the real issues in the application.

(2)   A chronology.

(3)   A questionnaire of further information and documents requested from the other party. This must be drafted with reference to the issues raised in the statement of issues. In many cases it may be that the Form E and attachments leave no matters outstanding and, in these cases, the parties will file a statement that no further information and documents are required.

(4)   A notice in Form G stating whether that party will be in a position at the first appointment to proceed on that occasion to an FDR appointment. This will be the case where both parties feel that they have all the disclosure they need and it allows a form of 'fast tracking' in these cases.

These four documents must be filed and served by both parties at least 14 days before the first appointment. In addition, immediately before the first appointment, the solicitors for both parties must produce a written estimate of the costs incurred so far in Form H. Note that this is something separate from the schedule of costs required by CPR 1998 (see **9.10**). Thus, if the solicitor wishes to claim the costs of the First Appointment, he must complete and serve a schedule of costs at least 24 hours before the hearing.

9.8   COURT HEARINGS

9.8.1   The first appointment

The court will fix a date for this when the applicant files Form A (see **9.6.1**). The short timetable is to allow the court to monitor the application and its progress from an early stage with a view to limiting the issues and saving costs. Both parties and all legal representatives must attend. At this appointment, the district judge will give directions and decide how the application should proceed from then on.

The directions will deal with:

(a)   the extent to which the questionnaires need to be answered;

(b)   documents to be produced;

(c)   valuations or other expert evidence (joint independent experts should be instructed where practicable);

(d) the production of other evidence, such as schedules of assets or, in some cases, affidavits.

Particular considerations which may arise at this stage

VALUATION OF THE HOME

Directions will usually require that the parties agree a valuation and, if they are unable to agree, that they appoint a joint expert valuer. If they cannot agree on a valuer, then the court will appoint one.

VALUATION OF THE FAMILY BUSINESS

There may be a family business which the client wants to be valued. The court will not order a sale of the family business, nor make an order which would mean in effect that the owner was forced to sell to comply with the order (see **7.2.1**). The court will also be anxious to ensure that the family assets are not needlessly wasted on expensive valuations of the business (*Evans v Evans* [1990] 1 FLR 319). Therefore, an approximate valuation is all that is needed.

Again, the court is likely to restrict the use of experts by giving a direction for joint appointment or, in default, only allowing one per party.

NEW PARTNERS

One party may claim that the other party has a new partner who is working and who, therefore, is able to contribute to the outgoings, thus freeing more cash for the former family or reducing the new family's needs. Say, for example, that the wife had a new partner. The husband might want to know what that partner's assets were. Although the district judge is empowered to order the attendance of any person at the hearing (FPR 1991, r 2.62(4)), in practice this power has been restrictively interpreted. Accordingly, the court will not order a non-party to attend for cross-examination unless he has filed an affidavit (*W v W* (1981) *The Times*, 21 March). In addition, it has been held that the court cannot order a non-party to file an affidavit (*Wynne v Wynne* [1980] 3 All ER 659).

In such a situation, it may be possible to persuade the court to order the non-party to attend an 'inspection appointment'. FPR 1991, r 2.62(7) provides that any party may apply to the court for an order that any person attend an inspection appointment, bringing with him such documents as are specified in the order and the inspection of which appears to the court to be necessary for disposing fairly of the case. The case of *Frary v Frary* [1993] 2 FLR 696 makes it clear, however, that FPR 1991, r 2.62(7) does not change the law relating to *who* the court can order to disclose their assets, it simply allows the court to order disclosure at an earlier date, ie before the hearing.

The district judge will then usually give a date for a Financial Dispute Resolution (FDR) appointment unless, exceptionally, he decides this is not appropriate. In these exceptional cases (which are likely to be those which are very complicated), the district judge must give one of the following directions:

(1) that a further directions appointment be fixed;
(2) that an appointment be fixed for an interim order;
(3) that the case be fixed for a final hearing; or
(4) that the case be adjourned for mediation or negotiation or (in exceptional cases) generally.

Alternatively, unless there are considerable assets involved or the assets require further investigation, the district judge will treat the first appointment as an FDR appointment.

Both parties' representatives will produce their written costs estimates. The district judge must consider whether he should make a costs order at this stage, depending on the circumstances and the extent to which the parties have adhered to the rules. Thus if, for example, one party fails to provide the relevant documentation with Form E and this wastes the opportunity of having an FDR, they are very likely to have a costs order made against them.

9.8.2 From first appointment to FDR

Both parties should comply with all directions made at the first appointment before the FDR. Neither party can insist on any further disclosure without leave of the court.

The applicant must inform the court of all offers or proposals and responses made to them at least 7 days before the FDR. This should give the lawyers sufficient time to consider any proposals and ensure that their clients are not surprised by them at the hearing. Although there is no statutory requirement, the court will expect the parties to make offers and proposals, to give them proper consideration and not attempt to exclude their consideration at the FDR (*Practice Direction (Ancillary Relief Procedure)* [2000] 2 Fam Law 509).

Immediately before the FDR, both parties must produce a second written costs estimate.

9.8.3 The FDR appointment

The aim of the FDR is to produce a settlement. Both parties and all legal representatives must attend. The FDR will be conducted by a district judge who will then have nothing more to do with the case. The district judge will attempt to help the parties towards settlement by exploring common ground. Any offer made so far can be referred to at the FDR, even 'without prejudice' offers. All discussions at the FDR will be completely privileged. Documents referring to prior offers must be returned to the party who filed them at their request and not kept on the court file.

Where a settlement is reached at the FDR, the district judge may make a consent order reflecting the agreement. The district judge may also adjourn the FDR to allow one or both parties time to consider their position.Where there is no agreement reached, the judge may make further directions, including, where appropriate, setting a hearing date. In cases involving large sums of money, the district judge may make a direction that narrative affidavits be filed by the parties at this stage to give a broader presentation of the historical background of the application than that allowed for in the Form E. These might cover, for example, the respective contributions of the parties, the genesis of current resources and the standard of living during the marriage (*W v W (Ancillary Relief: Practice)* [2000] Fam Law 473).

9.8.4 From FDR to hearing

Any directions made at the FDR should be complied with. Either party can apply for further directions, and the court may direct a further FDR.

Before the hearing, both parties must draft a statement of proposed orders, file this at court and serve it on the other party. The applicant must do this at least 14 days before the hearing and the respondent within 7 days of being served with the applicant's proposals. These statements are open and no privilege will attach to them. However, this new rule has no effect on the without prejudice offer and such offers may continue to be made at any time (see **9.10**).

The parties must both produce a costs estimate at the final hearing.

9.8.5 The final hearing

The hearing is usually before a district judge, in chambers and in private. The district judge has power to refer the case to a judge if necessary (FPR 1991, r 2.65).

In theory, the hearing should follow the same course as ordinary civil proceedings. However, they are often much more informal. Having read the papers, the district judge may open by letting the parties know what he has in mind and inviting them to discuss and negotiate around this for a while.

If this does not succeed, or if the district judge wishes the proceedings to follow a more formal course, then the applicant's solicitor (or counsel) will open. He will outline the case and then call his evidence. The evidence will often consist only of that of the applicant, but other witnesses, for example, a new partner or valuer may be called. The witnesses will then be cross-examined by the respondent's solicitor. He will then present his own client's case. Once all the evidence has been given, the district judge will make the order (or may reserve his judgment until a later date). A careful note should be taken of exactly what is said in case it should be necessary to appeal.

It is possible that the district judge will not feel able to make a final order at this time, for example, because it appears that the respondent is about to obtain (or lose) a job, or because the respondent has not turned up to the hearing. In such a situation, the district judge could make an interim order on such terms as he thought just.

Copies of any order made are sent to both parties by the court.

9.9 INTERIM ORDERS

Despite the fact that one of the aims of the procedure is to save time, it may still be many months before a final order is made. Thus, the Rules allow a party to apply at any stage of the proceedings for an order for maintenance pending suit (see **4.3.1**), interim periodical payments or an interim variation order. The application will be made by notice of application. If the application is made before filing Form E, it must be accompanied by a draft of the order requested, together with a short sworn statement explaining why the order is necessary and giving necessary information about means. On filing the notice of application, the court will give a hearing date which must be at least 14 days later. The applicant must then immediately serve the respondent with a copy of the notice of application (and accompanying documents where relevant). Where the respondent has not already filed Form E, he must file and serve a short sworn statement setting out his means at least 7 days before the hearing.

9.10 COSTS

9.10.1 Costs generally

Introduction

The importance of costs in ancillary proceedings cannot be over emphasised. It is essential that the question of costs is kept in sight and in proportion to the overall assets in dispute. In the case of *Re T (Divorce: Interim Maintenance: Discovery)* [1990] 1 FLR 1, FD, the entire litigation costs were said to exceed £1.2m. The impact of costs on the family finances is so significant that, under FPR 1991, r 2.69F, each party must produce to the court at each court appointment, a written estimate of costs (see **9.7.2**). In addition, adherence to the overriding objective and active case management by the courts under the new ancillary relief procedure should help to ensure that costs are kept in proportion to the overall assets.

Whilst the Civil Procedure Rules 1998 (CPR 1998) do not directly affect family law and procedure generally, the new Rules, as they relate to costs, do apply to family proceedings. The relevant Parts are Part 43, Part 44 (except rr 44.9–44.12), Part 47 and Part 48, which provide for summary assessment and detailed assessment of costs when a costs order is being made (see Family Proceedings (Miscellaneous Amendments) Rules 1999, SI 1999/1012, and also *Practice Direction (Family Proceedings: Costs)* [1999] 1 FLR 1295).

One important modification, however, is that the general rule set out in r 44.3(2) – that costs follow the event – does not specifically apply to family proceedings. The case of *Gojkovic v Gojkovic (No 2)* [1991] 2 FLR 233 suggests that this should still be the starting point in family cases but that it can be displaced much more easily than in other civil proceedings. One of the key difficulties in family proceedings is that the task of determining who has 'won' and who has 'lost' is not always as straightforward as in ordinary civil actions. For example, a wife applies for a transfer of the home into her sole name plus maintenance for herself. The husband objects as he wishes the house to be sold immediately. If the court orders that the wife should only have the right to remain in the house for life under a trust of land in return for paying the husband a small lump sum, it is difficult to see which party is the victor.

In exercising its discretion on costs the court may take into account a party's conduct towards the financial proceedings. Therefore, if a party fails to co-operate with the *Evans* guidelines, uses unnecessary delaying tactics or refuses to disclose relevant documents he may be penalised by a costs order against him (see *Gojkovic v Gojkovic (No 2)* and now also r 44.3(4) of CPR 1998).

The incorporation of the cost rules contained in CPR 1998, together with the FPR 1991, means that the solicitors for both parties must file and serve a schedule of costs containing the information required by the Practice Direction to Part 44, para 4.5(2) at least 24 hours before any hearing.

9.10.2 Offers to settle

Offers to settle are an important part of ancillary relief cases. The new Family Proceedings Rules, rr 2.69 and 2.69A–2.69E superimpose on the basic costs structure set out in CPR 1998, specific rules relating to family proceedings in relation to offers to settle.

The Rules provide that either party may at any time make a written offer to settle which is 'without prejudice except as to costs' (FPR 1991, r 2.69). This reflects in legislation the so-called '*Calderbank*' offer (named after *Calderbank v Calderbank* [1975] 3 All ER 333) and is a means of putting pressure on the other party to settle. Such an offer will not be disclosed to the court, except in the context of an FDR (see **9.8.3**), until all the issues have been resolved and the question of costs is being considered.

Such an offer can be made at any time, but to be effective there must have been full relevant disclosure (*Gojkovic v Gojkovic (No 2)* [1991] 2 FLR 233). This means that, in most cases, such an offer will not be appropriate until exchange of Form Es (see **9.7.2**). What is the effect of such an offer?

Judgment more advantageous than offer made by the other party

Where the recipient beats the offer made, the court must award her costs (from 28 days after the offer was made) unless it considers it unjust to do so (FPR 1991, r 2.69B). This is clearly designed to focus the mind of the person making the offer to ensure that his offer is reasonable.

Judgment more advantageous than offers made by both parties

What if, as is usually the case, offers are made by both parties? In this situation, if either party does better than both offers the court may order, where it considers it just:

(1) the other party to pay costs on the indemnity basis;
(2) interest on those costs at up to 10 per cent above base rate; and
(3) interest on any lump sum awarded.

In each case, this would run for some or all of the period beginning 28 days after 'the offer' was made. It is not clear which of the offers this refers to, presumably the last.

Note that whether the court makes all (or any) of these orders is in its discretion.

Just or unjust?

FPR 1991, r 2.69D sets out factors which the court should take into account in deciding whether it would be just or unjust to make the orders outlined above. The court must take into account all the circumstances of the case including the terms of any offers; the stage in proceedings that any offer was made; the information available to the parties at the time of the offer; and the conduct of the parties and the means of the parties.

9.11 NEGOTIATIONS

One of the key features of the ancillary relief procedure is the promotion and facilitation of settlements. Most cases do, in fact, settle by agreement, often during informal discussions following the FDR. However, negotiations are an on-going process and may well commence at a very early stage. This is generally to be encouraged as it will probably be quicker and will cost the parties less, so leaving more of the assets available to be divided between them. Further, it may help to lessen any ill-feeling caused by the breakdown of the marriage and, therefore, aid the parties' future relations, in particular with the children. In addition, the respondent is more likely to comply with an order which he has agreed to, thus avoiding the need for enforcement proceedings.

However, beware of settling at any price. Any agreement represents a compromise but the solicitor must ensure that negotiations are carried out with full knowledge of all material facts. Both parties are under a duty of full and frank disclosure (see **9.7.1**). Do not be afraid to ask the other party for the same level of disclosure as he would give if the matter was to proceed to a hearing.

In addition, the solicitor should be aware of the type of order which the court might be expected to make, thus ensuring that he does not allow his client to accept too little or offer too much. Take care to check that the client is not willing to accept a very low offer simply because he is in an emotionally vulnerable state following the breakdown of the marriage.

If a settlement is reached, heads of agreement should be drawn up and signed by the parties and their legal representatives to evidence the necessary consensus. However, as was made clear in *Xydhias v Xydhias* [1999] 1 FLR 683, although the court will usually uphold the agreement, it is not enforceable in its own right.

9.12 CONSENT ORDERS

Once the parties have reached agreement, the applicant's solicitor should draw up a draft consent order and send it to the respondent's solicitor. To enable the court to investigate the parties' means, a statement of information must also be completed. This statement must include:

(1) the duration of the marriage, the age of each party and of any minor children of the family;

(2) an estimate of the approximate value of the capital resources and net income of each party and of any minor child of the family;

(3) what arrangements are intended for the accommodation of the parties and any minor child of the family;

(4) whether either party has remarried or has any present intention to remarry or to cohabit with another person;

(5) where the order includes a transfer of property, whether any lender has been served with notice of application and whether they have objected to the transfer;

(6) where the order includes a term which imposes any requirement on the person responsible for a pension arrangement, whether they have been served with the notice of application and whether they have objected to the order;

(7) any other specially significant matters.

However, if the application is only to vary a periodical payments order or for an interim periodical payments order, the statement of information can be restricted to an estimate of the net income of the parties and any minor children (FPR 1991, r 2.61).

Often the applicant's solicitor will insert the applicant's details in the statement and then send it to the respondent's solicitor with the draft order. The respondent's solicitor will then complete the statement with the respondent's details, indorse his consent on the order and return both to the applicant's solicitor. However, the statement of information does not have to be on one document, so each party can complete their own.

The applicant's solicitor should then file the draft order plus a copy together with the statement of information. He must also file Form A if agreement was reached at such an early stage that this has not yet been done.

The district judge will then peruse the filed documents and, if satisfied, can make an order in the agreed terms. In the rare event that he is not satisfied, he can order the parties to attend a hearing.

If agreement is reached at a hearing, the district judge can dispense with the need for filing a statement of information.

The consent order is then drafted immediately by both parties' solicitors and approved and made by the district judge.

9.13 DRAFTING ANCILLARY FINANCIAL AND PROPERTY ORDERS

It is very important for a family solicitor to be able to draft orders which give effect to any financial agreement between husband and wife (or order of the court) in the way intended. It is equally important for the solicitor to be able to spot any errors in a draft order that is sent to him for his approval. At **9.13.13**, there are three specimen orders: Shah, Levy and Brown. These should be read carefully as they will be referred to throughout **9.13** to illustrate a variety of drafting points.

9.13.1 Form of order

The order should be set out in three parts as follows:

Title of suit

PREAMBLE

This can deal with matters the court has no power to order, for example, mortgage payments, paying for outgoings on the house (but see **9.13.5** – deferred trusts of land). It:

(1) states whether the order is made by consent (as in Shah and Levy) or (in a contested case) after hearing representations from the parties (and their solicitors/counsel) (see Brown);

(2) may indicate the basis on which the order is made, for example, on the basis that the applicant pays the mortgage instalments out of her maintenance payments (see Levy);

(3) recites any undertakings given by either party, for example, to keep the property in good repair (see Levy).

OPERATIVE PART OF ORDER

This is prefaced by the words 'It is ordered'. It must be couched in clear and unambiguous terms so that each party can see, for example, what he or she is required to do, by when and/or until when. It must also reflect what the court's powers under MCA 1973, ss 22–24A actually are. Even by consent, the court cannot order a party to do something which it has no power to do (eg order the husband to pay school fees).

Note that third parties cannot be ordered to do anything, for example, a building society cannot be ordered to grant or transfer a mortgage.

9.13.2 Undertakings

An undertaking given to the court would appear to take effect (for all practical purposes) as if it were an order (see, for example, Lord Brandon in *Livesey (formerly Jenkins) v Jenkins* [1985] FLR 813 at 829). It is contempt of court to fail to comply with an undertaking, and the obligation can be enforced like an order, for example, if it is to pay money, garnishee or other methods of enforcement can be used (see **10.2.2**). The court may accept undertakings to do things which it cannot itself expressly order. The terms of an undertaking will be set out in the preamble to the order. Common examples would include provisions for one party:

(1) to make payments to a third party, for example, the husband to pay mortgage instalments to the building society direct in addition to, or instead of, periodical payments, or to pay debts;
(2) to take out a life insurance policy for the benefit of the other;
(3) to seek the release of the other party from mortgage or leasehold covenants, or to indemnify him/her in respect of them;
(4) to guarantee a mortgage;
(5) to purchase property.

9.13.3 Periodical payments

The order must indicate in relation to the payments:

(1) by whom payable;
(2) to whom payable;
(3) period by reference to when calculated, for example, £2,000 per annum;
(4) period by reference to which payable, for example, monthly in advance;
(5) from what date or event payments are to commence; and
(6) until what date or event they are to continue (remember the age limits for children (see **4.3.2**)).

Example
'That the respondent makes or causes to be made to the petitioner periodical payments for herself during their joint lives or until she remarries or until further order as from 1 April 2000 at the rate of £5,000 per annum payable monthly in advance on the first day of each calendar month.'

Spouse and child provision (if any) should appear in separate clauses. In cases where maintenance for a child is not covered by the Child Support Act 1991, child provision should clearly indicate whether payer is to:

(1) pay direct to the child; or
(2) pay to a third party (usually the other parent) for the child's benefit.

Where (as is usual) the order provides for payment to continue until the child reaches 17 (or 18) or ceases full-time education, the words 'whichever is the later' should be added.

Note that where the Child Support Agency makes an assessment, this will not appear in the court order.

9.13.4 Lump sums

Remember that an order may provide for more than one sum and that payment may be deferred until a later date or an event and/or be by instalments (see **4.4.1**). The order must indicate in respect of each sum:

(1) by whom it is payable;
(2) to whom it is payable;
(3) by what date or contingency it is to be paid;

For example, 'on or before the 30th day of June 2001'.

9.13.5 Property adjustment orders (not requiring an immediate sale)

Remember that although such orders usually affect only the home, any property may be covered such as furnishings, stocks and shares, other land, cars (see Shah). The following points primarily relate to land, including the home.

Preliminary considerations

The order must make sense from a conveyancing and property law point of view. The solicitor will need to ascertain the following.

(1) Where is the legal estate now? Is it in joint names, or his or hers alone?
(2) Where is the legal estate going? Is it to stay in joint names or to be put into joint names for the purposes of a deferred trust of land? Or is it to be transferred into the sole name of one? This will be so for an outright transfer (with or without a lump sum in return), or a deferred charge.
(3) What are the equities now, and what are they going to be? This is relevant in two main cases:

   (a) where the house is in one spouse's sole name but the other spouse may have an equitable interest from contributions to purchase or improvement. If the owning spouse is to keep the home outright, perhaps paying the other a lump sum, the non-owner should be ordered to transfer her equitable interest to him;
   (b) a *Mesher* or *Martin*-type order creating a deferred trust of land, where the new equities will be set out in the order.

Outright transfers (with or without lump sums in return)

The legal estate and/or equitable interests must be ordered to be transferred to one party as appropriate (see, eg, Shah, clause 2) and a date or event for compliance must be inserted. This date/event must be after the decree absolute (see **4.2**).

Deferred trusts of land (see Levy)

The legal estate must be vested in trustees (usually but not necessarily the parties) and ordered to be transferred if need be, with a date for compliance if that is so. The terms of the trust must be set out including:

(1) a statement of who has the right to occupy until sale;
(2) the determining (or 'triggering') event(s) for sale to take place, for example, the occupying spouse's remarriage;
(3) the proportions of the sale proceeds to which the parties will be entitled on sale.

Other provisions may be included, for example, detailed provisions to enable the original property to be sold and another bought on the same trusts if the occupier wishes to move, or as to who should have responsibility for repairs.

Contrary to the usual position, where there is a deferred trust the wording of MCA 1973, s 24(1)(b):

> 'an order that a settlement of such property ... be made to the satisfaction of the court ...',

is wide enough to allow the court to actually order a party to, for example, pay the mortgage or insurance on the property, rather than having to deal with it by way of undertaking (see, eg, Levy, clause 2.3).

Deferred charge (see Brown)

If necessary, the legal estate must be ordered to be transferred into the sole name of the intended occupier with a date for compliance. She will then be ordered to execute a legal charge (within a specified time) to secure payment to the non-occupier of a sum representing a proportion of the value of the property as defined in the order or a fixed sum (as agreed).

The order will require the charge deed to specify the events which will make the statutory power of sale arise and become exercisable, and may provide for matters such as removal and repairs to be covered by covenants to be set out in the deed.

Transfer of tenancies

The court also has power to order the transfer of most types of tenancy (see **8.5**). The wording of an order to effect this is relatively straightforward, for example, 'The Respondent do transfer his tenancy in Flat 2, The Broadway, Guildshire, to the Applicant within one month of decree absolute'. Remember that the landlord should be contacted at an early stage so his consent can be obtained.

Further points

The orders do not operate to vest or transfer legal estates nor to create legal charges. Conveyancing documents will be required to do this. The order should state who is to pay for the conveyancing costs (eg Brown, clause 1).

9.13.6 Orders for sale

In some cases, property may need to be sold in order to realise and divide the cash value. Where the home is in the sole name of one party this will most commonly be achieved by ordering the property owner to pay a lump sum to the other party equivalent to the desired share. The owner may raise the sum either by borrowing against the property or selling it, at his option. The non-owner is unaffected either way so long as the cash is paid.

Where property is in joint names, the court has power under the Married Women's Property Act 1882 (MWPA 1882), s 17 to order simply that the trust of land be executed and the proceeds divided. On divorce, the court may exercise its powers under MWPA 1882, s 17 without a separate formal application.

9.13.7 Pensions (from 1 December 2000)

The order must state that there is to be a provision by way of pension arrangement (or earmarking) or pension sharing in accordance with an annex or annexes to the order. This annex must contain must contain the information prescribed in FPR 1991, r 2.70(14) and (15) (as amended).

9.13.8 Dismissals

Just as an application for a particular type of order may be granted by the making of an order, for example, for the payment of a lump sum, so an application may be dismissed. Any application by either party which is not granted by the making of an order should be dismissed. The dismissal may be of an individual application or the order may provide for the dismissal of all outstanding applications (see, eg, Levy, clause 5).

However, an application can be dismissed only if it has been made. If the husband is the respondent in the divorce, he may not have made any applications. Some courts will require that he files Form A so that his applications can be dismissed. However, no fee will be required if Form A is marked 'for dismissal purposes only'.

9.13.9 Clean break orders

Remember that such orders involve either an immediate dismissal of all maintenance claims or an order that maintenance should be paid for a finite term only (see **4.6.2**).

Where an application for periodical payments for a spouse is dismissed to effect a clean break the order should go on (under MCA 1973, s 25A) to direct that she 'shall not be entitled to make a further application in relation to the marriage' for a secured or unsecured periodical payments order (as in Shah, clause 4).

Where the order is for term maintenance, it should direct that the applicant 'shall not be entitled to apply for an extension of the term' (see Levy, clause 4(a)).

The order should normally state that neither party, on the death of the other, shall be entitled to apply for an order under the Inheritance (Provision for Family and Dependants) Act 1975 (see Shah, clause 5).

9.13.10 'Liberty to apply'

The words 'Liberty to apply' are conventionally included in an order. They simply envisage that the parties may need to come back to the court to resolve any difficulties over the interpretation of the order in the light of circumstances which may occur or putting it into effect, for example, if when the house is sold there is a dispute over which/how many estate agents to use. They do not in any way affect the court's power to vary an order and the restrictions on that power.

9.13.11 Costs

The costs of each ancillary matter is a separate matter distinct from the main suit and any other application. When considering the costs of the ancillary relief proceedings, remember that the cost provisions in CPR 1998 apply, with slight amendment, to family proceedings (see **9.10**). On an earlier hearing, there may already have been a summary assessment of costs. Alternatively, if the order was silent as to costs, no party is entitled to costs in relation to that order (CPR 1998, r 44.13).

Where the court orders one party to pay the costs of the other party, it may either make a summary assessment or order a detailed assessment of the costs (for further details, see LPC Resource Book *Civil Litigation* (Jordans)).

If each side is to bear its own costs, the order will say that there be 'no order as to costs' (see, eg, Shah, clause 7). Where it is an application for a consent order (see **9.12**), the parties should agree a figure for costs to be inserted in the order or agree there should be no order as to costs as otherwise it will be necessary for attendance at the hearing.

If the receiving party is publicly funded:

(1) there must be a detailed assessment of costs, if not agreed (see, eg, Brown, clause 8); and

(2) where property or cash 'recovered or preserved' is intended to provide a house, a statement to that effect must be included in the body of the order to enable the Legal Services Commission to exercise its discretion to postpone the enforcement of the statutory charge. The Lord Chancellor has prescribed the following clause:

> 'And it is certified for the purpose of the Community Legal Service (Financial) Regulations 2000 [that the lump sum of £X has been ordered to be paid to enable the applicant/respondent to purchase a home for himself/herself (or his/her dependants)] [that the property (address) has been preserved for/recovered by the applicant/respondent for use as a home for himself/herself (or his/her dependants)].'

See Brown, clause 1.

Finally, remember to deal with the costs of implementing the order, for example, conveyancing costs.

9.13.12 Side-letters

In some cases, it may be useful to record in a side-letter the background to the order and the result that it is trying to achieve. This can aid the court if at a later date one of the parties seeks to vary the order (see **10.8.3**).

9.13.13 Specimen orders

There follow three specimen orders: Shah, Levy and Brown. These should be read carefully as they are referred to throughout **9.13** to illustrate a variety of drafting points.

SHAH v SHAH

[Order for transfer of property with lump sum back or sale in default.]

There follows an outline of the facts of the case which resulted in the order below (note these facts are *not* part of the order):

H and W are both working and self-supporting. There are no children. The matrimonial home is owned in joint names and is subject to a mortgage to the Halnat Building Society. It has been agreed that W (respondent) will transfer to H her half share in the property in return for £15,000, being approximately ½ the net equity. H will finance this by a second mortgage. Should it not be possible for him to raise the money within 3 months of decree absolute the house will be sold and the proceeds divided equally. Each party is to pay their own costs.

IN THE HULLPOOL COUNTY COURT		2001	No ....
BETWEEN	RAJ SHAH		Applicant
	AND		
	GITA SHAH		Respondent

ORDER

UPON the Applicant UNDERTAKING to the court to indemnify the Respondent against any future liability under the mortgage dated ... in favour of the Halnat Building Society ('the Mortgage') secured on the property at 93 Brook Court Hullpool ('the Home') and to use his best endeavours to obtain her release from her covenants under the Mortgage and to pay for the costs of transfer of the Home as set out in clause 2

BY CONSENT IT IS ORDERED THAT:

1. The Applicant shall within 3 months of decree absolute in this cause ('the Payment Date') pay or cause to be paid to the Respondent the sum of £15,000 (the 'Lump Sum').

2. On payment of the Lump Sum on or before the Payment Date the Respondent shall execute such document or documents as may be required to transfer to the Applicant

    (i) all her legal and equitable interest in the Home
    (ii) all fixtures and chattels now in the Home which belong to her alone and her interest in any such items which are jointly owned.

3. If the Lump Sum is not paid by the Payment Date then the Home shall be sold and the proceeds of sale (after redemption of the Mortgage and payment of the costs of the sale) shall be divided as to £15,000 to the Respondent, and the balance to the Applicant.

4. Upon compliance with clauses (1)–(3) and the Applicant's undertakings to the court and upon the making of a final decree herein, the Applicant's and the Respondent's claims for financial provision and property adjustment orders do stand dismissed and neither the Applicant nor the Respondent shall be entitled to make any further application in relation to the marriage for an order under s 23(1)(a) or (b) of the Matrimonial Causes Act 1973.

5. Pursuant to the Inheritance (Provision for Family and Dependants) Act 1975, s 15, the court considering it just so to order, neither the Applicant nor the Respondent shall be entitled on the death of the other to apply for an order under s 2 of that Act.

6. There be liberty to apply.

7. There be no order as to costs.

Dated the   day of   2001.

…………………………………..

Signature (on behalf) of the Applicant

…………………………………..

Signature (on behalf) of the Respondent

    Signed:

        District Judge

LEVY v LEVY

[Mesher order: periodical payments to wife (linked to payment of mortgage) and step-child; dismissal of prayer for lump sum and respondent's application.]

Background information (note this is *not* part of the order): Michelle Levy has recently obtained a decree absolute against Michael Levy under MCA, s 1(2)(d). The parties have agreed that the 3 children of the family, Anthony (7) (who is Mrs Levy's child by her first husband who is now dead) Robert (5) and Peter (3), will remain with Mrs Levy. The parties are in their mid-thirties. Mr Levy is a partner in a firm of surveyors. Mrs Levy has not been in paid employment since the birth of their first child. The former matrimonial home is in joint names and subject to a mortgage. Mr Levy has agreed that Mrs Levy and the children will remain in the home while the children are being educated. Mr Levy now lives in a flat. A consent order has been negotiated. Neither is publicly funded.

IN THE HIGHBRIDGE COUNTY COURT   2001   No ....

BETWEEN   MICHELLE ANN LEVY   Applicant

AND

MICHAEL JAMES LEVY   Respondent

ORDER

BY CONSENT IT IS ORDERED:

1.   That the property known as Twintrees, Hill Road, Highbridge ('the Property') is held by the Applicant and Respondent upon a trust of land for themselves as beneficial tenants in common.

2.   That the trust be subject to the following terms and conditions:

2.1   The Applicant shall be entitled to occupy the Property to the exclusion of the Respondent until sale

2.2   The Property shall not be sold without the Applicant's written consent until

2.2.1   the Applicant remarries, dies or (subject to clause 2.6) voluntarily leaves the Property; or

2.2.2   all the children of the family reach the age of 18 or finish full-time undergraduate education if later; or

2.2.3   further order of the court;

whichever first occurs

2.3   The Applicant shall with effect from the date of this order be solely responsible for all payments of capital and interest on the mortgage in favour of [ ]

2.4   The Applicant shall be responsible for all routine maintenance and decorative repairs to the Property

2.5   The cost of insuring the Property and of any structural repairs shall be shared equally between the Applicant and the Respondent

2.6   So that the Applicant shall be able to move to another house during the subsistence of this trust:

      (i)   the trustees shall, if requested by the Applicant, sell the Property and re-invest the proceeds in the purchase of such other dwelling ('the Substitute Property') as she shall direct for her occupation

      (ii)   the Applicant shall pay the costs of and incidental to such sale and purchase

      (iii)   the Substitute Property shall be held on the same trusts terms and conditions as the Property and the trustees shall have full power as if they were beneficial owners to execute such mortgage deed as may be necessary to enable the purchase to be completed

      (iv)   if the purchase price of the Substitute Property shall be less than the net proceeds of the Property the difference shall be divided as to 75% to the Applicant and 25% to the Respondent

3.   That upon sale (except in accordance with clause 2.6), the proceeds shall be applied in redeeming the mortgage, and paying the costs of the sale. The balance remaining shall be divided in the proportion of 75% to the Applicant and 25% to the Respondent.

4.   The Respondent shall make or cause to be made to the Applicant:

    (a)   for herself, periodical payments at the rate of £X per month the first payment to be made on   , subsequent payments to be made monthly in advance on the first day of each calendar month, these payments to continue until

      (i)   the Applicant remarries, dies or (subject to clause 2.6) voluntarily leaves the property; or

      (ii)   all the children of the family reach the age of 18 or finish full-time undergraduate education if later; or

      (iii)   further order of the court,

    whichever occurs first, whereupon the Applicant's claims for periodical payments and secured periodical payments shall stand dismissed and the Applicant shall not be entitled to make any further application under the Matrimonial Causes Act 1973, s 23(1)(a) or (b) in relation to the marriage AND IT IS DIRECTED pursuant to the Matrimonial Causes Act 1973, s 28(1A) that the Applicant shall not be entitled to apply for an extension of the term of the above order

[handwritten margin note: only if capable of supporting self at this stage, if not leave it out.]

    (b)   for Anthony Levy periodical payments at the rate of £Y per month, the first payment to be made on   , subsequent payments to be paid monthly in advance on the first day of each calendar month until Anthony reaches the age of 18 or finishes full-time secondary education if later, or until further order.

5.   Save as aforesaid, the applications by the Applicant and the Respondent for financial provision and property adjustment orders do stand dismissed and the Respondent shall not be entitled to make any further application in relation to their marriage under the Matrimonial Causes Act 1973, s 23(1)(a) or (b).

6.   Liberty to each party to apply.

7.   That the Respondent shall pay the Applicant's costs of this application in the sum of £   .

Dated the   day of   2001.

…………………………………..

Signature (on behalf) of the Applicant

…………………………………..

Signature (on behalf) of the Respondent

     Signed:

          District Judge

BROWN v BROWN

[Deferred charge on Martin contingencies; order for nominal maintenance]

Background information (note this is *not* part of the order): Eileen and Arthur Brown are in their fifties, and were married for 35 years. Mr Brown is an office manager and Mrs Brown is a typist. The children of the family are married and self-supporting. Mrs Brown has obtained a decree absolute based on Mr Brown's adultery with a woman with whom he now lives permanently. Mrs Brown continues to live at the former matrimonial home, a small 3 bedroomed terraced house which is in Mr Brown's sole name. The mortgage was paid off 2 years ago, and Mrs Brown can afford to pay the outgoings from her earnings. Mrs Brown has arthritis and has been advised that she will probably have to stop work in about 3 years' time. Mr Brown wants the house sold, and has offered Mrs Brown 1/3rd of the net proceeds. Mrs Brown, who has registered a notice under the Family Law Act 1996, has rejected the offer, saying this will be insufficient to rehouse herself. She wishes to remain in the house. Mrs Brown obtains public funding and applies to the court. The District Judge makes the following order.

IN THE LOKE COUNTY COURT	2001	No ....

BETWEEN   EILEEN AUDREY BROWN   Applicant

AND

ARTHUR GEORGE BROWN   Respondent

ORDER

UPON the basis that the Property (described below) be used as a home for the Applicant AND UPON the Applicant UNDERTAKING to the court to discharge all outgoings and expenses on the Property

IT IS ORDERED:

1. That the Respondent shall on or before the   day of   transfer all his legal and beneficial interest in the property at 34, Lower Lane, Loke ('the Property') into the name of the Applicant, the Respondent to pay for the costs of such transfer AND it is hereby certified for the purpose of the Community Legal Service (Financial) Regulations 2000 that the Property has been preserved for the Applicant for use as a home for herself.

2. The Applicant shall within one month of the transfer of the Property execute a legal charge ('the Charge') to secure the payment to the Respondent of a sum equivalent to one half of the Net Value of the Property as defined in clause 3 below.

3. The Net Value of the Property shall mean the open market value of the property with vacant possession between willing seller and purchaser at the date of redemption of the said legal charge or, if the said property is to be sold, on completion of the sale of the property the gross sale price including any consideration paid for fixtures and fittings. The open market value of the property as between willing seller and purchaser as at the date of redemption of the said legal charge shall in default of agreement between the Applicant and the Respondent be determined by a chartered surveyor appointed on the application of either party by the President for the time being of the Royal

Institution of Chartered Surveyors who shall act as an expert and not as an arbitrator and whose costs shall be borne equally by the Applicant and the Respondent.

4. The Charge shall not become exercisable until:–

    (a) the death or remarriage of the Applicant; or
    (b) upon her voluntary removal from the Property; or
    (c) upon such earlier date as a further order of the court may provide

    whichever occurs first.

5. That the Respondent shall make or cause to be made periodical payments to the Applicant of 5 pence per annum during their joint lives until the Applicant shall remarry or further order.

6. Save as aforesaid, the applications by the Applicant and the Respondent for financial provision and property adjustment orders do stand dismissed and the Respondent shall not be entitled to make any further application in relation to their marriage under the Matrimonial Causes Act 1973, s 23(1)(a) or (b).

7. That there be liberty to both parties to apply.

8. The Respondent shall pay the Applicant's costs to be determined by detailed assessment, if not agreed.

Dated the   day of   2001.

      Signed:

          District Judge

9.14 SUMMARY OF COURT PROCEDURE

Ancillary finance procedure can be effectively illustrated by way of checklists. Two such checklists follow. One shows the contested procedure and the other the procedure to be followed where the parties have reached agreement.

9.14.1 Application to the court for financial relief

Applicant (A)	Court	Respondent (R)
(1) Files at court:		
– Form A		
– court fee		
– public funding certificate		
– notice of issue of public funding, (where appropriate)		
– notice of acting (Legal Help divorce cases only)		
	(2) Fixes first appointment (FA) 12–16 weeks ahead (Form C)	

	Applicant (A)		*Court*		*Respondent (R)*
		(3)	Serves on Respondent within 4 days:		
			– Copy Forms A and C		
(4)	Serves on respondent				
	– notice of public funding, where appropriate				
	– copy notice of acting (Legal Help divorce cases only)				
	Serves on lender and person responsible for any pension arrangement Copy Form A				
(5)	Completes, files and exchanges Form E at least 35 days before FA			(5)	Completes, files and exchanges Form E at least 35 days before FA
(6)	Drafts, files and serves:			(6)	Drafts, files and serves:
	(a) statement of issues;				(a) statement of issues;
	(b) chronology;				(b) chronology;
	(c) questionnaire and documents requested;				(c) questionnaire and documents requested;
	(d) notice in Form G				(d) notice in Form G
	at least 14 days before FA				at least 14 days before FA
(7)	Produces costs estimate immediately before FA in Form H			(7)	Produces costs estimate immediately before FA in Form H
(8)	Attends FA with client			(8)	Attends FA with client
		(9)	Makes directions; usually fixes FDR		
(10)	Complies with directions			(10)	Complies with directions
(11)	Gives notice to court of all offers and responses 7 days before FDR				

Applicant (A)		Court		Respondent (R)
(12)	Produces costs estimate immediately before FDR			(12) Produces costs estimate immediately before FDR
(13)	Attends FDR with client			(13) Attends FDR with client
		(14)	May:	
			(a) make consent order;	
			(b) give directions;	
			(c) fix final hearing;	
			(d) adjourn	
(15)	Complies with directions made at FDR			(15) Complies with directions made at FDR
(16)	Drafts, files and serves on R statements of open proposals 14 days before hearing			
				(17) Drafts, files and serves on A statement of open proposals 7 days after receipt of A's proposals
(18)	Produces costs estimate immediately before hearing			(18) Produces costs estimate immediately before hearing
(19)	Attends hearing with client			(19) Attends hearing with client
		(20)	Makes order	

9.14.2 Consent orders

There are two possible procedures. Which is appropriate depends on how far (if at all) the application has progressed on a contested basis when the parties reach agreement. Whichever is used, Form A must be filed before an order can be made. This will either have taken place before the steps described below or (if not) can be incorporated into para 3 (see note (ii) below).

Normal consent procedure (no court attendance)

Applicant (A)	Court	Respondent (R)
(1) Completes Statement of Information Prepares draft order and submits it to R for approval/ amendment		
		(2) Completes Statement of Information. Endorses consent on draft order. Returns both documents to A
(3) Files at court:		
(a) Draft order, endorsed with R's (and A's) consent, plus		
(b) copy;		
(c) Statement of Information		
	(4) If satisfied, makes order. Sends copy to A and R. If not satisfied, may require parties to attend	

Notes

(i) Where appropriate, public funding certificate; notice of issue of certificate and notice of acting should be filed and/or served.

(ii) If A has not yet filed Form A, the draft order can conveniently be incorporated into that application which will be endorsed with R's consent.

Where attendance at court

The normal contested procedure will be followed up to the date of the hearing.

Once agreement has been reached, provided the district judge has the prescribed information as to parties' resources etc, an order may be made despite the lack of a draft order and written statement of information.

9.15 MAINTENANCE ASSESSMENTS

To apply for a maintenance assessment the parent with care must complete a maintenance assessment form giving details of her finances and information to enable the Child Support Agency to trace the absent parent. If the parent with care is in receipt of means-tested welfare benefits and she does not give the information required about the absent parent (and there is no risk of harm etc), she will be penalised by having her benefit reduced. The reduction will be 40 per cent of the adult personal allowance for 3 years (see **7.3.1**). The parent with care will not be required to give this information about the absent parent if there is a risk of harm or undue distress to her or any children living with her as a result of providing such information.

On receipt of the application form, the Agency will send a maintenance enquiry form to the absent parent which asks for details of his means. The absent parent has 14 days in which to complete and return this form. Maintenance is payable from the date the form is received by the absent parent. If the absent parent does not return the form, or returns it without having given all the information required, the Agency has a number of powers under the Act to enable it to obtain the information. If, after using these powers the Agency still does not have the information, it has the power to make an interim assessment.

The maintenance enquiry form will allow the absent parent to dispute paternity. Should the absent parent do so, the maintenance assessment will usually be deferred until the court has determined paternity (Child Support Act 1991, s 27). If the court declares the absent parent to be the natural parent and when the Agency has sufficient information, it will make its assessment and notify the applicant and the absent parent. Liability to pay will be backdated to the date the maintenance enquiry form was received by the absent parent.

9.16 FURTHER READING

Black and Bridge *A Practical Approach to Family Law* 6th edn (Blackstone Press, 2000)
Blair et al *Practical Matrimonial Precedents* (Longmans, 1994)
Butterworths Family Law Service (looseleaf)
The Family Court Practice (Family Law, 1999)

Chapter 10

ENFORCEMENT, APPEALS, SETTING ASIDE AND VARIATION

10.1 INTRODUCTION

Frequently, the respondent to an order for financial relief will fail to comply with some, or all, of the provisions of that order. It is essential, therefore, that the solicitor should be aware not only of the methods of enforcement which are available but also which of those methods is most appropriate in the circumstances.

A client may wish to appeal against an order which he thinks is unfair. In certain situations an order may even be set aside. If the circumstances have changed since the order was made, the client may wish to have that order varied. This chapter deals with what action the solicitor can take on these occasions.

10.2 FINANCIAL ORDERS IN THE COUNTY COURT

Financial orders in the county court comprise all orders apart from property adjustment orders (which are considered later), but most commonly will be spouse periodical payments orders or lump sum orders. Enforcement of child maintenance assessments will be effected by the Child Support Agency (see **10.4**), but where a child maintenance order has been made by the court, enforcement will generally be through the court in the usual way. However, the Child Support Agency can collect and enforce 'top up' child maintenance orders made by the court under CSA 1991, s 8.

Payments of money orders made by the county court are made direct between the parties. This can sometimes lead to problems since not only may the parties have to remain in direct contact (which could result in continued acrimony) but, as there is no independent record of payments, proof of payment (or non-payment) may be difficult. These problems can be mitigated by use of the Maintenance Enforcement Act 1991. This Act provides that when granting or varying a periodical payments order the High Court or county court can order:

(1) payment by standing order;
(2) the payer to open a bank account;
(3) attachment of the payer's earnings (see **10.2.2**).

10.2.1 Preliminary steps

When the order is first obtained the solicitor should tell his client to contact him immediately if the respondent defaults. This is particularly important in the case of periodical payments because leave will be required to enforce arrears that are more than 12 months old. The court may refuse leave, remit the arrears and give the respondent a fresh start.

If the client was in receipt of public funding for the ancillary proceedings and the certificate has not been discharged, the solicitor will need to extend the certificate to cover enforcement proceedings. If the certificate has been discharged, then the solicitor must apply for a new certificate.

Before proceedings are issued to enforce an order for payment of money, the applicant must file an affidavit setting out the amount due (ie the arrears of the periodical payments or the unpaid amount of any lump sum). This is because the court will have no independent record of this.

The method of enforcement used will depend upon the decision as to which method would be most effective. This in turn will usually depend upon the assets the respondent owns. The applicant will already have this information where the respondent has defaulted shortly after the order was made. However, in other cases, the applicant can apply to the district judge to have the respondent orally examined as to his means and assets. If the district judge agrees to the application, the respondent will be summoned to court and asked to bring any relevant documents with him. He will then be thoroughly examined by the district judge or other court officer as to his means and may be cross-examined by the applicant's solicitor.

10.2.2 Methods of enforcement

Attachment of earnings

Under an attachment of earnings order the respondent's employer will deduct a specified sum from his earnings. This sum will represent the amount of the maintenance order plus, possibly, a proportion of the arrears. The order must also specify a minimum amount, known as the 'protected earnings rate', below which the respondent's wages cannot fall. This rate is generally the amount that the respondent would be entitled to if he was reliant on welfare benefits. The employer will forward the money deducted from the respondent's wages to the court.

An attachment of earnings order is probably the best method of enforcement for a periodical payments order. It can be applied for either when the order is first made or later when the respondent defaults. However, the drawback of this method of enforcement is that the respondent must be in employment. It cannot be used if the respondent is self-employed or unemployed and can be administratively difficult if the respondent frequently changes jobs.

Warrant of execution

A warrant of execution enables the county court bailiff to seize and sell assets belonging to the respondent sufficient to meet the outstanding amount. The solicitor applies to the court for a warrant, no hearing is needed. This method is most useful for unpaid lump sums but could also be used for substantial arrears of maintenance.

Garnishee proceedings

A garnishee order enables the applicant to receive payment direct from someone who owes the respondent money, for example, a bank or building society. Garnishee proceedings involve two stages. At first, an order to show cause (obtained without notice) will freeze the account. At the subsequent 'on notice' hearing the district judge can make the order absolute which will require the bank or building society to pay the applicant the amount outstanding. This method is most useful for unpaid lump sums.

MCA 1973, s 24A

Under s 24A of MCA 1973, the court can make an order for sale to enforce, for example, a lump sum or secured periodical payments order (see **4.4.3**). The s 24A order for sale can be made at the same time as the original order as a type of precaution. Thus, for example, an order could provide that the respondent is to pay the applicant a lump sum of £30,000 (representing her share in the home) and that if that sum is not paid within 3 months of decree absolute the home is to be sold and the £30,000 paid to the applicant out of the proceeds of sale. Alternatively, the order for sale can be made later, if the respondent defaults.

Charging order

The applicant can apply to charge land (and/or certain securities) which the respondent owns or in which he has an interest with the amount outstanding. However, the procedure involved is protracted. The applicant needs to apply without notice for an order to show cause which can be made absolute at the subsequent on notice hearing. This will give the applicant security for the debt but a further hearing is needed to obtain an order for sale. At that further hearing, the court will have total discretion as to whether to order sale and it may decide not to, for example, if the charging order is over the respondent's home and the amount owed is relatively small. It is usually far better to utilise s 24A.

Judgment summons — threat it could have paid & didn't.

A judgment summons provides that the respondent must attend before the judge to be examined as to his means. The judge may then make such order as to payment of the outstanding amount as he deems fit, for example, that the outstanding lump sum is paid within 28 days. The judge also has power to commit the respondent to prison for non-payment, but any committal order made is usually suspended on condition that the respondent complies with the judge's order. This procedure is rarely used, partly because public funding is not available in the county court.

10.3 ENFORCEMENT IN THE FAMILY PROCEEDINGS COURT

Where orders for maintenance have been made in the family proceedings court the respondent must usually make payments to the clerk to the justices (although under the Maintenance Enforcement Act 1991 the family proceedings court can direct payments to be made in other ways, for example, by standing order between the parties). The court clerk will then forward the payments to the applicant. Thus, the court will have a complete record of all payments made and the parties need not be in contact with each other.

Before enforcement proceedings are commenced, and if the client is eligible, the solicitor should apply for public funding.

10.3.1 Methods of enforcement

If it becomes necessary to enforce the order, four methods are available:

(1) An attachment of earnings order. This has already been considered (see **10.2.2**).

(2) Committal to prison. This is very much a last resort. Three conditions must be fulfilled (MCA 1980, s 93(6)). These are:

> (a) the court must inquire, in the respondent's presence, whether the default was due to his wilful refusal or culpable neglect, and impose imprisonment only if satisfied that either was the case; and
>
> (b) the court must be satisfied that an attachment of earnings order is either not possible or not appropriate; and
>
> (c) the respondent must be present when committal is ordered.

> The arrears will not continue to accrue while the respondent is in prison (unless the court directs that they should), although imprisonment does not discharge the arrears. The respondent can obtain his release if he pays the whole amount due, or reduce the length of detention if he makes part-payment. Imprisonment lasts for a maximum of 6 weeks. The committal can be suspended on condition that the respondent pays the order in future together with gradual repayment of the arrears.

(3) A warrant of distress. This is similar to a warrant of execution. It is an order to the police to seize and sell goods belonging to the respondent, using the proceeds of sale to repay the arrears. It is not an appropriate method for enforcing maintenance and is rarely used.

(4) The order can be registered in the High Court or county court so that the methods of enforcement available in that court can be used. However, the arrears will rarely be substantial enough to make this course of action appropriate.

As in the county court, the family proceedings court has power to remit all or part of the arrears and will generally not enforce arrears which are more than 12 months old.

10.3.2 Registration of county court maintenance orders

Once a periodical payments order has been made in the county court, it can be registered in the family proceedings court. To do this, the solicitor lodges a standard form in duplicate plus a copy of the maintenance order at the court which made the order. Some district judges will not agree to the order being registered unless there are arrears of maintenance.

Once registered, payments under the order will be made to the clerk to the justices so there will be a full record of all payments. Another consequence of registration is that if the applicant is on income support and the respondent is a persistently poor payer, the applicant may be able to take advantage of the diversion procedure (see **6.9.1**).

Finally, once registered, the family proceedings court has power to vary the order thus possibly making subsequent variation quicker and cheaper than in the county court.

10.4 COLLECTION AND ENFORCEMENT BY THE CHILD SUPPORT AGENCY

The Child Support Agency will collect maintenance assessments for applicants. Applicants who are not on benefit can request this service. For those on benefit it will be provided automatically.

In cases where the Agency collects payments, it will consult both parents to decide which method of payment should be used. The most common method is likely to be by standing order. The Agency has power to compel the absent parent to open a bank account for this purpose (CSA 1991, s 29).

The Agency may instead serve a deduction from earnings order on the absent parent's employer (CSA 1991, s 31) and can use this as a method of enforcement. This will work in the same way as an attachment of earnings order.

Where one or more payments remain unpaid and a deduction from earnings order is inappropriate or has proved ineffective, the Agency can apply to the family proceedings court for a liability order (CSA 1991, s 33). Once a liability order has been obtained, the debt can be recovered by distress. If this proves ineffective, the Agency can apply to the county court for a garnishee or charging order. In the last resort, the Agency can apply to the family proceedings court to have the absent parent committed (CSA 1991, s 40).

10.5 PROPERTY ADJUSTMENT ORDERS

If the respondent fails to execute the documents required to effect a property adjustment order then the court has power to order the document to be executed by another person, usually the district judge, on his behalf (County Courts Act 1984, s 38). Should there be a problem with drafting the documents, the court can refer the matter to conveyancing counsel. In such a case, the court can direct that the granting of any decree be deferred until the documents have been executed.

10.6 APPEALS

10.6.1 County court orders

If either party is dissatisfied with an order made by the district judge after a contested hearing, he can appeal against that order to a judge in chambers within 14 days of the district judge's order (FPR 1991, r 8.1). On appeal, it seems that the judge must usually adopt the district judge's findings of fact and not admit any new evidence unless there are good reasons for doing otherwise, but he still retains a discretion to amend the original order.

10.6.2 Orders in the family proceedings court

A right of appeal lies from the magistrates making the order to the High Court (DPMCA 1978, s 29). The appeal should usually be made within 14 days of the order.

10.6.3 Maintenance assessments

Any person affected by a decision of the Child Support Agency can ask for a full reconsideration of the decision. If still dissatisfied, they can usually appeal to an independent appeal tribunal run by the Appeals Service. A decision of that tribunal can be appealed on a point of law to a child support commissioner.

10.7 SETTING ASIDE

One of the parties may attempt to have the order set aside. One advantage of this procedure over an appeal is that there will be no time-limit, so that the application could be made several years after the original order (although this would be very unusual). However, the court is reluctant to set aside orders for reasons of certainty; divorcing couples should be able to organise their future lives without fear of their divorce settlement being reopened. An application to set aside, therefore, can only be made on narrow grounds, the scope of which are not totally clear. These grounds include:

(1) Non-disclosure of material evidence. In the case of *Livesey (formerly Jenkins) v Livesey* (see **9.7.1**) the House of Lords stated that each party owed to the other a duty of full and frank disclosure. Where this duty is breached the order may be set aside. It must be emphasised, however, that not every non-disclosure will justify setting an order aside. The non-disclosure must have resulted in the court granting an order substantially different from that which it would have granted had the true facts been known or the court will not agree to set the original order aside.

(2) Fraud, for example, if one party deliberately misrepresents the size of his assets.

(3) Events occurring after the order is made. The House of Lords in *Barder v Barder* [1988] AC 20 laid down four conditions which must be fulfilled before the order will be set aside:

   (a) the subsequent events must have invalidated the basis upon which the order was made; and

   (b) these events must have occurred within a relatively short time of the original order; and

   (c) the application to set aside must be made promptly; and

   (d) the granting of the application must not prejudice the rights of a bona fide purchaser for value of any property in question.

The facts of *Barder v Barder* provide a useful example of the extreme circumstances which are necessary for the court to set aside an order on this ground. As part of a consent order, Mr Barder agreed to transfer the home to his ex-wife within 28 days so that she could live in it with their children. Before he had done so, Mrs Barder killed both children and committed suicide. Under her will, all her property would go to her mother. The House of Lords agreed to set the order aside.

The case of *Heard v Heard* [1995] 1 FLR 970 suggests how this approach may be of use in times of falling house prices. In this case, the house was valued at £67,000 at the time of the hearing. The wife was awarded £16,000 with the balance of the equity going to the husband. The house was sold some 6 months later for only £33,000. The Court of Appeal held that the basis of the original order, under which the district judge had intended to allow the husband enough money to rehouse himself, had been invalidated. However, in other cases, a fall in value of the home was found insufficient to set aside an order (see, eg, *B v B* [1994] 1 FLR 219).

Remember that a subsequent maintenance assessment by the Child Support Agency will not be sufficient grounds for setting aside a clean break order (see **7.3.7**).

10.8 VARIATION

10.8.1 Types of county court order which can be varied

It is possible to apply to the court to vary an order not only where that order was made after a contested hearing but also where the order was made by consent. However, it will not be possible to vary an order which effected a clean break.

Orders which can be varied are set out in MCA 1973, s 31(2) and include orders for:

(1) Maintenance pending suit and interim maintenance.

(2) Periodical payments and secured periodical payments. Periodical payments orders are the type of order most commonly varied. Applications are made either by the payee to increase the amount being paid or by the payer to reduce or extinguish the payments. Several points should be noted:

    (a) where the court makes an order for fixed-term maintenance, the term can usually be extended, provided that the application for an extension is made before the original order has expired (although the actual hearing may take place after enquiry). However, this can be prevented by the court including a direction in the original order that no application for an extension can be made (see MCA 1973, s 28(1A) and **4.6**);

    (b) when the court discharges a periodical payments order or varies such an order to make it last for a further limited term only, it may also make a lump sum order or one or more property adjustment orders or (after 1 December 2000) one or more pension sharing orders. It may also include a direction that no application for an extension of a limited-term periodical payments order can be made. These provisions allow the court to impose a 'deferred clean break'. Whether a deferred clean break is appropriate will depend on much the same factors as those taken into account when deciding whether a clean break is appropriate (see **4.6**). In particular, the payer should consider whether the payee is likely to remarry in the near future. If publicly funded, the payee should be reminded that a lump sum payment will attract immediate enforcement of the statutory charge unless the money is to be used to purchase a home and the order includes the necessary clause to enable the Legal Services Commission to postpone the charge (see **2.6**);

    (c) when varying a periodical payments order the court has power to remit any arrears due under the order (MCA 1973, s 31(2A)). This power could be used, for example, where the payer had become unemployed and arrears had built up before he had a chance to apply for a downward variation.

(3) Payment of a lump sum by instalments. Generally, this power will only enable the court to vary the number and amount of the instalments so that the amount

payable overall will remain the same. However, it was held in *Tilley v Tilley* [1979] Fam Law 89 that in exceptional circumstances this power could be used to order the complete discharge of the remaining instalments thus reducing, possibly substantially, the total amount payable. In *Tilley v Tilley*, payment of the final instalment outstanding would have rendered the four children of the marriage homeless and thus the order was varied to exclude the final payment.

(4) Payment of a lump sum ordered in relation to pensions under s 25B(4) or s 25C of MCA 1973.

(5) The sale of property under MCA 1973, s 24A. This could be used, for example, where the order for sale was made as a way of enforcing a lump sum order. If the payer could find some other means to pay, he could then apply to have the order for sale discharged.

10.8.2 Types of county court order which cannot be varied

Orders for capital provision usually cannot be varied. This is to avoid uncertainty and so that the parties can make plans for the future on the basis that the distribution of capital is permanent.

(1) Lump sum orders cannot be varied unless they are payable by instalments or ordered in relation to a pension (see **10.8.1**).

(2) Transfer of property and settlement of property orders cannot be varied. So, for example, if the court orders a deferred trust of land on *Mesher* contingencies, the occupier will not be able successfully to apply to court at a later date to have the sale further postponed. However, it may sometimes be possible to obtain a sale at a date earlier than that set out in the original order by applying for an order for sale under MCA 1973, s 24A. The court can make an order for sale either at the same time as making the original order or at a later date (see **4.4.3**). It is totally in the court's discretion whether to make such an order, but it may do so if, for example, it is the spouse in occupation who is seeking the sale against the wishes of the non-occupying spouse (see, eg, *Thompson v Thompson* [1986] Fam 38).

(3) Pension sharing orders (when they become available from 1 December 2000) cannot generally be varied. The only exeption to this is when the variation takes place before the order comes into effect and before the decree absolute. Once the decree has been made absolute, or if the order is in effect, it cannot be varied.

Many orders contain a clause which gives the parties 'liberty to apply'. This does not allow the parties to return to court to vary the order. Instead, it gives the parties the opportunity to return to court if they experience trouble implementing the order, for example, due to conveyancing difficulties or misunderstanding of minor terms where property is settled (see *Practice Direction* [1980] 1 All ER 1008).

10.8.3 Factors to be considered on a variation

The factors to be considered on a variation are set out in MCA 1973, s 31(7) which requires the court to have regard to all circumstances of the case, giving first consideration to the welfare of any child of the family who is not yet 18. This subsection also states that 'all the circumstances of the case' includes any change in the matters which the court was required to consider when making the original order, ie any change in the s 25 factors. Where the party against whom the order was made has died, 'all the circumstances of the case' include the change in circumstances as a result of his death. This will generally be relevant only in the case of secured periodical payments orders. However, case law makes clear (see, eg, *Flavell v Flavell* [1997] Fam Law 237) that the court is not restricted to considering changes in the matters which were taken into account when making the original order, but can consider the case afresh.

The court must also consider on a variation application (even if it decides not to vary the amount of the order) whether the term of any payments ordered could be limited without causing undue hardship to the payee.

The court will need to take into account the 'package' made by the original order for financial relief. For example, perhaps the wife received less maintenance than she otherwise would have done in return for a greater share in the home. This must be taken into consideration on the variation application in order to maintain the balance achieved by the original order.

Finally, remember that it is possible to record in a side-letter the reasons why a particular order has been made (see **9.13.12**). Any side-letter should be drawn to the court's attention on a later variation application and, although it will not bind the court, it is likely that the court will uphold its terms (see *N v N (Consent Order: Variation)* [1993] 2 FLR 868).

10.8.4 Procedure

The procedure to be followed is very similar to that used for the original order (see Chapter 9). Where appropriate, an application for public funding should be made. If both parties agree to the variation sought, then the normal consent procedure must be followed (see **9.12**).

10.8.5 Variation in the family proceedings court

Either party can apply to vary or revoke a periodical payments order made in a family proceedings court. Either party can also apply for a lump sum order or further lump sum order. In deciding whether or not to grant the application, the court will have regard to any change in the circumstances since the original order was made (DPMCA 1978, s 20).

10.8.6 Review of maintenance assessments under CSA 1991

Maintenance assessments will automatically be reviewed bi-annually. Either parent can also apply for a review where there has been a material change of circumstances. Generally, a new assessment will not be made unless the review would result in a change of more than £10 per week.

Until existing child maintenance orders are taken on by the Child Support Agency, the court will retain power to vary those orders.

10.9 CHAPTER SUMMARY

(1) Financial orders can be enforced by the county court or the family proceedings court.

(2) The order will usually be enforced in the court that made it; however sometimes it can be advantageous to register an order obtained in the county court with the family proceedings court and then enforce it in the family proceedings court.

(3) The following methods of enforcement are available in the county court:
- attachment of earnings;
- warrant of execution;
- garnishee proceedings;
- s 24A of MCA 1973;
- charging order;
- judgment summons.

(4) The following methods of enforcement are available in the family proceedings court:
- attachment of earnings;
- committal to prison;
- warrant of distress.

(5) The Child Support Agency will enforce payments of child maintenance where the carer is on benefit.

(6) The county court can execute documents to transfer property where the respondent fails to do so.

(7) It may be possible to appeal an order for ancillary relief, but this must be done without delay.

(8) In exceptional circumstances the court may set aside an order. This may happen if, for example, the respondent did not disclose the existence of certain of his finances.

(9) Orders for maintenance can be varied, as can instalments of a lump sum and lump sum orders made in relation to a pension.

(10) Other lump sum orders, pension sharing orders and property adjustment orders cannot be varied.

10.10 FURTHER READING

Rayden and Jackson *Divorce and Family Matters* 17th edn (Butterworths, 1997 (and service))

Black, Bridge and Bond *A Practical Approach to Family Law* 6th edn (Blackstone Press, 2000)

The Family Court Practice (Family Law, 2000)

Butterworths Family Law Service (looseleaf)

Chapter 11

PRE-MARITAL AGREEMENTS AND SEPARATION AGREEMENTS

11.1 INTRODUCTION

This chapter looks at the ways in which married couples can achieve a binding agreement to cover maintenance and other matters without starting court proceedings. It looks at the validity of agreements entered into before marriage. It then examines how a spouse can enter into a maintenance or separation agreement as an alternative to starting divorce proceedings or obtaining an order under DPMCA 1978.

11.2 PRE-MARITAL AGREEMENTS

11.2.1 General

An increasing number of unmarried couples are entering into 'cohabitation agreements' governing the ownership of property and chattels (see Chapter 15). Subject to general contractual principles, cohabitation agreements are binding.

What if a couple wish to enter a pre-marital agreement? At present, such agreements are not binding. At most, the court may take them into account as 'one of the circumstances of the case' under s 25 of MCA 1973, but it is unlikely to attach much weight to them (see, eg, *F v F (Ancillary Relief: Substantial Assets)* [1995] 2 FLR 45). However, some couples do choose to use them and there are precedents available to use (see 'Agreements between Husband and Wife' (SFLA, 1993)). The agreement would assist to sort things out if the breakdown was amicable.

A pre-marital agreement will need to comply with general contract principles. There will need to be offer and acceptance, intention to create legal relations, certainty and consideration. Unless the contract is by deed there could be a problem in establishing consideration. The agreement would also be set aside if a party could show that undue influence was exerted over him or her when the agreement was entered into.

The only type of agreement that the law will definitely give weight to is a reconciliation agreement, which can be entered into when spouses have already separated, but have decided to cohabit again to give the marriage another chance. In an agreement made at this stage the parties will agree to resume cohabitation, but can also make provision for maintenance and property division should they separate in future.

11.2.2 Law of Property (Miscellaneous Provisions) Act 1989, s 2

The Law of Property (Miscellaneous Provisions) Act 1989, s 2 provides that all the terms of any contract for the disposition of any interest in land must be in writing and signed by all the parties. This means that any informal agreement between spouses relating to ownership of the home will not be enforceable unless it is properly recorded.

11.2.3 Reform

The Government announced in May 1998 that it intended to introduce legislation to make pre-marital contracts binding. There are likely to be some exceptions to this, for example, where children have been born following the making of the agreement or where either or both of the parties failed to receive independent legal advice before entering the contract. In such situations it is likely that the court will retain full discretion over the making of financial orders.

11.3 SEPARATION AGREEMENTS

11.3.1 General

If spouses separate, they can, as an alternative to divorce or other court proceedings, enter into an agreement which provides for maintenance, care of the children and division of any property (for precedents, see 'Agreements between Husband and Wife' (SFLA, 1993)). These agreements are known as either separation agreements or maintenance agreements. The only distinction is that a separation agreement will always include a clause in which the parties agree to an immediate separation. If a married couple have decided to separate but are still living together at the time of the agreement, it is essential to use a separation agreement as the inclusion of this clause agreeing to separate immediately will ensure that the agreement will not be void on grounds of public policy, as it will establish that the marriage had broken down before the agreement was made. If the parties have already separated, either type of agreement can be entered into depending on whether the parties agree to the separation. If one party has deserted the other, it is important that, if the parties have agreed on financial matters, a maintenance agreement is used. This will ensure that there is no suggestion that the other spouse is agreeing to the separation which would end the desertion and the possibility of obtaining a divorce using Fact C.

The rest of this chapter uses the term separation agreement to include both types of agreement.

A separation agreement, like any other contract, must be formed in accordance with contract principles. A vital element is an intention to create legal relations. The agreement can be challenged by a party on the grounds of fraud, mistake, duress or undue influence. It is, therefore, important that both parties have independent legal advice before entering into this type of agreement.

11.3.2 Contents

The matters that typically are covered by a separation agreement are as follows.

Agreement to separate
The parties can state that they are going to live apart. Their agreement releases them from the duty married persons have to cohabit and effectively prevents either party being in desertion (but see **11.3.1** above for the use of maintenance agreements). The agreement is also evidence that the parties are treating the marriage as at an end so

that a period of separation can begin to run for the purposes of divorce on the grounds of 2 or 5 years' separation (Fact D or E).

Periodical payments

The agreement can contain provision for the payment of maintenance to the parties and any children. In relation to children, any agreement to pay money will be binding. However, a separation agreement cannot oust the jurisdiction of the Child Support Agency under CSA 1991, so either party can at any later time apply to the Agency to determine the amount of maintenance payable (see **7.3.4**). Any agreement to pay maintenance to a spouse cannot prevent either party applying to the court for ancillary relief as part of divorce, nullity or judicial separation proceedings. However, were this to happen, the separation agreement would be one of the factors that the court would consider under s 25 of MCA 1973 in the ancillary relief proceedings. Care must also be taken to draft maintenance provisions for spouse and child clearly, making provision for how long the maintenance is to last and what will happen if the parties resume cohabitation.

Property

If appropriate, an agreement about the home can be included. Often, as the parties may have only recently separated and not yet decided whether the separation will be long term, it is too soon to decide matters concerning the home and other property. However, the agreement could cover matters such as payment of the mortgage, outgoings and repairs in the short term.

Children

There is no need for any arrangements to be included relating to the children. Both parents still share parental responsibility and can make decisions jointly or alone relating to the children. However, if the parents wish, any agreement about where the children should live and how much contact is to be given to the parent with whom they do not live can be included. This would not prevent either parent from making an application under the Children Act 1989 at any later date.

11.3.3 Advantages of a separation agreement

The parties' decision to enter into a separation agreement will usually be based largely on a desire to avoid court proceedings including applying to court for a consent order. They should also take into account the following factors.

Speed

A separation agreement can be entered into quickly; a contested court order may not be made for a considerable time. It is, therefore, cheaper. It may also assist the parties by avoiding the confrontation and bitterness that is often caused by protracted court proceedings.

Flexibility

Anything can be agreed and included in a separation agreement. So, for example, a husband could agree to pay the outgoings and repairs on the home in which the wife and family remained living, or to pay off outstanding hire-purchase debts. Neither of these matters can be ordered by the divorce courts under MCA 1973 even if the parties apply for a consent order.

11.3.4 Disadvantages of a separation agreement

Enforceability

A separation agreement is enforced in the same way as any other contract. The usual remedies for breach of contract must, therefore, be sought, ie damages to cover any loss from arrears of maintenance payments and the equitable remedies of specific performance or an injunction to force the other party to carry it out. This means that by comparison with a court order (see Chapter 10), a separation agreement is much more difficult to enforce.

Finality

A court order for a 'clean break' can prevent either party from applying to court again and achieves a once and for all settlement. A separation agreement can never be a guaranteed final solution. A party to a separation agreement can always apply at a later date, for example, on divorce, for further provision from the court. However, on a later application the separation agreement will be taken into account under MCA 1973, s 25 and may be followed (see *Edgar v Edgar* [1980] 3 All ER 887). In the more recent case of *G v G (Financial Provision: Separation Agreement)* [2000] 2 FLR 18, the court confirmed that an earlier separation agreement between the parties should be taken into account, either as part of 'all the circumstances of the case' (MCA 1973, s 25(1)) or as 'conduct which it would be inequitable to disregard' (MCA 1973, s 25(2)(g)). Such an agreement may be strongly persuasive in deciding what orders to make, but not conclusive, as all the s 25 factors must be considered. In deciding what weight to attach to an agreement, the court said that the most relevant questions to ask are:

- how did the agreement come to be made?
- did the parties themselves attach importance to it?
- have the parties themselves acted upon it?

Variation

A court order for periodical payments can always be varied by the court by an application by either party at a later date. All written separation agreements can also be varied by the court (see **11.3.5**). However, if the agreement is not in writing it can only be varied by agreement between the parties.

11.3.5 MCA 1973, ss 34–36

Despite the fact that separation agreements are made between the parties and do not involve the court, MCA 1973 does contain provisions giving the court power to vary them.

The court will have jurisdiction if the agreement comes within the wide definition of 'maintenance agreement' under MCA 1973, s 34(2). This will include any written agreement containing financial arrangements, or any written agreement to separate which does not contain any financial arrangements (where no other document exists which does contain such arrangements).

The court's jurisdiction

Any provision in a maintenance agreement which restricts the right of either party to apply to court for financial provision is void. However, any other provision in the agreement will still be binding.

Variation

If the parties can agree a variation, the original separation agreement can be varied by them without application to the court. If they cannot agree, either party can apply to court and the court has jurisdiction to vary or to insert financial arrangements in a written maintenance agreement during the lives of the parties under MCA 1973, s 35. It will vary the agreement only if there has been a change in circumstances justifying this. The court can then make such order as it thinks just having regard to all the circumstances.

The court can also in certain circumstances vary a written maintenance agreement after the death of one of the parties (MCA 1973, s 36). The application should be made within 6 months of the grant of representation being taken out in respect of the estate, otherwise leave of the court is required (see FPR 1991, r 3.3).

11.4 CHAPTER SUMMARY

(1) Pre-marital agreements (ie agreements made *before* marriage dealing with what will happen on divorce) are unlikely to be binding (although there are reform proposals to change this).
(2) Separation agreements (ie agreements made when a couple *actually* separate) CAN be binding contracts.
(3) A separation agreement can be made as an alternative to a court order.

Advantages of a separation agreement:
- speed;
- flexibility.

Disadvantages of a separation agreement:
- difficult to enforce;
- not final;
- variation by court.

11.5 FURTHER READING

Jackson *Splitting-up Precedents* (Sweet & Maxwell, 1999)
Agreements Between Husband and Wife (SFLA, 1993)

Chapter 12

CHILDREN

12.1 INTRODUCTION

The Children Act 1989 (CA 1989) has been described as 'the most comprehensive and far reaching reform of child law ... in living memory' (Lord Mackay, Hansard, House of Lords, 6 December 1988). The aim of the Act is to simplify the law relating to children, making it more consistent and more flexible and to make the law more appropriate to the needs of children by making it more child-centred. CA 1989 deals with both public and private law. Most of the existing legislation concerning children was repealed when CA 1989 came into force on 14 October 1991.

Children are sometimes described as a solicitor's invisible clients in divorce proceedings. The client is the parent, not the child, but a solicitor must consider the effect of his client's actions on the child involved. A solicitor may often feel that the client would be helped by mediation in relation to decisions about the children and should recommend that an appropriate agency is consulted (see **1.3.2**).

CA 1989 enables a child to apply for an order himself. The requirements involved are considered in this chapter. Provisions dealing with financial orders for children are summarised at the end of the chapter.

The Solicitors Family Law Association Code of Practice sets out useful reminders of how to approach children matters and how to deal with the conflicts which can arise. The SFLA has also produced a *Guide to Good Practice for Solicitors Acting for Children* 5th edn (2000) which should be referred to when representing a child. This sets out general guidance as well as dealing with particular problems, for example, interviewing and taking instructions from a child. It also provides very useful guidance to further reading.

A recent development is the Criminal Justice and Court Services Bill, which establishes a new Children and Family Court Advisory and Support Service (CAFCASS). CAFCASS will be a non-departmental body, accountable to the Lord Chancellor. In respect of family proceedings in which the welfare of children is in question, the Service has the principal function of safeguarding and promoting the welfare of the children, giving advice to any court about any application made to it in such proceedings, making provision for the children to be represented in such proceedings, and providing information, advice and other support for the children and their families. The Service's 'case workers' will fulfil the roles of court welfare officers (in private law proceedings) and guardians ad litem (in public law proceedings). The target date for bringing the new Service into operation is April 2001.

12.2 PARENTAL RESPONSIBILITY

12.2.1 What is parental responsibility?

CA 1989 introduced the concept of parental responsibility which was a deliberate shift away from the idea that parents have 'rights' over their child towards the idea that they have 'responsibilities' towards their child. Parental power to control a child is not for the benefit of the parents but for the child. The Act defines this term as 'all the rights, duties, powers, responsibilities and authority which by law a parent of a child has in relation to the child and his property' (CA 1989, s 3(1)). In reality, it gives the parent the responsibility of taking all the important decisions in the child's life, for example, education, religion and medical care. It also enables a parent to take day-to-day decisions, for example, in relation to nutrition, recreation and outings. The duties involved in parental responsibility will change from time to time with differing needs and circumstances and vary with the age and maturity of the child. It is important to bear in mind that a child will gradually become mature enough to take decisions himself. The House of Lords, in *Gillick v West Norfolk and Wisbech Area Health Authority* [1986] AC 112, HL, said that 'parental authority ceases in respect of any aspect of a child's upbringing about which the child himself is sufficiently mature to make decisions for himself'.

12.2.2 Who has parental responsibility?

Married parents have joint parental responsibility; if parents are not married, only the mother has parental responsibility. However, an unmarried father can acquire parental responsibility in any one of five ways:

(1) by entering into a 'parental responsibility agreement' with the mother (CA 1989, s 4(1)(b)); this must be on a prescribed printed form;
(2) by applying to the court for a parental responsibility order (CA 1989, s 4(1)(a));
(3) by being appointed a guardian either by the mother or the court, although in these cases he will assume parental responsibility only on the mother's death;
(4) by obtaining a residence order from the court (see **12.3.1**);
(5) by marrying the mother.

For further discussion of an unmarried father's position, see **15.4.1**.

Various other people may also acquire parental responsibility towards the child. A local authority will acquire parental responsibility if a care order is made in relation to the child, or anyone who is granted a residence order in relation to the child, or even the court if the child is made a ward of court.

12.2.3 How can you lose parental responsibility?

There is no limit to the number of people who can have parental responsibility at any one time and no one will lose parental responsibility just because another person acquires it (CA 1989, s 2(5)). If, on divorce, a residence order is made in favour of a grandparent this will mean that the child's mother, father and grandparent will all have parental responsibility. The parents 'lose' the responsibility of having the child living with either of them because of the residence order but retain all other responsibilities. If a care order is made, the local authority acquires parental responsibility but the parents still, in theory, retain parental responsibility. However, in practice the local authority is given the discretion to determine the extent to which a parent may meet his or her parental responsibility (CA 1989, s 33(3)).

Two situations in which parents will lose parental responsibility are:

(1) the parent's death; and
(2) the child's adoption. The Adoption Act 1976, s 12 provides that an adoption order will automatically extinguish the parental responsibility which any person had before the making of the order.

An unmarried father, who has acquired parental responsibility by a parental responsibility order (CA 1989, s 4(1)(a)) can lose it if the court makes a further order ending it. (See *Re P (Terminating Parental Responsibility)* [1995] 1 FLR 1048, where an unmarried father who had acquired parental responsibility then lost it under a court order, having inflicted serious injury on the child.)

Anyone other than an unmarried father, who has acquired parental responsibility by being granted a residence order, will lose it automatically when the residence order terminates.

The acquisition and loss of parental responsibility in the case of unmarried fathers raises potential issues of discrimination under the Human Rights Act 1998. However, in *McMichael v UK* (1995) 20 EHRR 205, the European Court of Human Rights accepted that discrimination between married and unmarried fathers could be justified as identifying 'meritorious' fathers who might be accorded parental rights, thereby protecting the interests of the child and the mother. The position of unmarried fathers is set to improve following the government's stated intention to amend CA 1989, to give parental responsibility to all unmarried fathers who register the birth of their children.

12.2.4 Exercising parental responsibility

Even though several people may have parental responsibility for a child, it is possible for each to act alone with no duty to consult anyone else (CA 1989, s 2(7)). However, in *Re C (Change of Surname)* [1998] 1 FLR 549, the court held that even when there was joint parental responsibility, this did not confer the right to unilaterally change the child's surname. Also, in *Re J (Child's Religious Upbringing and Circumcision)* [2000] 1 FLR 571, CA, the court held that there are a small group of important decisions made on behalf of a child which, in the absence of agreement by all those with parental responsibility, ought not to be carried out or arranged by the one-parent carer, notwithstanding s 2(7). Instead, they should be referred to the court for the court's determination, on the facts of the case each time, by way of a specific issue order. As well as change of a child's surname, the court gave sterilisation and circumcision as examples of such decisions.

Subject to these exemptions, one parent can determine questions such as certain medical treatment, religion and education without consulting the other. The only way to challenge a decision is to make an application to court, for example, for a specific issue order or a prohibited steps order. If a child is being adopted, or taken out of the UK there are specific provisions requiring both parents' consent or the consent of the court (see **12.3.1** and **12.9.1**).

It is not possible to transfer or surrender parental responsibility (CA 1989, s 2(9)). However, parents can delegate responsibility for a child on a temporary basis, for example, to a school for a school trip, or to a nanny, or childminder. Temporary carers do not acquire parental responsibility but 'may do what is reasonable in all the circumstances of the case for the purpose of safeguarding or promoting the child's welfare' (CA 1989, s 3(5)). This could cover emergency medical treatment for the child if needed when the parent is absent, for example, during a school trip or when the parent is at work during the day and a nanny is in charge.

12.3 SECTION 8 ORDERS

The CA 1989, s 8 enables four orders to be made in relation to children:

(1) residence orders;
(2) contact orders;
(3) prohibited steps orders;
(4) specific issue orders.

Each of these orders will determine a particular matter relating to the child's upbringing.

12.3.1 Residence order

A residence order is an order settling the arrangements to be made as to the person with whom the child is to live.

Following a divorce, parents will share parental responsibility and, therefore, the making of a residence order will only decide where a child will live.

A residence order can be made in favour of non-parents and, if this is done, the non-parent will automatically have parental responsibility as well, but only for so long as the residence order is in force (CA 1989, s 12(2)). The parental responsibility acquired in this way also has two limitations as first, no agreement or refusal to an adoption order or freeing for adoption can be given and, secondly, no guardian can be appointed by the non-parent.

A residence order can be made in favour of two or more persons who do not all live together. The order can specify the periods during which the child is to live in the different households involved (CA 1989, s 11(4)). This means that a court could order that a child lives alternate weeks with each parent, or lives during term-time with one parent and during the holidays with the other, or spends a fixed period say, the summer holidays, with one parent. A residence order is, therefore, a flexible power which can be adapted to the needs of a particular family. Obviously, the court will only make a split residence order if it feels it is in the welfare of the child to do so. In *Re H (A Minor) (Shared Residence)* [1994] 1 FLR 717, the Court of Appeal recognised that in some circumstances a shared residence order could reduce bitterness between the parents but stressed that, almost invariably, the circumstances require that the child should make his settled home with one parent; giving him two competing homes would only lead to confusion and stress.

The court is given wide powers to attach directions, conditions, incidental and supplementary provisions to the residence order. These could, for example, direct where the child is to be educated or impose a ban on removing the child from the country or could direct that the non-resident parent be informed if the child requires medical treatment in circumstances where the parent with whom the child is living has religious objections to blood transfusions.

When a residence order has been made, two aspects of parental responsibility are automatically affected.

Change of surname

Where a residence order is in force, the order will provide that no person can cause the child to be known by a new surname without either:

(1) the written consent of every person who has parental responsibility; or
(2) the leave of the court (CA 1989, s 13(1)).

However, following *Re C* (see **12.2.4**), it seems that where there is joint parental responsibility, regardless of whether there is a residence order, the same conditions will apply.

If a divorced mother wants to change her child's surname, perhaps following remarriage or reverting to a maiden surname herself, she will have to obtain the permission of her former spouse and, if this is not given, she will have to apply to court. The court will base any decision on the welfare principle (see **12.4**). The court is generally reluctant to authorise a change of surname unless it is in the interests of the child to do so. Factors to weigh up include embarrassment to the child and parent of having different surnames, the child's wishes and the extent to which the child's original surname is important to maintain links with the parent and other relations with whom he does not live. In *W v A (Child: Surname)* [1981] 1 All ER 100 both parents had remarried. The mother wanted to emigrate to Australia with her second husband who was Australian, and take the two children (aged 12 and 14) from her first marriage with her. The mother wanted to change the children's surnames to the new husband's surname. The children, who were interviewed by the judge, also wanted to change their surname. The judge decided that the children should keep their natural father's name. He stressed that change of name was a serious issue and, in this case, it had not been shown that it was in the children's best interests to change their name. He did not place great weight on the children's wishes in this case as he felt that they had been influenced by their mother and were merely reflecting her view.

This case was followed in *Re F (Child: Surname)* [1993] 2 FLR 837, where it was stated that allowing a child to be known by a different surname is an important matter which is not to be undertaken lightly. In *Dawson v Wearmouth* [1999] 1 FLR 1167, the majority of the House of Lords considered that there had to be particular circumstances to justify a change of name; effectively, there is a presumption in favour of the status quo.

Leaving the UK

Where a residence order is in force, no person may remove the child from the UK without either:

(1) the written consent of every person who has parental responsibility; or
(2) leave of the court (CA 1989, s 13(1)).

The Act does allow the person in whose favour the residence order is made to take the child out of the UK for periods of less than one month without such consent.

Thus, the parent with whom the child lives can take the child abroad as many times as he or she likes provided each individual trip does not last more than one month. The parent without the residence order needs to seek consent every time he or she wants to take the child abroad for whatever period. However, at the time that the residence order is granted, the court can add a direction authorising removal to avoid repeated applications to court. This would be sensible in a situation where the non-residential parent lives abroad so that regular trips to stay with the parent will be permitted without consent being needed.

If no residence order is in force, either parent can (in theory) take their child abroad without any restriction or need for consent under CA 1989. However, the parent proposing the trip could be prevented from going by the other parent obtaining a prohibited steps or specific issue order forbidding the child being taken abroad. Additionally, a criminal offence under the Child Abduction Act 1984 will be committed by the parent taking the child if permission of the other parent, or the court, is not obtained.

If a parent needs to apply to court to seek permission to take the child abroad, the court will again base its decision on the welfare principle. It will, therefore, seldom be difficult to persuade the court that a holiday abroad is in the best interests of the child, unless, for example, it is a cover for an abduction. Where emigration is intended, if the child's future must inevitably lie with the parent seeking to leave the jurisdiction then, provided that the proposals for the child's living arrangements and upbringing are realistic and sensible, the court is likely to permit the application to remove. In *Re H (Application to Remove from Jurisdiction)* [1998] 1 FLR 848, the Court of Appeal indicated that there had to be some compelling reason to justify a court preventing the custodial parent from taking a reasonable decision to live outside their jurisdiction. Where there is concern over future contact arrangements, the court could impose conditions. For example, in *Re S (Removal from Jurisdiction)* [1999] 1 FLR 850, prior to authorising removal, the court required the custodial parent to deposit a large sum of money pending authentication of the English contact order by the Chilean Supreme Court.

When either parent, at any time before or after a residence order, is intending to take a child abroad, reference must be made to the Child Abduction Act 1984 which makes it a criminal offence in certain cases for a parent to remove a child from the UK without the consent of the other parent or the court (see **12.9.1**).

12.3.2 Contact order

A contact order is an order requiring the person with whom the child lives or is to live to allow the child to visit or stay with the person named in the order, or for that person and the child otherwise to have contact with each other.

A contact order can authorise physical contact but can also cover contact by letter or by telephone (or even by video). The amount of contact can either be specified in the order, to cover weekend visits or holidays, or the order could be for 'reasonable contact' in which case the arrangements can be made by the parents. The latter is obviously preferable as the parents can make and alter arrangements to suit the circumstances. A contact order can also be made preventing contact with someone (*Nottingham CC v P* [1993] 3 All ER 815, CA). The alternative way to achieve this is by a prohibited steps order.

Since the order can be made in favour of a parent or any other person, it could enable contact to be maintained with more distant relatives or other friends of the child.

A contact order can contain conditions and directions. These could be used to build up contact gradually between a young child and a parent who had not seen the child for a while, or to ensure supervised contact to protect the child. This could take place at a local Child Contact Centre. These centres have been set up across the county to provide an opportunity and setting for contact to take place in circumstances where arranging contact might otherwise be difficult.

The court's approach is that the child has a right to know both parents and therefore the starting point is that a child should have contact with the absent parent (*Re D (A Minor) (Contact)* [1993] 1 FCR 9, CA). However, the court will always consider all the circumstances and may decide that because of factors such as the parent's conduct, the emotional welfare and stability of the child, or even the attitude and behaviour of a step-parent, it is in the best interests of the child not to grant a contact order (*Re T (A Minor) (Parental Responsibility: Contact)* [1993] 2 FLR 450).

Although there is a presumption that a child should have contact with both parents (unless there are cogent reasons to the contrary), that is not necessarily the approach towards any other member of the family, such as a grandparent. In *Re A (Section 8 Order: Grandparent Application)* [1995] 2 FLR 153, the Court of Appeal stressed that just because the grandmother had succeeded in obtaining leave to apply for a contact order, that did not mean that there was a presumption that she should actually be granted a contact order; the court had to consider what was in the child's best interests (although see also the case of *Re W* [1997] 1 FLR 793).

In *Re O (A Minor) (Contact: Imposition of Conditions)* [1995] 2 FLR 124, the Court of Appeal confirmed that the court had a wide and comprehensive jurisdiction to make contact orders, including for indirect contact, such as the absent parent being sent school progress reports and any cards or letters sent by him being read to the child. The court rejected the mother's argument that it was wrong in principle to compel her to read the father's communications when she was unwilling and hostile to such contact, saying that would mean that the mother was being given a power of veto. She was subject to an enforceable duty to promote contact if the court considered that that promoted the child's welfare: that was a decision for the court, not for the mother. However, a practical problem with contact orders is how to enforce them if the parent with day-to-day care is determined that contact will not occur. The court has power to enforce contact orders (FLA 1986, s 34 and see **12.9.1**). However, in practice, this is often ineffective in contact disputes. The court can penalise in costs the party who is breaching the contact order (*Re B (Contact Application: Costs)* [1995] Fam Law 650). Ultimately, contempt proceedings can be used, or at least threatened, when a parent with whom the child lives consistently and unreasonably refuses contact (*Re N (A Minor) (Access: Penal Notices)* [1992] 1 FLR 134 and *Re N (A Minor)* (1997) *The Times*, 11 October, CA). However, these proceedings are often inappropriate and could cause the child added trauma, especially if the unfortunate result is the imprisonment of the parent with whom the child lives. Nevertheless, in *F v F (Contact: Committal)* [1998] 2 FLR 237, the Court of Appeal, concluding that the mother had sabotaged contact which was clearly in the interests of the children, confirmed a sentence of 7 days' imprisonment, suspended for 6 months on condition that she complied with the contact order.

A distinction must be made between cases where a parent is opposed to contact for no good reason, when the court will be very slow to conclude contact would harm the child, and those where there are genuine and rational reasons for opposing contact. A particular difficulty arises where, during the relationship, the custodial parent has been subjected to violence by the other parent. In *Re H (Contact: Domestic Violence)* [1998] 2 FLR 42, the Court of Appeal stated that domestic violence was not, of itself, a bar to contact, but one factor in a very complex equation. While the courts have re-emphasised the presumption in favour of contact, recent cases have shown a willingness to hold that the presumption is rebutted on the facts. See, for example, *Re M (Contact: Violent Parent)* [1999] Fam Law 380, where Wall J stated:

> 'Too often, notwithstanding that domestic violence had been found, the mother was none the less ordered to arrange for contact with the father, the courts neglecting the other side of the equation which was that such a father should first demonstrate by changing his behaviour, that he was a fit person to have contact and would not destabilise or upset the children.'

See also *Re K (Contact: Mother's Anxiety)* [1999] Fam Law 527, where the court found that the mother had been so traumatised by the father's behaviour that direct contact would bring about a state of heightened anxiety and fear which would inevitably be conveyed to the boy, causing him significant emotional harm.

Most recently, the issue came before the Court of Appeal in four cases, heard together, where, in each case, the father's application for direct contact was refused because of a background of domestic violence between the parents (*Re L (Contact: Domestic Violence)* [2000] 2 FLR 334, CA). The Court of Appeal eschewed any presumption either for or against direct contact in cases involving domestic violence. The balancing exercise required to determine what was best for a child's welfare had to be carried out in the usual way. However, the court should particularly consider the following points:

- the past and present conduct of both parties;
- the effect on the child and the residential parent; and
- the motivation of the parent seeking contact.

The Court of Appeal also pointed out the need for family judges and magistrates to have a heightened awareness of the effects on children of being exposed to domestic violence by one parent against the other. (See the Children Act Sub-Committee of the Advisory Board on Family Law's report to the Lord Chancellor on the question of parental contact in cases where there is domestic violence.)

12.3.3 Prohibited steps order

A prohibited steps order is an order that no step which could be taken by a parent in meeting his or her parental responsibilities for a child and which is of a kind specified in the order shall be taken by any person without the consent of the court. This order deals with a specific problem which has arisen. However, it cannot overlap with a residence or contact order. Section 9(5) of CA 1989 provides that the court cannot make a prohibited steps order or a specific issue order with a view to achieving a result that could be achieved by a residence or contact order. For example, the court could not grant an order prohibiting the child living with anyone other than the applicant as this would in effect be a residence order. It can be used to restrict anyone, not just a parent. So, it could be used to prevent a grandparent with whom the child lived from removing the child from the jurisdiction.

Another situation in which the overlap between the various s 8 orders must be considered is child abduction. If, in an abduction case, the result that is required is for the abducted child to be returned to live with the non-abducting parent, then the correct order for this parent to seek is a residence order (with appropriate conditions and directions) and not a specific issue order ordering return of the child coupled with a prohibited steps order to prevent further removal (*Re W (A Minor) (Residence Order)* [1992] 2 FLR 332). If the required result is to obtain the return of the child to the UK and prevent further removal but the child is to remain living with the abducting parent, then a prohibited steps order is the correct order to obtain (*Re D (A Minor) (Child: Removal from Jurisdiction)* [1992] 1 FLR 637).

If no residence order were in force, a prohibited steps order could be used to prohibit the removal of the child from the country or prevent a change of surname.

If it is desired to prevent anyone having contact with the child, this is the appropriate order to seek as it is widely believed that a contact order can only authorise contact and not prevent it. However, in *Nottingham CC v P* [1993] 3 All ER 815, CA, it was held that the court could make a contact order providing for no contact. Therefore, the person with whom a child lives could be prevented from allowing contact with an abusing parent or anyone else who the court considered was harming the child in any way. However, in *Re H (Prohibited Steps Order)* [1995] 1 FLR 638, CA, where the mother's cohabitee had abused the children, the court decided that a 'negative' contact order preventing the mother from allowing contact would only afford partial protection. Instead, the court made a prohibited steps order against the cohabitee, even although he was not a party to the proceedings and had not been given notice.

An important restriction on a prohibited steps order is that it can only relate to matters which are included within parental responsibility. If an order is needed to restrict publicity for example, the wider powers of wardship are needed as this is not one of the matters included within parental responsibility.

12.3.4 Specific issue order

A specific issue order is an order giving directions for the purpose of determining a specific question which has arisen or which may arise in connection with any aspect of parental responsibility for a child.

It does not give a parent a general power, it just makes a decision on one issue over which there is a disagreement which cannot be resolved. It could be used to decide which school a child should attend, whether a child should have a particular operation (including, for example, sterilisation or circumcision) or course of treatment, or the religion a child should adopt.

It can be used by non-parents, for example, the local authority or doctor or relation, to resolve issues involving the child, for example, over abortion or life-saving medical decisions. In *Re R (A Minor) (Blood Transfusion)* [1993] 2 FLR 757, a specific issue order was used to deal with a situation where a child needed a blood transfusion and his parents refused to give consent due to their religious beliefs.

Again, it cannot be used to achieve a 'back-door' residence or contact order, for example by ordering a child to attend a particular school thereby necessitating a change of residence (see **12.3.3**).

12.3.5 Family assistance order

A family assistance order is not a s 8 order at all, although it is closely connected. CA 1989, s 16 allows the court in any family proceedings where it has power to make a s 8 order to make an order requiring a probation officer or local authority officer to be made available to advise, assist and befriend any person named in the order.

It can only be made in exceptional circumstances and only if everyone named in the order, excluding the child, consents.

The aim of the order is to support the family in the immediate aftermath of a family breakdown and to help everyone to adjust to the changed circumstances. The order can only be made by the court of its own motion and is likely to be made in conjunction with one or more s 8 orders.

12.3.6 Local authority investigation

If exceptional circumstances are revealed in family proceedings, for example, in divorce proceedings serious neglect is discovered which makes it unlikely that either parent should look after the children, the court may not be prepared to grant either parent a s 8 order. The court does not have the power to make a care order relating to the children and what it will have to do is to make an order under CA 1989, s 37 to direct the local authority to investigate the child's circumstances. It is then up to the local authority to decide whether or not to bring care or supervision proceedings depending on the outcome of their inquiries. The court can, when making a s 37 order, make an interim care order to protect a child pending the investigation (see **13.3.3**).

12.4 WELFARE PRINCIPLE

Section 1(1) of the CA 1989 states:

> 'When a court determines any question with respect to –
>
> (a)   the upbringing of a child; or
> (b)   the administration of the child's property or the application of any income
>   arising from it,
>
> the child's welfare shall be the court's paramount consideration.'

The welfare principle will determine any contested proceedings under s 8 of CA 1989 and it will also extend to care proceedings (CA 1989, s 31) and related public law orders.

It is a concept that has been used for many years in cases concerning children and is summarised by the words of Lord McDermott in *J v C* [1969] 1 All ER 788, HL:

> 'More than that the child's welfare is to be treated as the top item in a list of items relevant to the matter in question, [the words] connote a process whereby, when all the relevant facts, relationships, claims and wishes of parents, risks, choices and their circumstances are taken into account and weighed, the course to be followed will be that which is most in the interest of the child's welfare as that term has now to be understood... . [It is] the paramount consideration because it rules upon or determines the course to be followed.'

12.4.1 Human Rights Act 1998

Article 8 of the European Convention on Human Rights provides that 'everyone has the right to respect for his private and family life, his home and his correspondence'. Although the welfare of the child is paramount under the Children Act, under Article 8 the starting point is that each family member is on an equal footing.

There is a debate as to whether the welfare principle is incompatible with Article 8 and an individual's right to respect for family life. In other words, placing the child's welfare as paramount does not involve balancing the family rights of the other relevant individuals. In the past, the European Court has tended to adopt more of a straightforward balancing exercise and the idea of paramountcy has not been supported.

Any inconsistency between the approach of the English courts and the minimum standards required by the Convention may need to be reconciled, particularly if the English courts continue to interpret 'paramount' to mean 'sole' consideration (as opposed to 'pre-eminent' or 'particularly important' consideration). For example, in contact applications, it may be argued that the court must consider the right of the parent and other family members to contact as opposed to this being the right of the child.

Similarly, where an application is made to remove a child from the jurisdiction, the welfare of the child is paramount and the courts have held that leave should not be withheld unless the interests of the child and the custodial parent are incompatible (*Re H (Application to Remove from Jurisdiction)* [1998] 1 FLR 848). In theory, it is arguable that this approach may not give sufficient weight to respect for the family life of the parent remaining under Article 8. However, in a recent Court of Appeal decision (*G-A (A Child)* [2000] 3 UKHRR 572), where the mother wished to return to New York to work there, taking with her the parties' young child, the court held that although the father and the child had a right to family life, the mother also had a right to her private life which included the freedom to work where she reasonably chose to. The court was therefore not prepared to interfere with the established line of authorities and doubted that matters would be decided any differently under the HRA 1998.

12.5 CHECKLIST OF FACTORS

Section 1(3) of CA 1989, directs the court to pay particular attention to seven factors when it is applying the welfare principle in contested s 8 proceedings and any proceedings for care and supervision orders.

The aim of the checklist is to promote a consistent approach by providing a framework to use when solicitors are preparing evidence and when courts are making decisions. It could sometimes be a very useful tool to use to explain to clients the approach that they should, and that the court certainly will, take in making a decision.

It provides a minimum that must be considered in every case. The Act gives no indication of the relative importance of the factors so the court is left to assess the relative importance of each factor in the circumstances of each case. The checklist is not exhaustive and the court can also take any other relevant factors into account. For example, in *Re R (Residence Order: Finance)* [1995] 2 FLR 612 it was confirmed that a judge was entitled to look at the case in the round, which could include taking into account financial considerations, such as a possible assessment by the Child Support Agency.

12.5.1 The ascertainable wishes and feelings of the child concerned (considered in the light of his age and understanding)

This factor reflects the importance of allowing the child's wishes to be given a place in deciding what is in his or her welfare (see the *Gillick* case at **12.2.1**). Lord Justice Butler-Sloss in the Cleveland Report made the point that 'a child is a person, not an object of concern'.

There are a number of cases where, on the particular facts, the court not only considered but also followed the wishes of children. In *M v M (Transfer of Custody: Appeal)* [1987] 1 WLR 404, CA, the trial judge said that it was wrong to order that a 12-year-old girl should live with her father instead of her mother without taking proper account of her adamant and strong opposition to this. In another case, the wishes of a 'sensible and mature' boy aged 14 years were the deciding factor in ordering that he should go to a local day school enabling him to live with his father rather than go away to a boarding school. The boy was very anxious to build a relationship with his father with whom he had not lived for 5 years (see *Re P (A Minor) (Education: Child's Views)* [1992] 1 FLR 316). In *S v S (Child Abduction: Child's Views)* [1992] 2 FLR 492, the Court of Appeal said that there was no age below which a child was to be considered as not having attained sufficient maturity for his views to be taken into account.

However, the child's wishes do not necessarily take precedence and the court may feel that the children's wishes are not in their best interests (*Re DW (A Minor)* [1984] Fam Law 17).

There are a number of ways in which the child's wishes and feelings can be made known. The court will place great importance on the welfare report prepared by the court welfare officer which will consider the child's wishes as well as the maturity of the child and the extent to which the parents may have exerted influence over the child in forming any views. In some cases, a judge may interview a child privately during the case to form his own opinion. This is not common and will not be done in relation to children under 8 years of age. (See *B v B (Minors)* [1994] 2 FLR 489, CA.) Magistrates can also see a child in private but this power must be exercised only in rare and exceptional cases and should not be used if the child's wishes are adequately dealt with in the welfare report.

A wider issue involving a child's wishes is the extent to which a child can consent to or refuse medical treatment (see *Re W (A Minor) (Consent to Medical Treatment)* [1993] 1 FLR 1). If a child is sufficiently mature, he can consent to treatment and only the court can override his consent. If such a child refuses consent to treatment, then either the court or anyone with parental responsibility can give consent.

12.5.2 The child's physical, emotional and educational needs

This factor focuses on the child and will look at accommodation, medical needs and education as well as how close the child is to brothers and sisters and others with whom he may lose touch if a particular order is made.

The court will not equate welfare with material advantages and the fact that one parent can offer more is of little weight, particularly because the court could compensate for this when making financial orders.

The court will consider the circumstances very carefully before splitting brothers and sisters (*C v C (Minors: Custody)* [1988] 2 FLR 291, CA). This will mean that it will be unusual to separate siblings especially when they are close in age, although the larger the age gap, especially if linked with the fact that one child is at boarding school, could mean that children might be happier separated with generous contact during holidays.

12.5.3 The likely effect on the child of any change in circumstances

If the current arrangements for a child are working satisfactorily the court will be very unlikely to change them. This attitude, which is often referred to as maintaining the 'status quo', was explained in *Allington v Allington* [1985] FLR 586, CA:

> 'It is generally accepted by those who are professionally concerned with children that particularly in the early years, continuity of care is a most important part of a child's sense of security and that disruption of established bonds is to be avoided whenever it is possible to do so.'

A result of this attitude is that the person with whom the child is living is at a considerable advantage and it may encourage them to increase this advantage by delaying the proceedings. This problem is tackled by the Act where it provides that any delay is 'likely to prejudice the welfare of the child' (CA 1989, s 1(2)) and it further discourages delay by its imposition of a litigation timetable (CA 1989, s 11(1) and see **12.7**).

12.5.4 The child's age, sex, background and any characteristics of the child which the court considers relevant

Age may be important as very young babies tend to need to live with their mothers whereas a 15-year-old child can generally cope with living with either parent. Also, age has a decisive influence on the importance a court will attach to a child's wishes but there is no presumption of law that a child of any age should be with one parent or the other (*Re W (A Minor) (Residence Order)* [1992] 2 FLR 332, CA).

The sex of the child can be taken into account. In *Re H (A Minor)* (1990) *The Times*, 20 June, CA, the court agreed that a 2-year-old girl should live with her father and stated that 'It may be natural for young children to be with their mothers but this is merely one consideration not a presumption'. Obviously, the needs of a teenager might best be met by living with a parent of the same sex. The factor also refers to the background of the child. This can cover race, culture, and religion. The needs of a mixed-race child are of particular difficulty when deciding where a child should live. The court will look at how the child has been brought up and the influence of each culture and make appropriate residence and contact arrangements (see *Re P (A Minor) (Adoption)* [1990] 1 FLR 96).

12.5.5 Any harm that the child has suffered or is at risk of suffering

This factor will cover any past or future harm to the child. Harm is a very broad term and will cover both physical and psychological injury.

The court will also consider the harm caused to a child by not seeing both parents. In the case of *Re S (Minors: Access)* [1990] 2 FLR 166, the court said that contact 'is the right of the child not of the parent ... The child has a right to know his other parent'.

12.5.6 How capable each of the child's parents and any other person in relation to whom the court considers the question relevant is of meeting the child's needs

This factor involves the court looking at the parents or other proposed carers to assess their ability to care for the child. The parents' conduct will be relevant to the extent that it may affect their suitability as a parent. Any criminal record, say, for violence or dishonesty, will be relevant.

In disputes between a natural parent and another, for example a grandparent, the courts tend to presume that, unless there is positive evidence to the contrary, it is in the child's interests to live with his natural parent. The question was not which household would provide the best home (*Re D (Care: Natural Parent Presumption)* [1999] 1 FLR 134).

Whether a parent works will influence the care of the child. A parent's lifestyle and sexual orientation may be relevant. Issues of homosexuality and lesbianism can affect the child, especially if this causes problems, for example teasing or bullying, at school.

A parent who suffers from a mental or physical illness which could mean sudden or long-term stays in hospital might also be less suitable as a full-time carer. Religion, too, may have an influence on a court's decision, especially if it may adversely affect a child's health or have a harmful influence on the child's development. In *Re R (A Minor) (Residence: Religion)* [1993] 2 FLR 163, CA, the court said that there was no rule of law or legal principle that it could never be right to force a child to abandon his religious beliefs. The court made a residence order that a child of 9 years of age live with his father even though the child had been brought up in a strict religious sect from which the father had been excluded. The court took the religious issue into account but felt that it was in the child's best interests to be with his father.

If a parent is proposing to share care with someone else that person's capabilities will also be considered. This means that new partners or spouses, relatives and friends may be relevant as well as nannies and childminders.

12.5.7 The range of powers available to the court under this Act in the proceedings in question

This factor encourages the court to think laterally and consider every option open to it, including that of not making an order at all.

The court has the power to make any order in favour of any person irrespective of who has applied and for what. Thus, in the course of an application for a residence order by a parent, the court may decide that the child would be better off living with a grandparent. They can make this order even though the grandparents were not parties to the application. The deciding factor is the welfare of the child.

The court could also adjourn s 8 proceedings brought by a parent if they felt that a care or supervision order would be the best thing for the child (CA 1989, s 37(1)).

This section enables the court to direct the local authority to investigate the circumstances of the child and following this the local authority could start care proceedings. The divorce courts do not have the power to make a care or supervision order themselves.

12.6 THE 'NO ORDER' PRESUMPTION

Section 1(5) of CA 1989 states:

> 'Where a court is considering whether or not to make one or more orders under this Act with respect to a child, it shall not make the order or any of the orders unless it considers that doing so would be better for the child than making no order at all.'

This means that there is a policy that the court will not intervene and make an order unless it can be shown that there is a positive need and benefit to the child in doing so.

On divorce, the court should not make an order automatically for the children as part of the 'divorce package'. If the parties agree on where a child is to live after the divorce and when the other parent should see him, no court will make an order.

The aim of this presumption is to try to reduce the bitterness felt by a parent who may feel that he has 'lost' if a court order is imposed ordering the child to live with the other parent or allowing him contact at defined times. The long-term damage to a child following divorce is greatly reduced if bitterness can be minimised and the absence of unnecessary court intervention will help this. If parents are in dispute from the outset, or if agreed arrangements break down, the court can always be asked to make appropriate orders.

Other circumstances when the court will be likely to consider that an order is necessary include where there is a real danger that one parent may abduct the child and it is, therefore, an advantage to have in operation the restrictions on removal from the UK contained in a residence order or, perhaps, where both parents agree that an order is preferable. Another situation where the court made an order despite the fact that all parties were in agreement was where parents agreed with the maternal grandmother that the child should live with her. The court said that there was a reason to grant a residence order to the grandmother as it would give her parental responsibility for the child and give her important rights, for example, it would enable her to give consent to medical treatment and authorise school trips. The granting of a residence order also gave the arrangement more stability as the parents could not change their minds without going back to court (*B v B (A Minor) (Residence Order)* [1992] 2 FLR 327).

12.7 AVOIDING DELAY

Section 1(2) of CA 1989 states:

> 'In any proceedings in which any question with respect to the upbringing of a child arises, the court shall have regard to the general principle that any delay in determining the question is likely to prejudice the welfare of the child.'

Delay can be particularly damaging in children cases as a child's timescale is different from that of an adult. Six months is half a lifetime to a one-year-old child.

The object is to avoid drift or delay for no reason, which can be very damaging to a child. Sometimes delay can be positively beneficial, for example, an adjournment to see how the child is settling down to new arrangements.

Inappropriate delay may also now be a breach of Article 6 of the European Convention on Human Rights (the right to a hearing within a reasonable time).

12.8 PROCEDURE FOR SECTION 8 ORDERS

The procedure for making applications is governed by FPR 1991 in the county court or High Court and the Family Proceedings Courts (Children Act 1989) Rules 1991 in the family proceedings court.

12.8.1 Public funding

Legal Representation is available for Children Act proceedings. If an application is made both the means and merits test must be satisfied (see **2.5.4**). If a Legal Representation certificate has already been issued, for example, for ancillary financial proceedings in a divorce, the Legal Representation certificate issued in these proceedings will need to be amended. In urgent cases, emergency Legal Representation can be used.

12.8.2 Jurisdiction

Applications for s 8 orders can be made within any family proceedings; in fact the court can make an order of its own motion in such proceedings. Family proceedings are defined in the Act and cover divorce, nullity or judicial separation, financial relief applications (MCA 1973 and DPMCA 1978) and domestic violence applications under FLA 1996. Alternatively, 'freestanding' applications can be made where no order other than under CA 1989 is needed.

12.8.3 Is leave of the court needed?

The following can apply for *any* s 8 order without leave of the court:

(1) a parent (which includes an unmarried father whether or not he has parental responsibility); or
(2) a guardian; or
(3) any person with a residence order in his or her favour (CA 1989, s 10(5)).

The following can apply for a residence or contact order *only* without leave:

(1) a step-father or step-mother who has treated the child as a child of the family; or
(2) any person with whom the child has lived for at least 3 years out of the last 5 years; or
(3) any person who has obtained the consent of all those people whose legal position would be affected, ie anyone with parental responsibility or anyone with a residence order or the local authority if the child is in care.

All other people not within the above require leave.

Therefore, for example, grandparents will require leave unless the child has been living with them for 3 years or they have the necessary consents. However, grandparents will normally readily be given leave if they can show that they have a genuine interest and commitment to the child (*Re A (Section 8 Order: Grandparent Application)* [1995] 2 FLR 153). An application for leave must be made in writing.

It is unlikely that the requirement for certain categories of parties to apply for s 8 orders violates Article 6(1) of the European Convention on Human Rights as it is not a blanket denial of access to the court but rather a hurdle to overcome.

Application by the child

A child can apply on his own behalf for a s 8 order, but leave of the court is required. (See FPR 1991, r 9.2A(2).) There have been several cases where teenage children have been granted leave to apply and have gone on to obtain s 8 orders (see *Re AD (A Minor) (Child's Wishes)* [1993] 1 FCR 573). Even if a child obtains a residence order allowing him to live apart from his parents, his parents will still retain parental responsibility. Orders have been sought to enable a child to live with grandparents or the parents of the child's boyfriend and could also be used where a pregnant teenager did not want an abortion which her parents were forcing her to undergo.

The Solicitors Family Law Association *Guide to Good Practice for Solicitors Acting for Children* gives practical and very useful guidance for solicitors asked to act for children.

If a child wants to obtain a s 8 order, there are four hurdles to overcome.

(1) TO OBTAIN A SOLICITOR TO ACT FOR HIM

A minor can start proceedings without a next friend or guardian ad litem provided the court gives leave to proceed without a next friend or guardian ad litem *or* a solicitor considers that the child has sufficient understanding to give instructions. If the leave of the court is sought, it will base its decision on whether the child is mature enough to exercise a wise choice in his own interests in the circumstances that exist (*Re S (A Minor) (Independent Representation)* [1993] 3 All ER 36, CA). In complex cases, the court is likely to recommend that a third party such as the Official Solicitor or a guardian ad litem acts for the child. This could, of course, make it less likely that the order sought by the child is obtained.

If a child approaches a solicitor direct, that solicitor can take the decision whether to act for the child. The Solicitors Family Law Association guidelines (Section F: Assessing Understanding) point out that initially it is the solicitor's duty to assess the child's understanding. (See *Re CT (A Minor) (Wardship: Representation)* [1993] 2 FLR 278.) The solicitor must also be sensitive to his or her duty of confidentiality to the child.

(2) TO OBTAIN PUBLIC FUNDING

A child will usually need public funding and will have to convince the Legal Services Commission that his application has merit. The means test will not be a problem as it is the child's resources that are relevant when assessing financial eligibility. Legal Help is also available to a child to cover the cost of the initial interview.

(3) TO OBTAIN THE COURT'S LEAVE

The child will need to obtain leave of the court to start s 8 proceedings (CA 1989, s 10(8)). Leave will be given only if the court is satisfied that the child has sufficient understanding to make the application. All applications for leave in these circumstances must be dealt with by the High Court (*Practice Direction: Children Act 1989 – Applications by Children* [1993] 1 FLR 668).

In *Re H (Residence Order: Child's Application For Leave)* [2000] 1 FLR 781, a 12-year-old boy was refused leave to apply for a residence order in the course of his parents' divorce proceedings. The boy wished to live with his father and was worried that the court would not attach enough weight to his wishes unless he made his own application. The court decided that, although he had sufficient understanding to instruct a solicitor independently, the boy did not have a separate argument to make that would not be made on the father's behalf. The judge also said that the boy must be assured that experienced judges would take full account of his wishes and are conscious that it is not usually a good idea to impose a result contrary to a child's wishes, even though those wishes are not decisive.

(4) TO SHOW THAT THE MERITS OF THE CASE JUSTIFY THE ORDER SOUGHT

At the eventual hearing the court will consider the child's welfare and the statutory checklist when deciding whether to grant the order sought.

12.8.4 Which court?

If there are pending matrimonial proceedings, the application for a s 8 order must be made in the cause. Otherwise, the applicant has a free choice between the family proceedings court, a county court or High Court. One of the changes brought about by CA 1989 was to introduce this concurrent jurisdiction and to ensure that specially trained officials and judiciary are available at each level to deal with CA 1989 matters.

The family proceedings court

The family proceedings court can deal with private law applications for s 8 orders but it does not deal with divorce cases. In practice, as many s 8 applications will be linked to divorce proceedings they will be dealt with by the county court. Most public law cases, for example, for care or supervision orders, will start in the family proceedings court.

The work is mainly dealt with by lay magistrates who have had special training to deal with family cases and are therefore on a Family Panel. Sometimes, cases are dealt with by stipendiary magistrates.

County court

Any judge hearing family work in the county court must be nominated by the Lord Chancellor to hear family work and receive special training. There are various categories of judge who have been allocated particular areas of work. The detailed provisions are set out in *Practice Direction (Family Proceedings (Allocation to Judiciary) Directions 1997)* [1997] Fam Law 691:

District judges can only hear private law family work and have a limited jurisdiction. Although the CA 1989 originally suggested that district judges could hear contested as well as uncontested applications for s 8 orders, subsequent regulations provide for them to deal just with certain aspects of private law cases, ie interlocutory matters, uncontested hearings and interim orders in contested cases.

Nominated care district judges have a wider jurisdiction and can also hear uncontested public law cases and contested private law cases.

Circuit family judges have full private family law jurisdiction but cannot hear public law cases.

Nominated care judges have full private and public law jurisdiction.

Designated family judges have full private and public law jurisdiction and are based at care centres.

There are four classes of county court each with different types of jurisdiction.

(1) Non-divorce county courts

These courts have no family jurisdiction and therefore no involvement with the CA 1989, except for domestic violence injunctions.

The work is carried out by non-nominated circuit judges and district judges.

(2) Divorce county courts

These courts have jurisdiction to hear divorces and all uncontested private law CA 1989 cases. If any of these matters become contested they will be transferred to a family hearing centre.

The work is carried out by non-nominated circuit judges and district judges.

(3) Family hearing centres

These courts have jurisdiction to hear all private law CA 1989 cases whether or not contested.

The work is carried out by nominated circuit judges and (to a limited extent) district judges.

(4) Care centres

These courts have jurisdiction to hear all private and public law (eg, care and supervision orders) CA 1989 cases, both contested and uncontested.

The work is carried out by designated family judges, nominated care judges and nominated care district judges.

High Court

The High Court can hear all types of CA 1989 cases as well as appeals in CA 1989 cases from the family proceedings court. In practice, it will generally deal with the more complex cases which could either be started there or which are transferred from other courts.

Transfer of cases

Irrespective of where a case started, it can be transferred to another more appropriate court. This is essentially governed by the general principle that any delay is likely to prejudice the child's welfare, but other factors will be considered, such as the complexity of the case and the need to consolidate it with proceedings which may have been started in another court (see Children (Allocation of Proceedings) Order 1991, SI 1991/1677). It is possible for cases to be transferred either vertically or horizontally. Thus, a difficult case could be transferred from the family proceedings court up to the county court or, if a family proceedings court is too busy, it could transfer the case to another family proceedings court. If CA 1989 proceedings are commenced in a divorce county court ancillary to divorce, and the application is then opposed, the case will have to be transferred to a family hearing centre. In these circumstances, it is possible for the whole cause to be transferred rather than just the CA 1989 application. It is also possible for a case to be transferred down from the High Court to a county court. A case cannot be transferred down to a family proceedings court.

12.8.5 The application

The applicant must file Form C1 (or Form C2 if there are already family proceedings between the parents), together with sufficient copies for service (and a fee). The standard form enables the applicant to include the details of the order needed, any directions and the reasons for applying.

On filing, the court fixes a date for a preliminary hearing or directions appointment.

The applicant must join as a party every person whom he believes to have parental responsibility for the child. This would not cover a step-parent or putative father. However, any person may apply to be joined and the court has power to direct that anyone else be joined as a party. Therefore, all people with a genuine interest and active role in the child's upbringing can be involved in court proceedings.

12.8.6 Service

Copies of the application must be served on all parties at least 14 days before the hearing, together with a Notice of Proceedings (Form C6) showing the date for the directions appointment, and blank Acknowledgement (Form C7). The applicant must then file a Statement of Service (Form C9) at court, setting out how service was effected.

The FPR 1991 also provide that notice of the application must be given to a number of other interested people, so that they are given the chance to decide whether they want to be joined as a party. This will include anyone caring for the child or anyone who is a party to other proceedings which affect the child.

12.8.7 Ex parte applications

All s 8 orders can be made in an ex parte application. However, ex parte interim orders should only be made in exceptional circumstances where it is necessary to protect the child. For example, an ex parte application would be justified in a 'snatch' situation, where no order was made at the time of the divorce but a crisis arose when the parent failed to return the child to the other parent following a day's contact, or where an urgent medical problem arose and the parents were in dispute over a life-threatening decision. In *Re G (Minors) (Ex parte Interim Residence Order)* [1993] 1 FLR 910, the Court of Appeal granted an interim residence order to a father because of evidence that the mother was taking drugs and that the children needed to be removed from her care immediately.

When an ex parte application is made, the full application should be filed either at the same time or within 24 hours if the order is obtained by telephone. The application and order must be served on the respondent within 48 hours after the making of the ex parte order.

12.8.8 Acknowledgement

Within 14 days of service the respondent must complete the Acknowledgement (Form C7), file it at court and serve a copy on the other party.

12.8.9 First appointment

The court will fix a first directions appointment when an application is issued. The task of the court at the first appointment is to:

– investigate the issues;
– inquire into the possibility of settlement; and
– give directions in any case which has to proceed.

When giving directions, the court will normally consider the following issues.

A timetable for the proceedings

As a result of the 'no delay' principle, the court will want to ensure that the case proceeds as quickly as possible. By discussing the probable timing of the matter at the outset, problems and delays can be minimised.

Preparation of a welfare report by the court welfare officer

The court will often order a welfare report in contested s 8 proceedings. This will be prepared by the court welfare officer and must be filed with the court at least 14 days before the hearing and made available to the parties. The welfare officer will have access to the court file and will interview the parties and the child as well as anyone else who appears relevant, for example, schoolteachers, the family doctor, grandparents. A written welfare report will be prepared which will often include conclusions and recommendations as to which order should be made.

In some areas of the country there is a considerable delay in the preparation of these reports and it is, therefore, important to obtain a direction to prepare a report as early as possible in the proceedings.

Submission of expert evidence

The court must give its leave before any medical or psychiatric examination or other assessment of the child can take place. This is to protect the child from unnecessary and repeated assessment. The court tends to prefer to rely on the court welfare officer's report.

Exchange of witness statements

The court controls the time when evidence is submitted as no document can be filed or served without the court's leave. This is to prevent the parties from filing destructive documents which could lead them to take entrenched positions.

Attendance of the child

As the child is not a party to the proceedings, a child can only attend a hearing by direction of the court. Practice is normally not to direct the child's attendance.

Next appointment

Unless the issues are resolved, at the end of every court appointment a date must be fixed for the next appointment. Normally, even if only provisionally, the court will also fix the date of the final hearing.

Usually a final directions appointment will be timetabled to take place when any welfare report and all the evidence has been filed. This will consider what evidence can be agreed and what is in dispute, together with final arrangements for the hearing.

The parties cannot extend any time-limit ordered by the court by consent. This implements the 'no delay' philosophy and gives the court control of the litigation timetable.

12.8.10 Witness statements

All evidence must be filed at court in the form of written statements of the oral evidence which each party intends to use together with copies of the documents which will be relied on.

These statements can be filed only when the court gives a direction to do this. Hearsay evidence can be included (as in other civil proceedings). So, for example, a welfare officer in his report can include a remark made in a conversation he had with the child's schoolteacher that 'the child was always upset on the Mondays following a visit to his father'. The court can decide what weight to give to such evidence.

12.8.11 Judgment

The final hearing will be held in chambers before the appropriate judge (see **12.8.4**). *Practice Direction* [1994] 1 WLR 16 says that when a hearing is expected to last one day or more, the parties must provide the court with a written time estimate. Judgment must be delivered as soon as possible after the final hearing. Orders must be in writing and a record of any finding of fact and the reasons for the decision will be kept on the file. A copy of the order must be served on each party and on any person with whom the child is living.

It is general practice not to order costs in children cases, although it may be appropriate to do so if the parent goes beyond what is reasonable. This means unreasonableness in relation to the conduct of the litigation, rather than unreasonableness in relation to the child. In *Re G (Costs: Child Case)* [1999] 2 FLR 250, the court drew a distinction between 'hopeless' and 'unreasonable' applications. In that case, although the court considered the father's application for a residence order was hopeless, it was not in itself unreasonable. However, it is possible that the stage will be reached where the pursuit of a hopeless application becomes, in itself, unreasonable.

12.8.12 Duration of s 8 orders

Section 8 orders will normally be expressed to cease to have effect when the child reaches 16 years of age (CA 1989, s 91(10)). In any event, they will end when the child reaches 18 years of age (CA 1989, s 91(11)).

The court has power in exceptional circumstances to make or extend an order beyond the child's 16th birthday (CA 1989, s 9(6)).

If a residence or contact order is made in favour of a parent, these orders will automatically end if the child's parents live together for a continuous period of more than 6 months (CA 1989, s 11(5) and (6)).

12.9 PROTECTION OF CHILDREN

This section deals with emergency situations concerning children. It covers the threatened abduction of the child, recovering a child already removed from the UK, general emergency protection of a child by a parent or other interested person and, finally, an outline of how a local authority may protect children.

12.9.1 Abduction of children

If a child is not returned to the parent with whom he lives following an agreed visit to the other parent and abduction is suspected, a legal adviser needs to assess the situation quickly and obtain such protection as the law offers to try to ensure that the child is returned as soon as possible. Below is a list of relevant considerations.

Has a s 8 order already been made?

If the parent with whom the child normally lives already has a residence order in his or her favour, this will contain a provision preventing the other parent removing the child from the UK without consent of the parent with the residence order or consent of the court (CA 1989, s 13(1) and see **12.3.1**). This provision can be enforced by the court by an order that the child be produced to the parent with the residence order (CA 1989, s 14; FLA 1986, s 34).

If there is no s 8 order in force, an ex parte application for a residence order or prohibited steps order could be applied for and then enforced by the court.

A court has the power in proceedings for or relating to an order under s 8, to order any person who may have information as to the child's whereabouts to disclose it to the court (FLA 1986, s 33). This could be used to force relations or friends of the abductor to disclose addresses or likely destinations.

Family Law Act 1986

If a child has been removed from the jurisdiction of the English courts to another part of the UK, for example, to Scotland or Northern Ireland, this Act enables a s 8 order to be recognised and enforced by the local court. In order for this to be done, the s 8 order must first be registered with the appropriate court in the other part of the UK.

Child Abduction Act 1984

The Child Abduction Act 1984 (CAA 1984) contains criminal offences which will be committed if a child is removed without the appropriate consents irrespective of whether any residence order is in force.

(1) It is an offence for a parent of a child or any person with parental responsibility for a child to take or send that child out of the UK without either the consent of all persons with parental responsibility or the leave of the court (CAA 1984, s 1).

However, no offence is committed by a person in whose favour a residence order is in force who takes or sends the child out of the UK for a period of less than a month.

There are also provisions in the Act, which apply where no residence order has been made, which provide a defence if the person who removes the child either reasonably believes that he has consent or has taken all reasonable steps to obtain it.

If, following divorce, no s 8 order has been made, neither parent will be in contempt of court if they remove the child without the consent of the other under CA 1989 as each has parental responsibility. However, neither can take the child out of the UK for any time whatsoever without committing a criminal offence under CAA 1984, unless they obtain the appropriate consents.

(2) It is also an offence for any person, except a person with parental responsibility for a child, to take that child from any other person who has lawful control of the child without lawful authority or reasonable excuse (CAA 1984, s 2).

This will not affect married parents. However, a putative father who has not obtained parental responsibility will commit the s 2 offence but has a defence if he can show that he had reasonable grounds for believing that he was the child's father. He will nevertheless be liable under s 1 if he takes the child abroad unless he has the mother's consent.

Difficult ethical problems can arise for a solicitor if a client informs him that he intends to abduct his child from the mother. There is a duty of confidentiality towards a client, but a solicitor cannot ignore the interests of the child and must decide which duty prevails. (See Principle 16.02 of the Guide to the Professional Conduct of Solicitors.) It is important that a solicitor ensures that a client is made fully aware of the consequences of the crime he is proposing to commit and that the solicitor does not assist him to commit it.

'Port alert' procedure

The provisions in both CA 1989 and CAA 1984 may deter a potential abductor but do not contain any practical safeguards actually to prevent a determined abductor from removing the child. The 'port alert' procedure is designed physically to prevent a child from being taken abroad. The detail of this procedure is set out in *Practice Direction of 14 April 1986* [1986] 1 All ER 983, [1986] 1 WLR 475.

It is operated by the police on a 24-hour basis. If instituted, the police will liaise with immigration or security officials at ports and airports to try to find and stop the child from being taken abroad. The police have the power to arrest without warrant. There is no need for a s 8 order to have been obtained if the child is under 16, although if there is an order it should be produced to the police. The system is only available for children over 16 if, unusually, a s 8 order exists. The police will only operate the port alert procedure if they are satisfied that there is a real and imminent risk that a child will be taken out of the UK. 'Imminent' is taken to mean within 24 to 48 hours and 'real' means that the system is not being used just as insurance.

Application should be made to a police station (preferably the applicant's local station) with full details of the grounds for applying, the child, the person likely to remove the child, the applicant, the likely destination and the likely time of travel and port of embarkation. Any other helpful information should also be given as well as recent photographs of the child and the abductor. If the police feel that the requirements are satisfied, they will put the child's name on a stop list which is circulated to all ports and airports. The child will remain on this list for 4 weeks and will then be removed unless a further application is made.

Passports

PREVENTING ISSUE OF A PASSPORT

If the child does not have a passport already, it is possible for an interested party to give written notice to the Passport Department of the Home Office that a passport should not be issued to a child without the consent of the court or of both parents or others (*Practice Direction of 14 April 1986* [1986] 1 All ER 983).

SURRENDER OF PASSPORTS

If the above provision is not applicable as the child already has a passport, an order can be obtained for the surrender of the relevant passport. This can be done only if there is in existence an order prohibiting or restricting the removal of the child from the UK. An ex parte application for a residence order or a prohibited steps order may therefore need to be made. If a residence order or other s 8 order (eg a prohibited steps order), has been obtained, the court that made the order can order any person to surrender the child's passport or any other passport which includes details of the child.

If a contact order has been made, it is possible to include a direction that the parent exercising contact must lodge his passport with his solicitor during contact visits. Care must be taken by a solicitor acting for the parent with contact in these circumstances, as if this involves giving an undertaking to the court, there will be a conflict of interest if the client subsequently requests the return of the passport in breach of any undertaking given. If the solicitor returns the passport to his client, this will be a matter of professional misconduct as well as a contempt of court which could lead to a fine or imprisonment. If the client has given an undertaking to the court to lodge his passport with his solicitor, again the solicitor should not aid or abet his client to disobey a lawful court order (see Principle 21.14 (and commentary) of the Guide to the Professional Conduct of Solicitors).

Recovering a child abducted abroad

If the child has been removed from the UK, the abductor will have committed a criminal offence under CAA 1984 but this by itself will not bring about the return of the child. Provisions do exist to obtain an order from the country to which the child has been taken to return the child. The Child Abduction and Custody Act 1985 (CACA 1985) brought the provisions of the Hague Convention on International Child Abduction into force in this country. If a child is taken to a country which is a party to this Convention, it is possible to request the return of the child. This will usually be ordered if less than one year has elapsed since the removal. After this time the child will still be returned, unless settled in his new environment. CACA 1985 also brought the provisions of the European Convention on Recognition and Enforcement of Custody Decisions into force. This should also mean that provided the country to which the child has been taken is a party to the Convention an order can be obtained for the return of the child, although there are certain grounds on which the court in the country to which the child has been taken can decide that it is in the child's best interests to remain there.

Reference should be made to CACA 1985 and specialist textbooks for the detail of this area. A source of general advice and support for clients with problems in this area is an organisation called 'Reunite', the National Council for Abducted Children.

Practical advice

In considering the legal steps which can be taken in this area, the solicitor must remind the client of the practical steps that can be taken to prevent an abduction occurring. These could include notifying the child's school to ensure that the child will not be collected by the potential abductor, in serious cases refusing to allow unsupervised contact, ensuring that the child's passport is kept safe and ensuring that the telephone number of the local police station is kept to hand.

12.9.2 General protection of children

The protection a child needs may relate to a wide range of issues. It might concern a medical issue, an abortion, a proposed marriage, a change of name or religion, or protection from a violent parent. Those with parental responsibility may not be prepared to make a decision or may have made a decision with which another interested party disagrees. In this situation, a s 8 order may be used by parents and others to obtain a court decision. In urgent cases, all s 8 orders can be obtained ex parte.

The availability and flexibility of s 8 orders means that there is less need to resort to the High Court's wardship jurisdiction. However, there is no restriction on anyone (other than a local authority) making a child a ward of court. If this is done, parental responsibility will vest in the High Court. The High Court will also have the power to make any s 8 order, unless the child is also subject to a care order.

12.9.3 Protection of a child by the local authority

CA 1989 introduced a new legal framework for care and supervision orders (see Chapter 13).

A care or supervision order can be applied for only by the local authority or the NSPCC. The effect of a care order will be to vest parental responsibility in the local authority who will then take over responsibility for the child from his parents or other carers, including deciding where he lives. A supervision order gives someone, usually a social worker, the duty to oversee the child, who will generally remain living in his home.

CA 1989 also introduced new orders for the emergency protection of children. These are:

(1) emergency protection orders: these are usually obtained by the local authority to protect the child in an urgent case where, because of some neglect or abuse, it is essential to remove the child from his home immediately;

(2) child assessment orders: these can be used by the local authority to ensure that an essential examination or other assessment of the child, for example a medical examination can be undertaken in circumstances where the parents are unco-operative and where the local authority suspects some harm is occurring but does not have enough evidence to bring care proceedings.

12.10 FINANCIAL PROVISION AND PROPERTY ORDERS FOR CHILDREN

The law relating to financial provision and property orders for children is complex and is scattered throughout a number of statutes. This section summarises and cross-refers the main provisions as well as dealing with the financial provisions contained in CA 1989.

The following jurisdictions are relevant:

(1) maintenance under CSA 1991;
(2) maintenance and property orders in matrimonial proceedings under MCA 1973;
(3) maintenance and lump sums during marriage under DPMCA 1978;
(4) financial relief under CA 1989.

12.10.1 Maintenance under the Child Support Act 1991

The maintenance of most children will now be dealt with by the Child Support Agency using the statutory formula. CSA 1991 has ousted the court's jurisdiction to make maintenance orders in the majority of cases (see Chapter 7).

The Agency will have jurisdiction whether the parents are married or unmarried, but can make an order only if the parents are no longer living together. Orders can be made in favour of children under 16 years of age, and those under 19 years of age who are in full-time education. The Agency does not have jurisdiction to deal with step-children or children over 19 years still in full-time education, and in these cases application will have to be made to the courts to determine maintenance. Other situations where the courts can still be used include payment of school fees and, in wealthy families, when an amount exceeding the maximum figure payable by the Agency under the formula is sought.

12.10.2 Maintenance and property orders in matrimonial proceedings

If a parent is involved in divorce, judicial separation, or nullity proceedings, he could apply for a lump sum or property adjustment order for a child of the family as part of these proceedings (see Chapter 4). However, in practice, unless the family is wealthy, relatively few orders of this type are made in favour of children.

Apart from the situations mentioned above (see **12.10.1**), maintenance will generally be dealt with by the Child Support Agency.

12.10.3 Maintenance and lump sums during marriage

A married parent can apply during marriage for a maintenance order and a lump sum order of up to £1,000 for a child of the family from the other parent. This can be done using DPMCA 1978 in the family proceedings court (see **4.9.2**) or MCA 1973, s 27 in the county court (see **4.9.1**). However, in most cases, maintenance will be dealt with by the Child Support Agency under CSA 1991 as the courts will have no jurisdiction.

12.10.4 Financial relief under the Children Act 1989

CA 1989, s 15 and Sch 1 enables a parent (for these purposes, 'parent' includes an unmarried parent and a step-parent), guardian, anyone with a residence order in their favour and a child to apply for the following orders against one or both parents of a child:

(1) periodical payments to the applicant for the benefit of the child or to the child direct;

(2) lump sum to the applicant for the benefit of the child or to the child direct;

(3) settlement of property for the benefit of the child;

(4) transfer of property to the applicant for the benefit of the child or to the child direct.

Application can be made to the High Court or county court for any of the orders. An application to the family proceedings court can only be made for periodical payments and/or a lump sum up to £1,000.

The principles which the court must use in deciding whether to make an order are broadly similar to MCA 1973, s 25. This means that the child's welfare is not paramount when deciding financial provision (*K v K (Minors: Property Transfer)* [1992] 2 FLR 220).

The provisions in CA 1989 are rarely needed by married parents as they will normally apply only on marriage breakdown, when MCA 1973 can be used for lump sums and property adjustment orders, and CSA 1991 will be used for maintenance. However, CA 1989 can be very important to an unmarried parent as it can be used to obtain property orders for the benefit of the child which could secure the right for the child and the caring parent to occupy the home (*J v J (A Minor: Property Transfer)* [1993] 2 FLR 56).

The court can make any s 8 order it considers necessary in the financial proceedings.

12.10.5 Summary of financial orders for children

Parties divorcing
- CSA 1991 for maintenance
- MCA 1973 for lump sum/property adjustment order

Parties staying married
- CSA 1991 for maintenance
- DPMCA 1978 for £1,000 maximum lump sum
- MCA 1973, s 27 for lump sum
- CA 1989 for lump sum/property adjustment order

Parties never married
- CSA 1991 for maintenance
- CA 1989 for lump sum/property adjustment order

12.11 CHAPTER SUMMARY

(1) Issues concerning children are dealt with under CA 1989.

(2) Married parents have joint parental responsibility for their child. An unmarried mother has parental responsibility but an unmarried father does not, although he can acquire it in various ways.

(3) The court can make s 8 orders. These are:
- residence orders;
- contact orders;
- prohibited steps orders; and
- specific issue orders.

(4) When making any order, the court must consider:
- the welfare principle;
- the no-order presumption; and
- the principle of avoiding delay.

(5) When applying the welfare principle, the court must pay attention to the factors in s 1(3):
- the ascertainable wishes and feelings of the child;
- the child's physical, emotional and educational needs;
- the likely effect on the child of any change in circumstances;
- the child's age, sex, background, etc;
- any harm the child has suffered/may suffer;
- the capability of the parents (and other relevant people) to care for the child; and
- the range of powers available to the court.

(6) A checklist for the procedure for a contested s 8 application is set out below.

(7) There are various procedures available to try to prevent the abduction of a child. CAA 1984 is also relevant.

(8) Financial provision for children can be obtained under several different jurisdictions, including CA 1989.

Checklist for the procedure for a contested s 8 application in the county court

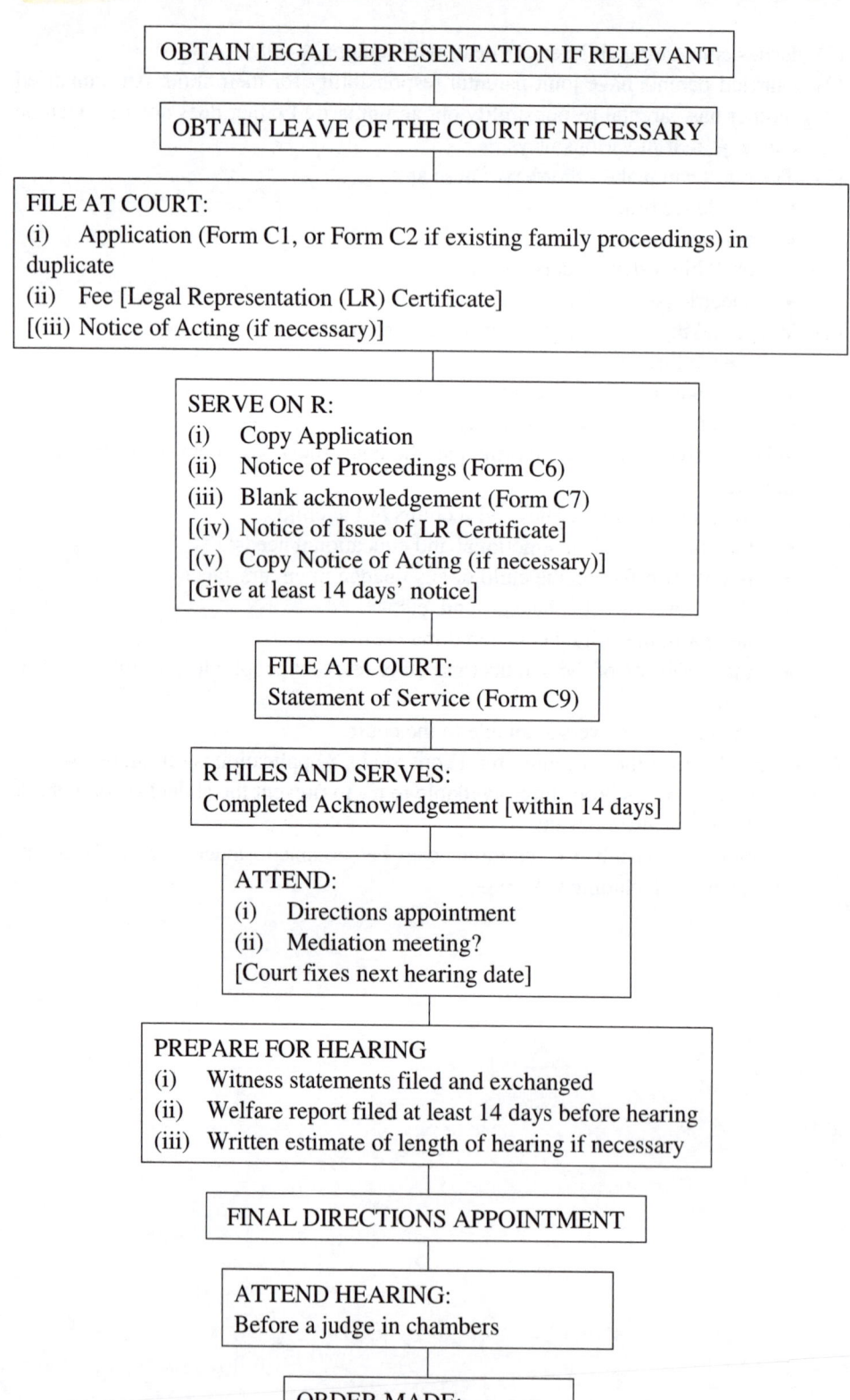

OBTAIN LEGAL REPRESENTATION IF RELEVANT

OBTAIN LEAVE OF THE COURT IF NECESSARY

FILE AT COURT:
(i)   Application (Form C1, or Form C2 if existing family proceedings) in duplicate
(ii)   Fee [Legal Representation (LR) Certificate]
[(iii) Notice of Acting (if necessary)]

SERVE ON R:
(i)   Copy Application
(ii)   Notice of Proceedings (Form C6)
(iii) Blank acknowledgement (Form C7)
[(iv) Notice of Issue of LR Certificate]
[(v)   Copy Notice of Acting (if necessary)]
[Give at least 14 days' notice]

FILE AT COURT:
Statement of Service (Form C9)

R FILES AND SERVES:
Completed Acknowledgement [within 14 days]

ATTEND:
(i)   Directions appointment
(ii)   Mediation meeting?
[Court fixes next hearing date]

PREPARE FOR HEARING
(i)   Witness statements filed and exchanged
(ii)   Welfare report filed at least 14 days before hearing
(iii) Written estimate of length of hearing if necessary

FINAL DIRECTIONS APPOINTMENT

ATTEND HEARING:
Before a judge in chambers

ORDER MADE:
Served on each party

Note: The procedure followed in the High Court or family proceedings court is broadly similar.

12.12 FURTHER READING

Hershman and McFarlane *Children Law and Practice* (Family Law, looseleaf)
Clarke Hall & Morrison on Children (Butterworths, 1994)
Masson and Morris *Children Act Manual* 2nd edn (Sweet & Maxwell, 2001)
Bainham *Children – The Modern Law* 2nd edn (Family Law, 1998)

Chapter 13

CHILDREN: PUBLIC LAW

13.1 INTRODUCTION

The Children Act 1989 introduced fundamental changes to child law, and this chapter considers those changes in relation to public law proceedings. The Act followed a number of reviews and reports, notably the *Cleveland Report*, which expressed concern that the local authority had acted too precipitately in removing children from their parents. Paradoxically, in other cases, the concern was that the authority had not acted promptly enough. One of the aims of the Act was to have a more balanced approach to the protection of children. Central to this is the concept of partnership: partnership between the local authority and parents and co-operation between all the agencies relevant to the child's well-being. To this end, the Act is supplemented by guidance in a document called 'Working Together to Safeguard Children' (together with various regulations). Although 'Working Together' does not have the force of statute, the guidance must be complied with and can only be departed from if good reasons can be shown.

13.2 LOCAL AUTHORITY SUPPORT FOR CHILDREN AND FAMILIES (CA 1989, Part III)

13.2.1 Introduction

The Act imposes responsibilities on local authorities to provide certain services, in particular for 'children in need' (see **13.2.3**). The local authority may discharge these responsibilities directly or by facilitating their provision by, for example, voluntary organisations.

13.2.2 Prevention of harm

Every local authority must take reasonable steps through the provision of services to prevent children in their area suffering ill-treatment or neglect. There is also a related duty to take reasonable steps to reduce the need to bring care or supervision proceedings.

13.2.3 Children in need

A child is to be taken to be 'in need' if:

(1) he is unlikely to achieve or maintain, or to have the opportunity of achieving or maintaining, a reasonable standard of health or development without the provision for him of services by a local authority; or
(2) his health or development is likely to be significantly impaired, or further impaired, without the provision for him of such services; or
(3) he is disabled (s 17(10)).

The definition therefore includes not just those children who are suffering, but also those who may be prejudiced in the future, if assistance is not provided for them.

'Development' is defined as physical, intellectual, emotional, social or behavioural development; 'health' as meaning physical or mental health; and 'disabled' as blind, deaf, dumb, suffering from mental disorder, or substantially and permanently handicapped by illness, injury or congenital deformity.

The definition of 'in need' is therefore very wide and reflects the Act's emphasis on local authorities taking preventative action through the provision of support services to families and only commencing court proceedings where absolutely necessary to protect the child.

The linking of 'need' to the provision of 'services' means that an authority could not identify a child as 'in need' and at the same time refuse to provide any service to meet that need. However, although the authority is obliged to provide some service to meet the child's needs, it has a discretion in deciding which service and at what level. In *R v London Borough of Barnet, ex parte B* [1994] 1 FLR 592, the court held that the obligations placed on a local authority to provide services must be subject to the ability to do so within its own budget restraints.

Duty to children in need (s 17)

It is the duty of every local authority:

(1) to safeguard and promote the welfare of children within its area who are in need; and

(2) so far as is consistent with that duty to promote the upbringing of such children by their families,

by providing a range and level of services appropriate to those children's needs.

Any service provided by the authority to the child can also be provided to the child's family or any member of the family, if it is provided with a view to safeguarding or promoting the child's welfare. 'Family' is widely defined to include any person with parental responsibility and any other person with whom the child is living.

A local authority could provide a range of services to help the parents cope with a child with disabilities: for example, a home help, day-care provision (whether for the disabled child or another child in the household) and a short-term placement for the child to relieve the carers.

13.2.4 Provision of accommodation (s 20)

A local authority must provide accommodation for any child in need within its area if there is no person who has parental responsibility for him, he is lost or abandoned, or the person who has been caring for him is prevented (whether or not permanently and for whatever reason) from providing him with suitable accommodation or care.

Limits on providing accommodation

A local authority may not provide accommodation if anyone with parental responsibility, who is willing and able to provide accommodation, objects. This means that if both parents have parental responsibility and one places the child in accommodation, the other parent can remove him.

The right of a person with parental responsibility to object does not apply if a person or persons with a residence order agrees to the child being accommodated.

Preventing removal from accommodation

The local authority should ensure that all those with parental responsibility are involved in the initial negotiations and agree on the provision of accommodation to avoid any subsequent problems. However, it is always open to a person with parental responsibility to remove the child at any time without notice.

If there is a risk that one parent may seek to remove the child, the authority may suggest that the other seeks a residence order (which may be granted ex parte) to prevent the removal (a local authority cannot itself apply for a residence order (s 9(2)).

If that is not appropriate or if both parents are seeking the child's return which the authority does not consider to be in the child's best interests, it could apply for an emergency protection order or interim care order.

13.2.5 Children 'looked after' by a local authority

Children who are in care (pursuant to a care order) or provided with accommodation (for a continuous period of more than 24 hours) are 'looked after' by the authority. This also includes children accommodated by a local authority under an emergency protection order, or in police protection (see **13.10**).

When an authority is 'looking after' a child, it is acting in a parental role. It is under a duty to safeguard and promote the child's welfare and to make use of services available for children (ie under Part III).

It is central to the philosophy of the Act that an authority should seek to act in consultation (and hopefully agreement) with all interested parties. Before making any decision with regard to the child it must find out, if reasonably practicable, the wishes and feeling of the child, parents, and other relevant persons. Any decision should give due consideration to those wishes and to the child's religious persuasion, racial origin and cultural and linguistic background.

Where the child is accommodated is of crucial importance. To foster the prospect of rehabilitation, the authority should first consider whether it is practicable for the child to live with a member of his family or other persons connected with him. If it is not practicable, consideration should be given to placing the child near to the family home.

13.2.6 Significance of the provision of services

As already seen, so far as it is consistent with the child's welfare, the local authority's duty under s 17 is to promote the upbringing of the child by his family through the provision of services. The authority should not initiate care proceedings unless there is clear evidence that the provision of services has failed to meet the child's needs or is unlikely to be successful in meeting them.

In most cases, it is better to advise the parents to co-operate and throw the onus onto the local authority to show it has done everything reasonable to assist the child and his parents.

Accordingly, in appropriate circumstances, a local authority should be required to explain:

(1)　what steps it took to identify the child as being in need;

(2)　what its plans are if a care order is made; in particular, what services it would then provide which it could not provide without a court order;

(3)　what evidence there is that what the authority is seeking to achieve by means of a court order could not be more satisfactorily achieved by the provision of appropriate services, with the child remaining at home.

In *Re K (Supervision Orders)* [1999] 2 FLR 303, the court said it was wrong to make a supervision order where the duties imposed on the local authority (under Part III) would sufficiently meet the child's needs.

13.2.7 Challenging the local authority

There is no provision in Part III for compelling a local authority to provide services. Nor can a specific issue order be used for that purpose. The courts have said that a local authority's powers and duties under Part III should not be subject to judicial scrutiny except by way of judicial review (*Re J (Specific Issue Order: Leave to Apply)* [1995] 1 FLR 669).

Complaints procedure (s 26)

Every local authority must establish a procedure for considering representations about the discharge of any of its functions under Part III.

If dissatisfied with the local authority's response, the complainant can require that the matter is referred to a review panel which must then make a recommendation. Although the ultimate decision remains with the local authority, if it ignores the panel's findings or fails to give satisfactory reasons for not implementing the recommendation, its actions may be subject to judicial review. In *Re T (Accommodation by Local Authority)* [1995] 1 FLR 159 the court quashed the refusal of the authority to ratify the recommendation of the panel on the basis that it had failed to take into account the correct considerations in deciding that the child's welfare would not be seriously prejudiced by not being accommodated.

Judicial review

Only in exceptional circumstances will the court consider an application for judicial review where the statutory right of appeal under the complaints procedure has not been exhausted (*R v London Borough of Barnet, ex parte S* [1994] 1 FLR 203). Even if the statutory procedures have been exhausted, judicial review is unlikely to be successful if there has been a genuine and fair consultation. In *R v London Borough of Barnet, ex parte B* [1994] 1 FLR 592 the court said that it is essentially a matter for the local authority, not the court, to decide what consideration and what weight should be given to the circumstances of any given child.

13.3 PREVENTING NEGLECT OR ABUSE

A central feature of the provisions for the protection of children is that this should be done in partnership with the family and in full consultation with other relevant agencies and professionals. Any assessment of the child should, wherever possible, be done following consultation and with the family's co-operation. The authority should seek to agree any protection plan for the child with the parents.

13.3.1 Court-directed investigation (s 37)

The court has no power to direct a local authority to commence proceedings for a care or supervision order. However, if in any 'family proceedings' where the court is considering the child's welfare, it appears to the court that it may be appropriate for a care or supervision order to be made, the court may direct the authority to investigate the child's circumstances. In deciding whether to make a direction under s 37, the child's welfare must be the court's paramount consideration.

'Family proceedings' include divorce, judicial separation, financial relief applications, domestic violence applications under FLA 1996 and all Children Act proceedings other than emergency provisions (see **13.11.1**).

When undertaking the investigation, the local authority must consider whether it should apply for a care or supervision order, provide services or assistance for the child or his family, or whether to take any other action with respect to the child. If the authority decides not to apply for a care or supervision order it must inform the court within 8 weeks (unless otherwise directed) of its reasons and other action, if any, it intends to take.

When directing an investigation, as an exception to the general rule, the court may make an interim care or supervision order without a formal application if satisfied as to the criteria in s 38 (see **13.9**). It would be usual in such circumstances for a guardian ad litem to be appointed for the child.

13.3.2 Local authority investigation (s 47)

When a child is subject to an emergency protection order, in police protection or where the authority suspects the child is suffering or likely to suffer significant harm, it must investigate the child's circumstances.

The enquiries should involve a detailed assessment of the needs of the child and his family and may lead to the provision of services under Part III, including an offer of accommodation. Alternatively, the authority may decide it is necessary to commence proceedings for a care or supervision order (or an emergency protection order if the child's immediate protection is in issue).

As part of its investigation, the authority should normally see the child. If access is refused or it is denied information as to the child's whereabouts, the authority *must* make an application to the court unless satisfied that his welfare can be safeguarded without such an order (s 47(6)).

13.3.3 Child protection conferences

Where, following an investigation, the local authority considers that there might be a risk of significant harm to the child, the local authority must consider convening a child protection convenience.

This is a formal meeting attended by representatives from all the agencies concerned with the child's welfare, ie social services, police, health and education, and often the child's parents. Its purpose is to gather together and evaluate all the relevant information about the child and plan any immediate action which may be necessary to protect the child.

Parents should be encouraged to attend and may bring a solicitor or other person to support them. Certainly, in the case of *R v Cornwall County Council, ex parte LH* [2000] 1 FLR 234, the court made it clear that it would be unlawful for a local authority to have a policy of a blanket refusal of attendance of solicitors.

The conference has to decide whether to place the child's name on the child protection register. They must do this if they decide that the child is at continuing risk of significant harm as a result of either physical, emotional or sexual abuse or neglect. If the child's name is to be put on the register, the conference must also formulate an outline child protection plan.

Categories of risk

Even if the decision is not to place the child's name on the register, the conference may decide what further support and services may be offered to the family.

13.3.4 Child protection register

A local authority should maintain a central register which lists all the children in its area who are considered to be suffering from or likely to suffer significant harm and for whom there is a child protection plan (following a child protection conference). If a child's name is placed on the register, this must be reviewed after 3 months and thereafter at no more than 6-monthly intervals.

The act of registration itself provides no protection and must always be supported by a child protection plan.

13.4 CARE AND SUPERVISION ORDERS (CA 1989, Part IV)

A care order is an order placing the child in the care of a designated local authority.

A supervision order is an order putting the child under the supervision of a designated local authority or of a probation officer.

13.4.1 Application

An application for a care or supervision order can only be made by a local authority (or NSPCC). The court has no power to require a local authority to commence proceedings, nor can it make an order unless there has been an application (*Nottinghamshire County Council v P* [1993] 1 FLR 115).

13.4.2 Grounds for a care or supervision order (s 31)

A court may only make a care order or supervision order in respect of a child under 17, if it is satisfied that:

(a) the child concerned is suffering, or is likely to suffer significant harm; and
(b) the harm or likelihood of harm is attributable to –
    (i) the care given to the child, or likely to be given to him if the order were not made, not being what it would be reasonable to expect a parent to give to him; or
    (ii) the child's being beyond parental control.

These conditions have become known as the 'threshold criteria' because they are not in themselves grounds for making a care or supervision order but the minimum circumstances which must be found before the court could be justified in making such an order.

Accordingly, in considering an application, the court must approach the matter in two distinct stages. First, whether the threshold criteria are satisfied and, secondly, if the criteria are satisfied, whether an order should be made and, if so, what type of order, bearing in mind the welfare principle. Note, however, that the court has power to make a s 8 order (eg a residence order) whether or not the threshold criteria are satisfied.

13.4.3 Interpreting the criteria

Significant harm

The central concept is whether there is harm which is significant. 'Harm' is defined as ill-treatment or the impairment of health or development. These terms are further defined:

(1) 'ill-treatment' includes sexual abuse and forms of ill-treatment which are not physical;
(2) 'health' means physical or mental health;
(3) 'development' covers physical, intellectual, emotional, social or behavioural development.

Where the question of whether the harm suffered by a child is significant turns on the child's health or development, it is necessary to compare his health or development with what could reasonably be expected of a similar child (s 31(1)). In *Re O (A Minor) (Care Proceedings: Education)* [1992] 4 All ER 905, it was held that, in relation to a truant child, the comparison should be made with a child attending school rather than one who was not. Where the child has learning difficulties or medical problems it would seem appropriate to compare with a child suffering similar difficulties.

The court must be satisfied that the child is suffering or is likely to suffer harm.

'Is suffering'

In *Re M (A Minor) (Care Order: Threshold Conditions)* [1994] 2 FLR 577, the House of Lords held that the relevant date for ascertaining whether the child is suffering significant harm is either at the hearing of the application for a care or supervision order or the date on which the local authority initiated 'protective arrangements' for the child, provided there has been no lapse in those arrangements before the hearing of the application. Protective arrangements could, for example, be an emergency protection order, an interim care order or being 'looked after' by the local authority. Accordingly, the court can find that the child is suffering significant harm at the date of the hearing or alternatively looking backwards, was so suffering when steps were taken to protect the child, provided these steps have continued in place until the hearing.

'Is likely to suffer'

This allows the court to consider whether a child is likely to suffer significant harm in the future and would enable the court to protect a child where, for example, an acknowledged abuser returns to the household or where another child has suffered in the same family.

In *Re H and R (Child Sexual Abuse: Standard of Proof)* [1996] 1 FLR 80, HL, the court stated that in assessing the evidence, the standard of proof is the balance of probabilities. However, when assessing the probabilities, it should bear in mind that the more serious the allegation, the less likely it is that the event occurred and therefore the stronger the evidence needed before the court could conclude that the allegation was established. In other words, the inherent probability or improbability of the alleged act or event was itself a relevant factor when weighing the probabilities.

The court also held that 'likely to suffer' meant 'a real possibility, a possibility that cannot sensibly be ignored having regard to the nature and gravity of the feared harm in the particular case'.

The approach which should therefore be adopted is that, first, the local authority must prove the disputed facts on the balance of probabilities. Secondly, on the strength of such facts as are proved, the authority must ask: is there a real possibility that future significant harm will occur?

Causation of the harm

A finding of significant harm or its likelihood is not sufficient. There must be a link between that finding and either the standard of parental care or the child being beyond parental control.

The standard of care against which parental care is judged is not what it would be reasonable to expect *this* parent to give, but what a hypothetical reasonable parent would give to meet the child's needs. Accordingly, the fact that the parents have their own particular problems (eg low intelligence, addiction, mental or physical disability) does not justify them in providing a lower standard of care.

Where the care of the child is shared between a number of individuals and the child has suffered serious harm through lack of proper care, there is no need to prove it was due to a failure by one or more indentified individuals before the court could make a care order. See *Lancashire County Council v A* [2000] 1 FLR 583, HL, where a baby had suffered non-accidental head injuries. The House of Lords held that the threshold criteria were met (and a care order was made) even though it was not possible to make a definitive finding of fact on whether the injuries were caused by the parents or the child minder. The court acknowledged that this might mean that innocent parents might face the possibility of losing their child but held that the factor which outweighed all others was the prospect that any unidentified, and unidentifiable, carers might inflict further damage on the child.

Concurrent applications

Where there has been an application for a care order, the court may be faced with a competing application for a residence order. Before considering the merits of making a residence order, the court should decide whether the criteria for a care order are satisfied and therefore whether the full range of orders are available to the court (see **13.4.5** and *Re M* (above)).

13.4.4 Welfare principle (s 1)

If the court is satisfied that the threshold criteria are met, it must then decide what order, if any, to make. In doing so, it must apply the principle contained in s 1: that the welfare of the child is the paramount consideration and that delaying a decision is likely to prejudice the child; consider the checklist; and not make an order unless it considers that doing so would be better for the child than making no order at all.

13.4.5 Orders available to the court

Even if the threshold criteria are satisfied and the court considers that it is in the child's interests to make an order, as applications under Part IV are 'family proceedings' it is not merely a question of whether to make a care or supervision order.

Under s 1(3)(g), the court is required to have regard to the range of orders available to it. On hearing an application for a care or supervision order, the court may make, inter alia:

(1) a care order *or* supervision order if the threshold criteria are satisfied;
(2) a residence or other s 8 order, whether or not the criteria are satisfied, (however, a residence or contact order cannot be made in favour of a local authority);
(3) a s 8 order in combination with a supervision order if the criteria are satisfied;
(4) a family assistance order under s 16, with the agreement of all the persons (other than the child) named in the order, whether or not the criteria are satisfied.

Care plans

In the application for a care order, the authority should outline what plans it has if a care order is made.

Guidelines on the structure, content and format of care plans for use in court proceedings are set out in Local Authority Circular LAC (99) 29 (12 August 1999) 'Care Plans and Care Proceedings under the Children Act 1989'.

Examples of some of the typical matters to be covered in the care plan include:

*   the child's identified needs (including needs arising from race, culture, religion or language, special education or health needs) and how those needs might be met;
*   the aim of the plan and the time-scale;
*   the proposed placement (type and details) and a contingency plan if the placement breaks down;
*   other services to be provided to the child and/or the family;
*   arrangements for contact and reunification; and
*   the extent to which the wishes of the child, his or her parents and anyone else relevant have been obtained and acted upon, or the reasons why such wishes have been discounted.

The care plan will be carefully scrutinised by the court. If it is not satisfied about material aspects of the care plan (eg where it is proposed to place the child with identified foster-parents, failure to give details as to the foster-parents and the proposed placement) it may refuse to make a care order (*Re J (Minors) (Care: Care Plan)* [1994] 1 FLR 253).

In addition, before making a care order the court must consider the authority's arrangements for contact and invite the parties to comment (s 34(11)).

13.4.6 Effect of a care order

The order remains in force until the child reaches 18, unless it is brought to an end earlier.

The local authority must receive the child into its care and provide accommodation and maintain the child for the duration of the order.

The care order gives the local authority parental responsibility jointly with any other holder. However, it is not an equal partnership. The authority has the power to determine the extent to which a parent may exercise parental responsibility, provided it is necessary to do so in the child's welfare. However, before making any decision, the authority should take into account the wishes and feelings of the child and parents.

While a care order is in force, as with a residence order, no person may change the child's surname without the written consent of every person with parental responsibility or leave of the court. In addition, the child may not be removed from the UK without similar consent or leave. This does not prevent the authority arranging for the child's temporary removal for a period of less than one month.

Most other court orders are incompatible with a care order and, accordingly, the making of a care order automatically discharges any s 8 order (but not a s 4 parental responsibility order).

On the making of a final care order, the court is effectively handing over responsibility for the child to the local authority. The court cannot impose any conditions on the local authority or seek to keep its management under review (see *Re T (A Minor) (Care Order: Conditions)* [1994] 2 FLR 423 and *Re B (Minors) (Care: Contact: Local Authority's Plans)* [1993] 1 FLR 543). This means that the court cannot, for example, direct where the child shall live or review the local authority's implementation of the care plan. However, this may be challenged in the future, using Articles 6 and 8 of the European Convention on Human Rights (see **13.12.1**).

13.5 CONTACT (s 34)

Regular contact with parents and other relatives can be important in enabling the child to adjust to its new environment and is essential if there is to be a successful rehabilitation with the family.

Section 34 is a self-contained section and provides a completely different structure from private law proceedings. Any s 8 contact order is discharged upon the making of a care order.

13.5.1 Initial considerations

Before making a care order, including an interim order, the court must consider the local authority's arrangements for contact and invite the parties to comment.

As contact is so important for a child, the local authority should, if possible, place the child with a member of his family or, if that is not appropriate, in accommodation near to the child's home. The local authority may also give assistance in travel and other expenses incurred in visiting the child to any person to whom there is a duty to promote contact.

13.5.2 Local authority duties

There is a general duty to promote contact between a child 'looked after' and his parents, others with parental responsibility and relatives, friends and other persons connected with him, unless it is not reasonably practicable or consistent with the child's welfare.

By s 34(1), the authority is also under a *positive* duty to allow a child in care reasonable contact with his parents (including a father without parental responsibility) and any person with whom the child previously lived by virtue of a court order, for example a residence order. The courts have said that reasonable contact is not the same as contact at the discretion of the local authority. 'Reasonable' means contact which is agreed or, in the absence of agreement, contact which the authority can demonstrate is objectively reasonable.

13.5.3 Application to the court

Any person mentioned in s 34(1), for example parents, can apply as of right to be allowed contact with the child. As there is a presumption of reasonable contact in this case, usually contact will be by agreement. It would only be necessary for the parents to apply if they were dissatisfied with the level of contact offered.

Any other person, for example, grandparents, can apply with leave. On an application for leave the court should apply the criteria set out in s 10(9) (*Re M (Care: Contact: Grandmother's Application for Leave)* [1995] 2 FLR 86). In particular, it should consider the nature of the contact sought, the connection of the applicant to the child, the risk of harm to the child and the wishes of the local authority and the parents.

A child in care has a right to apply for contact under s 34 with any named person. However, where contact is sought in relation to another child, then unless the local authority is opposing contact, the application should be under s 8 (requiring leave) rather than s 34, and it is the respondent child's welfare which is paramount (*Re F (Contact: Child in Care)* [1995] 1 FLR 510).

Refusal of contact

Where an application for a contact order under s 34 is refused, no further application can be made by the applicant for 6 months, without leave. Furthermore, on disposing of *any* application for an order, the court may direct that no application for any specified order may be made by a person without leave (s 91(14)). Such a direction would only be made in exceptional circumstances (*F v Kent County Council and Others* [1993] 1 FLR 432). Although the most likely reason for granting a restriction is where the applicant has made repeated and unreasonable applications with no hope of success, the court could make such an order, in the absence of repeated applications, if the welfare of the child requires it. In *Re M (Section 91(14) Order)* [1999] 2 FLR 553, the court imposed a restriction because it considered that the children urgently needed to settle down and make a permanent home away from their mother and that a premature application by her could disrupt them and hinder their permanent placement. Such a restriction is unlikely to infringe the Human Rights Act 1998 as, of course, it does not restrict access to the courts, but imposes a requirement for leave.

The local authority cannot refuse contact with persons to whom the presumption of reasonable contact applies. However, the authority can apply to the court for an order authorising it to refuse contact between the child and any person mentioned in s 34(1). In an emergency, the local authority can temporarily suspend contact without an order, for a period of not more than 7 days.

Although the court can authorise the refusal of contact by a local authority, it cannot, on the other hand, use its jurisdiction under s 34 to prohibit the local authority from allowing parental contact which the local authority considers to be advantageous to a child's welfare (*Re W (Section 34(2) Orders)* [2000] 1 FLR 502).

A contact order may be varied or discharged on the application of the child, local authority or the person named in the order. If the order is discharged, the presumption of reasonable contact with persons mentioned in s 34(1) still applies.

13.6 DISCHARGE OF CARE ORDERS (s 39)

A care order remains in force until the child reaches 18, unless it is brought to an end earlier. The order may be brought to an end by the making of a residence order (the only s 8 order which can be applied for), the substitution of a supervision order, or the making of an adoption order or a discharge order.

The application for a discharge can be made by any person with parental responsibility, the child or the local authority. There is no requirement for a child to seek leave before making an application.

On hearing an application to discharge the care order, the court may substitute a supervision order. The court must apply the welfare principle in s 1 but there is no requirement to find that the threshold criteria are still satisfied.

Where there has been a previous application to discharge a care order (other than an interim order) or to substitute a supervision order, no further application can be made for 6 months without leave.

If the care order is discharged without any other order being made, care of the child reverts to those having parental responsibility. A pre-care residence order will not be revived although on discharge the court has power to make any s 8 order.

13.7 EFFECT OF A SUPERVISION ORDER

Although the criteria are the same as for a care order, the effect of a supervision order is very different. The order places the child under the supervision of a local authority, but the supervisor does not acquire parental responsibility.

The basic duties of the supervisor are to advise, assist and befriend the child and to take steps to give effect to the order. Other powers of the supervisor depend on the order.

The order could include:

(a) a requirement for the child to live at a specified place, or participate in specified activities;

(b) with the consent of any 'responsible person' (any person with parental responsibility and any other person with whom the child lives), a requirement for that person to take all reasonable steps to ensure the child complies with any direction and also to comply with any directions to take part in specified activities. This has been used to require the responsible person to undergo treatment, for example in relation to sexual offences;

(c) a requirement that the child submits to specified medical or psychiatric examination or treatment. Where the child has sufficient understanding to make an informed decision, he may refuse to submit to the examination or assessment. However, it has been held that under its inherent jurisdiction, the High Court has power to override a child's refusal (*South Glamorgan County Council v W and B* [1993] 1 FLR 574).

The court decides on the broad structure of the supervision to take place, but the detailed implementation of any requirement in the order is left to the supervisor (ie the local authority). If the supervisor's directions are not complied with, the supervisor can only seek a variation or discharge of the order. The direction cannot be directly enforced either by the supervisor or the court.

A supervision order is normally made for up to one year, but it can be extended for a further period of up to 3 years from the date of the original order. An application to extend the supervision order is governed by the principles in s 1, but there is no need to consider whether the threshold criteria are satisfied.

13.8 CARE OR SUPERVISION ORDER

The protection of the child is the decisive factor when the court is deciding whether to make a care or supervision order. The court must weigh the likelihood of future harm to the child against the potential harm of removing the child from his parents under a care order. Note, however, that a care order can still be justified where the local authority intends for the child to remain at home (*Re T (A Minor) (Care or Supervision Order)* [1994] 1 FLR 103).

With a care order, the authority acquires parental responsibility and has an obligation to safeguard the child's welfare. In an emergency it can remove the child without recourse to a court.

In contrast, a supervision order is made to help and assist the child; responsibility for safeguarding the child's welfare rests with his parents. In an emergency, the local authority would have to apply to the court to remove the child. However, a supervision order does give the court a degree of control over the upbringing of the child.

13.9 INTERIM ORDERS (s 38)

Once care proceedings have been instituted, the court has the power to make:

(1) an interim care order;

(2) an interim supervision order;

(3) a residence and other s 8 orders for a limited period.

Where care or supervision proceedings are adjourned or the court in any proceedings (eg divorce proceedings) gives a direction to a local authority under s 37 to investigate the child's circumstances (see **13.3.3**), the court may make an interim care or supervision order.

It may not make the order unless satisfied that there are reasonable grounds for believing that the threshold criteria (s 31) are satisfied. At this stage, 'reasonable grounds' means that the court is likely to be relying to a large extent on the child's version of events or on medical evidence that certain symptoms are consistent with abuse. The fact that suspicion suffices at the interim stage should be contrasted with the position at the final hearing, where the court must be satisfied by proof that the threshold criteria are met.

Alternatively, if the court makes a residence order pending the outcome of the care/supervision application, it must also make an interim supervision order (unless satisfied that the child's welfare will be satisfactorily safeguarded without it).

An interim order has the same effect as a final care or supervision order except that the order can include directions as to the examination or assessment of the child and will be of limited duration.

It is common for a number of interim orders to be made pending a final hearing, although on each renewal the court must be satisfied that the criteria are still met.

In *Re G (Minors) (Interim Care Order)* [1993] 2 FLR 839, the court stated that an interim care order was an impartial step to preserve the status quo pending the final hearing and did not give a tactical advantage to the local authority.

It may be appropriate to delay making a final decision pending the outcome of an assessment of the child or a parent, or until the court is in possession of all material facts. The court must also be satisfied the local authority care plan is in the child's best interest. However, the Court of Appeal has said on a number of occasions that the court should not seek to exercise a supervisory role over the local authority by postponing a final decision.

Exclusion requirements

If the court makes an interim care order, it may include an 'exclusion requirement', provided there is reasonable cause to believe that if a person is excluded from the house where the child lives, the child will no longer suffer, or be likely to suffer, significant harm (s 38A(2)).

Before including such a requirement, another person (whether or not a parent) living in the house with the child must be able to look after the child and consent to the requirement being made. The 'exclusion requirement' may require the person to leave the dwelling house or not to enter the dwelling house. It can also require the person not to enter an area surrounding the house. A power of arrest can be attached to the exclusion requirement. The requirement will cease to have effect if the local authority removes the child to other accommodation for a continuous period of more than 24 hours.

Contact

The provisions regarding contact with a child in care apply equally on the making of an interim care order. However, as the issue is only being considered pending a final hearing, contact between a parent and child should be maintained unless there are exceptional circumstances.

13.10 EMERGENCY PROTECTION AND ASSESSMENT (CA 1989, Part V)

13.10.1 Emergency protection orders (s 44)

This is an order, initially limited to 8 days, to protect a child in an emergency where he is otherwise likely to suffer significant harm.

13.10.2 Grounds

The court may make an order on the application of any person, if it is satisfied that there is reasonable cause to believe that the child is likely to suffer significant harm if he:

(1) is not removed to accommodation provided by or on behalf of the applicant; or

(2) does not remain in the place where he is being accommodated.

The application will usually be made by a local authority, but anyone such as a police officer or a relative can apply. If the local authority is not the applicant, it has power to take over the order.

A local authority can also apply for an order where it is making enquiries because, for example, it suspects the child may be suffering significant harm and believes access is required as a matter of urgency, which is being unreasonably refused.

If the court finds that either condition applies, before making an order it must consider the welfare principle (s 1(1)) (and the no order presumption (s 1(5)), although there is no requirement to apply the checklist under s 1(3).

If the court makes an order under s 44, it may include an 'exclusion requirement' if there is reasonable cause to believe that if a person is excluded from the dwelling house in which the child lives, the child is unlikely to suffer significant harm (s 44A(2)). The exclusion requirements and conditions are the same as when made in conjunction with an interim care order (see **13.9**).

13.10.3 Application

The application must be made to a family proceedings court unless it arises out of a direction under s 37 to the local authority to investigate, when it should be made to the court which gave that direction. The application may not be transferred to a higher court and there is no appeal against the making or refusal of an order.

The application may be made ex parte with the consent of the justices' clerk and may be heard by a single justice. A copy of the application and order must be served on each party (every person with parental responsibility and the child) within 48 hours of the order. Alternatively, the application can be made on one day's notice.

The court will normally appoint a guardian ad litem for the child (see **13.11.8**). The court may take account of any statement contained in any report made to the court or any evidence given during the hearing, which is relevant to the application.

13.10.4 Effect of the order

The order operates as a direction to any person who is in a position to do so, to comply with any request to produce the child to the applicant and authorises the removal or prevention of removal of the child from his present accommodation. The order may authorise the applicant to enter specified premises and search for the child. If the applicant is likely to be refused entry, the court can issue a warrant authorising the police to assist, using reasonable force if necessary.

The order also gives the applicant parental responsibility for the child but this is limited to doing what is necessary to safeguard and promote the child's welfare.

13.10.5 Contact

During the currency of the order, the applicant must, subject to any direction of the court, allow the child reasonable contact with his parents, any other person with parental responsibility, any person with whom he was living prior to the order and any person in whose favour there is an existing contact order.

The court can give such directions and impose such conditions as it considers appropriate in relation to contact. However, where the applicant is a local authority, the court will usually leave contact to be negotiated between the parties unless the issue is clearly disputed.

13.10.6 Examination or assessment

The court may give directions as to a medical or psychiatric examination or other assessment of the child or may alternatively direct that there be no such examination or assessment. However, in an emergency, where the examination is required for medical reasons, this could be undertaken without the need for a court order under the applicant's parental responsibility.

A child of sufficient understanding to make an informed decision, may refuse to submit to an examination or assessment, but it has been held that the High Court may overrule the child and give consent under its inherent jurisdiction (*South Glamorgan County Council v W and B* [1993] 1 FLR 574).

13.10.7 Duration

The order may be granted for up to 8 days. The court can grant one extension for up to 7 days on the application of the local authority, if it has reasonable cause to believe the child is likely to suffer significant harm if the order is not extended.

An application to discharge the order can be made on one day's notice, but cannot be heard before the expiry of 72 hours from the making of the order. The application can be made by the child, a parent, any other person with parental responsibility or any person with whom the child was living prior to the order, unless that person was present at the hearing. As an application to extend the duration must be on notice, no one can apply for a discharge once the order has been extended.

13.10.8 Police protection (s 46)

A child may be taken into 'police protection' for up to 72 hours if a constable has reasonable cause to believe that the child is likely to suffer significant harm if he did not remove the child to suitable accommodation or take steps to prevent removal from his present accommodation (this is the same criteria on which the *court* must be satisfied to make an emergency protection order). This power could be used, for example, where a child has run away, been abandoned, is found in unsuitable home circumstances or alternatively to prevent his removal from, say, a hospital.

The police do not acquire parental responsibility but must do what is reasonable in the circumstances to safeguard or promote the child's welfare. They must inform the local authority who, if requested, must provide accommodation for the child. Following investigation, the police or local authority could, if appropriate, apply for an emergency protection order.

13.10.9 Child assessment order (s 43)

This is an order for the assessment of the child's health or development or of the way in which he has been treated. It is intended to deal with the situation where there is a suspicion that the child is suffering and there has been a denial of co-operation on the part of the child's carers. It is part of the 'planned responses' by a local authority rather than a device to provide emergency protection.

The grounds for the order are very specific. Essentially, the local authority must have reasonable cause to suspect the child is suffering, or is likely to suffer, significant harm. The court must be satisfied that an assessment is necessary to confirm or dismiss those suspicions and that the child's carers are unlikely to co-operate with such an assessment. Although the checklist in s 1(3) need not be applied, the court must have regard to welfare principle (s 1(1)) and no order presumption (s 1(5)).

13.11 PROCEDURE FOR CARE AND SUPERVISION ORDERS

The procedure for making applications in the family proceedings court is governed by the Family Proceedings Courts (Children Act 1989) Rules 1991 and in the county court or High Court by the Family Proceedings Rules 1991.

13.11.1 Jurisdiction

Proceedings under Part IV of CA 1989 (care and supervision orders, contact orders) are classified as 'family proceedings', allowing the court to make any of the orders under the Act, including s 8 orders. Proceedings under Part V (emergency protection orders, child assessment orders) are not included in the definition, but, by virtue of s 92(2), all Children Act proceedings in the family proceedings court are to be treated as 'family proceedings'.

13.11.2 Which court?

The jurisdiction of a particular tier of court to entertain an application is governed by the Children (Allocation of Proceedings) Order 1991.

An application for a care or supervision order (or for an emergency protection or child assessment order) must normally be made to a family proceedings court. However, the general rule is subject to two provisos. First, if the application arose in consequence of a direction under s 37 (eg during divorce proceedings) for the local authority to investigate, then the application should be made to the court which gave the direction. Secondly, any application to extend, vary or discharge an order under the Act, or where the outcome of the proceedings may have that effect, should be made to the court which made the original order.

13.11.3 Transfer of cases

Irrespective of where a case started, it can be transferred to another more appropriate court. It is possible for cases to be transferred either horizontally or vertically. The exception is an application for an emergency protection order which cannot be transferred from the family proceedings court to a higher court (see **13.10.3**).

Transfers between the same tier of court are essentially governed by the general principle that the child's welfare is the paramount consideration and any delay is likely to prejudice his welfare. Accordingly, if, for example, a particular family proceedings court is too busy to deal with the application or it is desirable to consolidate with other pending proceedings, the application could be transferred to another family proceedings court.

Applications commenced in the family proceedings court can be transferred to the county court under one or more of three heads:

(1) exceptional complexity, importance or gravity;
(2) the need to consolidate with other proceedings;
(3) the urgency of the case.

A transfer under the first head would be justified because of complicated or conflicting evidence about the risks to the child's welfare, the large number of parties involved or because of a difficult point of law. The courts have also indicated that cases with a time estimate of three days for the hearing should be transferred to the county court. If the magistrates refuse to transfer, application can be made to the county court for a transfer order.

The county court can transfer a case to the High Court if 'appropriate' and 'in the interests of the child'.

13.11.4 Public funding

Legal Representation is available for public law proceedings under the Children Act but is based on a special regime which depends on the nature of the proceedings and the status of the party.

Automatic Legal Representation for certain parties

Legal Representation must be granted, without regard to a means or merits test, to the child, the parents and any other person with parental responsibility in relation to proceedings for care, supervision, emergency protection or child assessment orders.

Other potential parties

Any other person who applies to be joined as a party to any of the above proceedings is subject to the usual means test. In addition, Legal Representation can be refused on the ground that representation is not necessary.

Other applications

Applications by anyone for s 34 contact orders, s 39 discharge orders or any s 8 order are subject to the usual means and merits test.

Related proceedings

In those cases where Legal Representation can be granted automatically, the certificate can cover proceedings relating to the application in question. A related matter is one where an order is sought at the same time as, and as an alternative to, the main proceedings. So, for example, applying for a s 8 residence order in the context of care or supervision proceedings would be covered by the Legal Representation certificate (although it should be formally amended).

Legal Representation is not available to a guardian ad litem, but the local authority must pay the guardian's reasonable expenses.

13.11.5 The application

The application must be made on Form C1 (or C2 if made in existing proceedings) together with supplement C13, with sufficient copies for service.

On filing, the court fixes a date for a preliminary hearing or directions appointment.

The applicant must join as a party the child and every person whom he believes to have parental responsibility. In the case of parents, consideration should always be given as to whether separate representation is appropriate because of a potential conflict of interest.

In addition, any person who is not automatically a respondent, may apply to be joined. A distinction is drawn between a putative father and other applicants. In the case of a putative father, his application should be granted unless there is some justifiable reason for not doing so (see *Re K (Care Proceedings: Joinder of Father)* [1999] 2 FCR 391). In the case of other applicants, the court will not join someone (other than a parent) where their interests and views are the same as an existing party. In *Re M (Minors) (Sexual Abuse: Evidence)* [1993] 1 FLR 822, the court held that, where the grandparents were offering a 'fall back' position to that of the mother, and were presenting the same case as her, there was no purpose in their separate representation and they should not have been made parties unless they had a separate point to advance.

13.11.6 Service

Copies of the application must be served on all respondents at least 3 days before the hearing, together with a Notice of Proceedings (C6) giving the date of the hearing. The applicant must file a Statement of Service (C9).

Within the same time period, the applicant must also give notice of the proceedings (C6A) to anyone caring for the child, an unmarried father who does not have parental responsibility and anyone who is a party to other relevant proceedings, so that they can consider whether to apply to be joined as a party.

In relation to a child, service must be on the solicitor acting for the child, or if none, on the guardian ad litem. The court has power to direct that a requirement as to service on anyone shall not apply or shall be effected in such manner as the court directs.

13.11.7 Answer

A respondent may file an answer, in which case it must be served on the other parties.

13.11.8 Appointment of guardian ad litem

As soon as practicable after commencement of the proceedings, the court must appoint a guardian ad litem for the child unless the court considers it is not necessary to safeguard the child's interests.

The guardian must be a member of the guardian ad litem panel (normally set up by the local authority). Guardians are usually self-employed social workers or employees of a local authority or voluntary organisation.

It is important to appreciate that the guardian is 'for the child', rather than to 'represent' the child. Accordingly, the guardian's role is to put forward what he considers to be in the best interests of the child even though that may not coincide with the child's views.

Duties of the guardian

The guardian must appoint and instruct a solicitor to represent the child (unless a solicitor has already been appointed), give the child appropriate advice, investigate the case and file a written report at least 7 days before the final hearing.

In addition, the guardian must attend all directions appointments and hearings (unless excused) and advise the court, inter alia, on:

(1) whether the child is of sufficient understanding for any purpose;
(2) the wishes of the child in respect of any relevant matter;
(3) the appropriate timing of the proceedings;
(4) the options available to the court in respect of the child;
(5) any other appropriate matter.

13.11.9 Appointment of solicitor for the child

Where a guardian ad litem has been appointed, he will appoint a solicitor to represent the child.

Alternatively, the court may appoint a solicitor in any of the following circumstances:

(1) where no guardian ad litem has been appointed;
(2) where the child has sufficient understanding to instruct a solicitor and wishes to do so;
(3) where the court considers it in the child's best interests.

Additionally, the child could appoint a solicitor directly where he is of sufficient understanding.

Duties of the solicitor

Where a guardian ad litem has been appointed, the solicitor must follow the instructions given by the guardian. However, in some cases it becomes apparent that the views of the child do not coincide with what the guardian considers to be in his best interests. In circumstances where the child wishes to give instructions which conflict with those of the guardian and the solicitor considers that the child is able, having regard to his understanding, to give such instructions, the solicitor must follow the child's instructions. Where this happens, the guardian must notify the court and may seek leave to have separate legal representation.

Children and Family Court Advisory and Support Service (CAFCASS)

It should be noted that clause 15 of the Criminal Justice and Court Services Bill (which introduced CAFCASS) provides that an authorised officer of the Service may conduct litigation in relation to any proceedings in any magistrates' or county court. This means that, in the future, a guardian ad litem (likely to be known as a 'case worker') could work without legal representation for a child throughout a case, and may well do so, in order to save costs.

13.11.10 First appointment

On the filing of the application, the court must fix a date for a preliminary hearing at which directions are likely to be given.

Directions may include:

(1) appointment of a guardian ad litem or solicitor for the child, if this has not already happened;
(2) transfer of the proceedings to another court;
(3) timetable for the proceedings;
(4) attendance of the child (though this would be unusual);
(5) submission of evidence, including expert reports.

The court can make an interim care or supervision order if the conditions in s 38 are met, or a s 8 residence order together with a supervision order.

Unless the proceedings are determined, the court must fix a date for the next appointment.

Timetable for the proceedings

Having regard to the 'no delay' principle, the court is required to draw up a timetable for the proceedings and give appropriate directions to ensure it is adhered to.

The fact that there are criminal proceedings pending (eg in relation to a parent) is not usually a reason to adjourn the application because the inevitable delay would not be in the child's best interests. A person cannot refuse to give evidence on the grounds of self-incrimination but any statement or admission made in the proceedings is not admissible in criminal cases (other than for perjury).

Attendance

The parties must attend any court appointments unless otherwise directed.

The court has power to direct that a child does not or need not attend. The general tendency is only to allow the child's attendance if satisfied that it would clearly be in his interests and, in practice, the courts tend to assume that the child will not attend without the need to make a formal direction.

13.11.11 Evidence

Admissibility

As in private law children proceedings, the general rules as to the admissibility of evidence are relaxed.

Of particular relevance is that any statement contained in a guardian ad litem's report and any evidence given in respect of matters referred to in it, are admissible. This provision is very wide in that 'any statement' is not restricted to one made by the guardian himself and could include a statement made by, for example, a home help or a school teacher. Further the court may allow 'any evidence' from any witness to be admitted if it relates to a matter referred to in the report.

A guardian ad litem has the right to examine and take copies of records held by a local authority. However, the local authority may claim, for example in relation to social work records, that public interest requires that the evidence should be excluded. In that case, the guardian would have to apply to the court for a direction as to its admissibility.

Witness statements

Each party must file and serve on the other parties and the guardian ad litem, written statements of the oral evidence it intends to use together with copies of any documents, including expert reports, which will be relied on, at or by such time as the court directs. Failure to do so means the evidence can only be admitted with leave.

Expert evidence

The court's leave is needed for any medical or psychiatric examination or other assessment of the child for the purpose of preparing expert evidence. In addition, no document relating to the proceedings can be disclosed, without leave, other than to a party, a legal representative, the guardian ad litem or the Legal Services Commission.

An application for leave should be made as early as possible, the applicant having identified the expert and relevance to the issues in question. Leave will only be granted on condition of disclosure of both the letter of instruction and the subsequent report.

13.11.12 Disclosure

In children cases, there is a duty to give full and frank disclosure (*Practice Direction (Case Management)* [1995] 1 FLR 456).

Although privilege from disclosure applies to solicitor/client communications, it does not apply in children cases to reports and other documents prepared for the purpose of the proceedings. Accordingly, where a party obtains an expert report, with or without the court's leave, no privilege will attach to the report and it must be disclosed to the court and to the other parties (*Re L (Police Investigation: Privilege)* [1996] 1 FLR 731).

13.11.13 The hearing

The guardian ad litem must file a written report at least 7 days before the final hearing. The court will then serve a copy on every party.

Prior to the hearing there will be a final directions appointment to determine the procedure to be adopted. This will seek to resolve what issues are still in dispute, the number of witnesses to be called and the length of the hearing.

Where all the parties are agreed that a care order should be made, the court's consideration may be limited to a perusal of the documentation and approval of the agreed order. On the other hand, where there are unresolved issues for example as to physical or sexual abuse, the court may order a split hearing (*Re S (Care Proceedings: Split Hearing)* [1996] 2 FLR 773): the first hearing to resolve these issues, the second substantive hearing to concentrate on what is in the child's best interests.

13.11.14 Judgment

Judgment must be given as soon as practicable after the hearing. The court must state any findings of fact and the reasons for its decision.

The order must be in writing (C32) and a copy served on each party and on any person with whom the child is living.

13.11.15 After a care order is made

Once a final care order has been made, the court has no future role in monitoring the local authority or the execution of its care plan unless some substantive issue comes before the court such as an application for contact or discharge of the order.

The local authority is required to draw up an individual plan for the child and review it on a regular basis. Before conducting such reviews, the authority should seek and take into account the wishes and views of the child and his parents.

13.12 HUMAN RIGHTS IMPLICATIONS

Taking a child into care clearly constitutes an interference with family life under Article 8 of the European Convention on Human Rights. The local authority, as a public body, must act in a way that is compatible with Convention rights. Taking a child into care will not breach Article 8 provided the interference is in accordance with the law, it pursues a legitimate aim (namely, the protection of children) and is necessary.

In the context of public law proceedings, the Convention has repeatedly emphasised that interference in the right to family life by taking a child into care should be regarded as a temporary measure to be discontinued as soon as circumstances permit (*Johansen v Norway* [1996] 23 EHRR 33).

The manner in which a child is taken into care may also be open to challenge. The European Court has emphasised that it is important to involve parents in the decision-making process leading to care proceedings. This would include being involved in child protection conferences.

As mentioned in Chapter 12, there is a debate as to whether the welfare principle in s 1(1) of the Children Act 1989 is incompatible with Article 8 and an individual's right to respect for family life. In other words, placing the child's welfare as paramount does not involve balancing the family rights of the other relevant individuals. But the decisions of the European Court make it clear that the rights of the parent may have to be deferred to the interests of the child. In *Johansen v Norway*, the court said that 'the parent cannot be entitled under Article 8 ... to have such measures taken as would harm the child's health and development'.

In the domestic case of *Dawson v Wearmouth* [1999] 2 FLR 308 the court said:

> 'It is submitted that the father's rights under Article 8 are infringed. There is no basis for this submission. The present case is concerned with the welfare of the child, not with the rights of the father. There is nothing in the Convention which requires the courts of this country to act otherwise than in the interests of the child.'

Also, in *KD (A Minor) (Ward: Termination of Access)* [1998] AC 806, there was an argument between the local authority and the parent as to contact. The mother relied on Article 8 of the Convention and submitted that contact was a parental right and not a child's right. Lord Oliver said it would not be inappropriate to describe a parent's claim to contact as a 'right' It was also a normal assumption that a child will benefit from continuing contact with his natural parents:

> 'But both the "right" and the assumption will always be displaced if the interests of the child dictate otherwise.'

These cases suggest that there is no conflict between s 1(1) and Article 8, because Article 8(2) contains the important qualification of the right to respect for family life that 'there shall be no interference except such as in accordance with the law and is necessary in a democratic society for the protection of health or morals or for the protection of the rights and freedoms of others' (ie the child involved).

13.12.1 The care plan

In care proceedings, the court is restricted to either making a care or supervision order or refusing to make such an order. Although the local authority's care plan is an important part of their strategy for meeting the child's needs, there is no judicial control of that plan and the local authority can change it at any time. If the parents are unhappy about the care plan, all they can do is apply to discharge the care order or apply for contact if the arrangements are unreasonable.

This would seem to conflict with the principle that the interests of the parent and of the child in the decision-making process should be given sufficient procedural protection.

Questions may also arise as to whether Article 6 (which guarantees the right to access to a court in determining civil rights and obligations) is breached by the inability of parents to question the care plan. Any future challenge to care plans is therefore likely to take into account Article 6 and Article 8.

13.13 CHAPTER SUMMARY

(1) There is a duty on local authorities to take reasonable steps through the provision of services to avoid the need for court proceedings.

(2) A care or supervision order can only be made on application by a local authority (or NSPCC).

(3) In contrast to private law proceedings, the child is always a party.

(4) Before making a care or supervision order, the court must be satisfied both that the threshold criteria are met and that such an order is in the child's best interests.

(5) Legal Representation for the main respondents is automatic.

(6) There is a presumption of reasonable contact for parents.

(7) In an emergency, anyone can apply for an emergency protection order.

(8) Checklists detailing grounds for a care or supervision order and the procedure are set out below.

Grounds for a care or supervision order – checklist

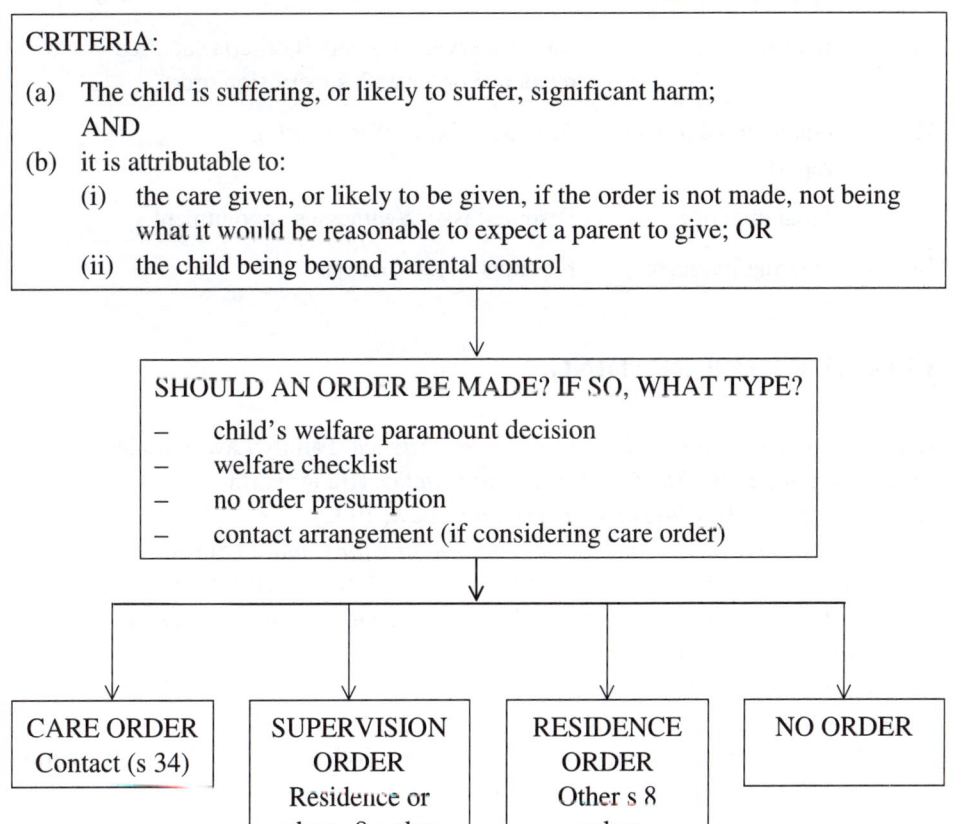

CRITERIA:

(a) The child is suffering, or likely to suffer, significant harm;
    AND

(b) it is attributable to:

    (i) the care given, or likely to be given, if the order is not made, not being what it would be reasonable to expect a parent to give; OR

    (ii) the child being beyond parental control

SHOULD AN ORDER BE MADE? IF SO, WHAT TYPE?

– child's welfare paramount decision
– welfare checklist
– no order presumption
– contact arrangement (if considering care order)

CARE ORDER
Contact (s 34)

SUPERVISION ORDER
Residence or other s 8 orders

RESIDENCE ORDER
Other s 8 orders

NO ORDER

Procedural checklist for a care order

1.	Applicant	Local authority (or NSPCC)
2.	Which court?	Family proceedings court (unless s 37 direction or effect existing order)
3.	Application	Form C1 and C13
4.	Guardian ad litem	Appointed by the court. Guardian appoints solicitor for child
5.	Respondents	Every person with parental responsibility and the child
6.	Notice	Parent without parental responsibility Person with whom child living
7.	Legal Representation	As of right for child, parents and others with parental responsibility.
8.	Service	3 days' notice
9.	Answer	A respondent may file and serve
10.	Directions appointment	Timetable/evidence/reports
11.	Interim orders	Care/supervision orders if criteria satisfied or s 8 residence order with supervision order
12.	Guardian ad litem's report	At least 7 days before hearing
13.	Final directions	Disputed issues/witnesses appointment
14.	Hearing/judgment	Findings of fact/reasons

13.14 FURTHER READING

Hershman and McFarlane *Children Law and Practice* (Family Law, looseleaf)
White, Carr and Lowe *The Children Act in Practice* (Butterworths, 1995)
King and Young *The Child as Client* (Family Law, 1992)
SFLA *Guide to Good Practice for Solicitors Acting for Children* 5th edn (2000)
The Children Act 1989 Guidance and Regulations Vols 1–4 (HMSO, 1991)
Working Together to Safeguard Children – Government Guidance on Inter-Agency Co-operation (The Stationery Office, 1999)
Framework for the Assessment of Children in Need and their Families (The Stationery Office, 1999)
Law Society Memorandum 'Attendance of Solicitors at Child Protection Conferences' (June 1997)
The Law Society's Protocol for the Working Relationship between Children Panel Solicitors and Guardians ad Litem (March 2000)
Swindells, Weaver, Kushner and Skilbeck *Family Law and the Human Rights Act 1998* (Jordans, 1999)

Chapter 14

DOMESTIC VIOLENCE

14.1 INTRODUCTION

This chapter is written on the basis that it is the wife or female partner who is seeking protection since this is the most common situation. However, men can be the victims of violence too and are entitled to the same legal remedies. Any children who are with the victim can usually be protected at the same time as their carer. However, if protection is needed specifically for the children alone this should generally be dealt with by using the procedures outlined in Chapters 12 or 13.

Although there is a variety of potential remedies available in situations of domestic violence, the solicitor must be careful not to raise the client's expectations too high. A court order may give limited protection but much will depend on the personality of the respondent. When the respondent is served with a court order, or arrested by the police (and later released), further violence may result. It is therefore crucial for the solicitor to adapt his advice to the particular circumstances of the applicant, taking into account the personalities of the parties, and to avoid giving the applicant a false sense of security.

The main emphasis here is on how to proceed in the civil courts, but the solicitor should be aware that court action is not the only possible remedy, and may not be the most appropriate one. For example, a solicitor's letter warning the perpetrator to desist from his behaviour or face court action may act as a deterrent. However, this would not be appropriate in cases of serious violence. In these cases the victim may consider going to the police. Some police forces are now becoming more involved in cases of domestic violence and may have their own domestic violence unit. Others may be less willing, or unable to help due to overstretched resources.

Finally, if the client is in such fear that she does not want to return home, the solicitor should consider the possibility of finding a place for her in a women's refuge or in temporary local authority housing (see **6.10**).

One of the most difficult features of this area of the law was that, until recently, there were a number of jurisdictions operating and the remedies available differed slightly in each. Part IV of the FLA 1996 is intended to codify the law in this area, making the same remedies available in any level of court. This part of FLA 1996 came into force on 1 October 1997. It extends protection to a wider group of people than before. In addition, s 60 of FLA 1996 (not yet in force) allows a 'representative' to apply for orders on behalf of a victim of domestic violence. Rules of court will set out who can be a representative, but it is thought that the police service will certainly be included.

Another relevant statute in this area is the Protection from Harassment Act 1997. This Act will be considered briefly, later in the chapter.

14.2 PROTECTION UNDER PART IV OF THE FAMILY LAW ACT 1996

FLA 1996 is likely to provide the remedies which will be most frequently utilised by the family law practitioner. Its provisions are therefore dealt with in some detail.

14.2.1 Types of order available

The types of order available fall into two main categories.

(1) 'Non-molestation orders' for the protection of parties and any children. These can be applied for by a wide range of 'associated persons'.
(2) 'Occupation orders' which exclude the other party from occupation of the home. They can extend to excluding that party from a specified area around the home if necessary. Occupation orders can be applied for by spouses and cohabitants. Other 'associated persons' can apply only in specified circumstances.

14.2.2 Who can apply?

One of the most important changes brought about by FLA 1996 is the extension of the right to apply for non-molestation and (sometimes) occupation orders to a wide group of associated persons. Section 62 states that a person is associated with another if:

(a) they are or have been married to each other;
(b) they are cohabitants or former cohabitants (ie they are or have been living together as husband and wife);
(c) they live or have lived in the same household, otherwise than by reason of one of them being the other's employee, tenant, lodger or boarder (this would, therefore, include gay relationships);
(d) they are relatives (this term includes immediate relations and other close relations such as grandparents, grandchildren, aunts, uncles, nieces, nephews, step-parents and step-children);
(e) they have agreed to marry one another (whether or not that agreement has been terminated. However, where the agreement has been terminated, any application must be made within 3 years of the termination date);
(f) in relation to a child, they are both parents or have, or have had, parental responsibility; where a child has been adopted or freed for adoption, two people will be associated if one is the natural parent and the other is the child or adoptive parent of the child;
(g) they are parties to the same family proceedings (other than proceedings under Part IV of FLA 1996 itself).

In addition, children (ie those under 18) can apply for non-molestation and/or occupation orders in their own right. However, if they are under 16 they will require leave of the court which will be given only if the court is satisfied that the child has sufficient understanding to make the application (s 43).

14.2.3 Non-molestation orders (s 42)

The court can grant an order prohibiting the respondent from molesting the applicant or a child. The word molestation covers not only violence and threats of violence but also pestering. Thus, such an order could be granted against a respondent who sends abusive letters to his wife, or persistently telephones his former partner in the middle of the night.

The court can grant a non-molestation order on the application of any associated person either within any family proceedings or the applicant may make a 'freestanding' application under FLA 1996. The court can also make such an order of its own motion in family proceedings.

Factors that the court must consider

Section 42(5) specifies that the court must have regard to all circumstances including the need to secure the health, safety and well-being of the applicant and any child. Thus, provided the applicant can show a genuine need for protection, a non-molestation order will be granted.

Duration

Section 42(7) states that the order may be made for a specified period or until further order.

The case of *M v W (Non-Molestation Order: Duration)* [2000] 1 FLR 107, makes it clear that, save in exceptional situations, non-molestation orders should be made for a specified period and should not be indefinite. An open-ended order could lead to arrest years later when circumstances had greatly changed.

14.2.4 Occupation orders (ss 33 and 35–38)

The provisions relating to occupation orders are quite detailed and complex. The status of the applicant (ie whether they have a right to occupy the home or are a former spouse, cohabitant or former cohabitant), will determine:

(a) whether the proposed applicant can apply for an order;
(b) the provisions of any order granted;
(c) the factors that the court will take into account in deciding whether to grant any order; and
(d) the duration of any occupation order.

An application for an occupation order can be made in the course of other family proceedings, or the applicant can make a 'freestanding' application under FLA 1996.

Applicant has an existing right to occupy the home (s 33)

An applicant will have a right to occupy the home for the purposes of this section if she is entitled to occupy by virtue of a beneficial estate, or interest, or contract or statutory entitlement (eg under s 30 of FLA 1996). The home in question must be, have been or have been intended to be, the home of the applicant and the person with whom she is associated (the respondent). Thus *any* associated person can apply under s 33 where he has an existing legal right to occupy the home.

Where the above conditions are satisfied, the applicant can apply for an occupation order which may:

(a) require the respondent to permit the applicant to enter and remain in the home or part of the home;
(b) regulate the occupation of the home by either or both parties;

(c)   prohibit, suspend or restrict the respondent's exercise of his right to occupy the home;

(d)   require the respondent to leave the home; or

(e)   exclude the respondent from a defined area in which the home is situated.

Where the applicant has matrimonial home rights and the respondent is the other spouse, the occupation order may further provide that those rights will not be brought to an end by the death of the other spouse or dissolution of the marriage. Unless such a provision is included in the order, it will cease to have effect on the death of either party or dissolution of the marriage.

FACTORS THAT THE COURT MUST CONSIDER

In deciding whether to grant the order sought, the court must take into account all circumstances including:

(a)   the respective housing needs and housing resources of the parties and any child;

(b)   the respective financial resources of the parties;

(c)   the likely effect of any order, or of any decision by the court not to make such an order, on the health, safety or well-being of the parties and any relevant child; and

(d)   the conduct of the parties in relation to each other and otherwise (s 33(6)).

[handwritten margin note: Apply to all applicants]

However, s 33(6) is subject to the 'balance of harm' test contained in s 33(7). This provides that if it appears to the court that the applicant or any child is likely to suffer significant harm attributable to the conduct of the respondent if an occupation order is not made, then the court shall make such an order unless it appears to the court that:

(a)   the respondent or any child is likely to suffer significant harm if the order is made; and

(b)   the harm likely to be suffered by the respondent or child is as great as or greater than the harm attributable to the conduct of the respondent which is likely to be suffered by the applicant or child if the order is not made.

[handwritten margin note: Balance of harm test. Relate test to facts.]

The case of *B v B (Occupation Order)* [1999] 1 FLR 715 illustrates the inter-relationship of s 33(6) and s 33(7) and the balance of harm test. The wife moved out of the matrimonial home with the couple's 2-year-old daughter due to the husband's violence. They were then temporarily rehoused by the local authority. The husband remained in the matrimonial home with his son (aged 6) from a previous relationship. Should the wife be granted an occupation order under FLA 1996, s 33? The Court of Appeal held that she should not. Although the wife and child would suffer significant harm attributable to the husband's conduct if an order were not made, the harm which the husband's child would be likely to suffer if an order were made was greater. This was on the basis of the housing needs of both parties and children. Whereas the wife was entitled to be rehoused by the local authority as she was not intentionally homeless, the husband would not be so entitled since he would be considered to be intentionally homeless on account of his violence. If the husband were forced to move out, then his son would also need to change schools.

The case of *Chalmers v Johns* [1999] 1 FLR 392, makes it clear that the applicant must show that she would suffer significant harm attributable to the respondent's conduct before the balance of harm test became relevant. Where such harm was not shown, the case would be determined on the basis of the factors in s 33(6) alone.

DURATION

An occupation order made under s 33 may be for a specified period, until the occurrence of a specified event or until further order. Thus, such an order can be for an indefinite period. In practice, it is likely, at least initially, to be for a specified period, probably 6 months.

Applicant has no existing right to occupy the home and respondent has such a right. Applicant is former spouse (s 35)

An applicant under s 35 must be the former spouse of the respondent. The respondent must be entitled to occupy the home (by virtue of a beneficial estate, or interest, or contract or by statute). The home must either be, or have been or have been intended to be, the matrimonial home.

Where these conditions are satisfied, the applicant can apply for an occupation order. Any order granted under s 35 *must* contain a provision (an 'occupation provision') stating:

(a) if the applicant is in occupation, that the applicant has a right not to be excluded from the home or part of it by the respondent for a specified period and prohibiting the respondent from excluding the applicant during that period;

(b) if the applicant is not in occupation, that the applicant be given a right to enter and occupy the home for a specified period and requiring the respondent to permit the exercise of that right.

In addition, the order *may* contain one or more provisions ('exclusion provisions'):

(a) regulating the occupation of the home by either party;
(b) prohibiting, suspending or restricting the respondent's right to occupy;
(c) requiring the respondent to leave the home or part of it;
(d) excluding the respondent from a defined area in which the home is situated.

FACTORS THAT THE COURT MUST CONSIDER

Note that the factors are slightly different for occupation provisions and exclusion provisions.

(1) Occupation provision

In deciding whether to make an occupation provision, the court must take into account all circumstances including:

(a) the respective housing needs and housing resources of the parties and any child;
(b) the respective financial resources of the parties;
(c) the likely effect of any order, or of any decision by the court not to make such an order, on the health, safety or well-being of the parties and any relevant child;
(d) the conduct of the parties in relation to each other and otherwise;
(e) the length of time that has elapsed since the parties ceased to live together;
(f) the length of time that has elapsed since the marriage ended; and
(g) the existence of any pending proceedings between the parties under s 23A or s 24 of MCA 1973 (NB: these section numbers refer to MCA 1973 as amended by FLA 1996, Sch 2) and Sch 1 to CA 1989 (financial orders relating to children), or relating to the legal or beneficial ownership of the home (s 35(6)).

S. 35

(2) Exclusion provision

The factors the court must take into account when making an exclusion provision are the same as (a)–(e) above for an occupation provision. However, for an exclusion provision, the exercise of discretion is subject to the balance of harm test mentioned above in relation to s 33.

DURATION

An occupation order made under s 35 must be made for a specified period not exceeding 6 months. The order can be extended any number of times, but any extension must be for a further specified period not exceeding 6 months. In addition, any order shall cease to have effect on the death of either party.

Applicant is cohabitant or former cohabitant (s 36)

An applicant under s 36 must be the cohabitant or former cohabitant of the respondent. Thus, other associated persons could not apply under this section. For example, a niece could not apply for an occupation order against her uncle under s 36. The respondent must be entitled to occupy the home (by virtue of a beneficial estate, or interest, or contract or by statute). The home must either be, or have been, or have been intended to be, the couple's home.

Where these conditions are satisfied, the applicant can apply for an occupation order. Any order granted *must* contain the same occupation provision as an order under s 35. In addition, it *may* contain any of the same exclusion provisions as an order under s 35.

FACTORS THAT THE COURT MUST CONSIDER

(1) Occupation provision

The relevant factors are in many ways similar to those under s 35. The court must take into account all circumstances including:

(a) the respective housing needs and housing resources of the parties and any child;
(b) the respective financial resources of the parties;
(c) the likely effect of any order, or of any decision by the court not to make such an order, on the health, safety or well-being of the parties and any relevant child;
(d) the conduct of the parties in relation to each other and otherwise;
(e) the nature of the parties' relationship;
(f) the length of time that they have lived together as husband and wife;
(g) whether there are or have been any children who are children of both parties or for whom both parties have or have had parental responsibility;
(h) the length of time that has elapsed since the parties ceased to live together; and
(i) the existence of any pending proceedings between the parties under Sch 1 to CA 1989 (financial orders relating to children), or relating to the legal or beneficial ownership of the home (s 36(6)).

It should be noted that s 41 requires the court to have regard to the fact that the parties have not given to each other the commitment involved in marriage. In practice, it is unlikely that this will have much effect on whether the court will make an order.

(2) Exclusion provision

In deciding whether to make an exclusion provision, the court must take into account all circumstances, including the factors (a)–(d) above in relation to an occupation provision and s 41. In addition, the court must consider the following questions:

(a) whether the applicant or any relevant child is likely to suffer significant harm attributable to the conduct of the respondent if the exclusion provision is not made; and

(b) whether the harm likely to be suffered by the respondent or child if the provision is included is as great or greater than the harm attributable to the conduct of the respondent which is likely to be suffered by the applicant or child if the provision is not included.

This is similar to the balance of harm test in ss 33 and 35. However, there is no duty on the court to make an order where the greater harm to the applicant or child is established, it is just one question to be considered.

Once an order has been made and for so long as it is in force, s 36(13) provides that the applicant will be afforded the same protection as a spouse under s 30(3)–(6). This means that a mortgagee or landlord must accept payments towards the mortgage or rent made by the applicant.

DURATION

An occupation order made under s 36 must be for a specified period not exceeding 6 months. The order can be extended only once, for a further specified period not exceeding 6 months. Thus the longest period for which a cohabitant or former cohabitant can obtain an occupation order is one year. In addition, any order shall cease to have effect on the death of either party.

Neither party has a right to occupy the home (ss 37 and 38)

These sections enable one spouse, former spouse, cohabitant or former cohabitant to obtain an occupation order against the other in relation to a home in which they both live or lived together but which neither of them has a right to occupy. These sections could be used, for example, to give the applicant a licence to occupy a home which is owned by the respondent's parents. Section 37 applies to spouses or former spouses; s 38 to cohabitants or former cohabitants.

As with ss 33, 35 and 36 such an order may, inter alia, exclude the respondent from the home or an area in which the home is situated.

FACTORS THAT THE COURT MUST CONSIDER

In deciding whether to grant an order under this section, the court must take into account similar factors to those under s 33 (where a spouse or former spouse is applying) or s 36 (where a cohabitant or former cohabitant is applying).

DURATION

Any order granted will last for a specified period not exceeding 6 months. Where the applicant is a spouse or former spouse, the order can be extended on one or more occasions, each time for a specified period not exceeding 6 months. Where the applicant is a cohabitant or former cohabitant, the order can be extended once only for a further specified period not exceeding 6 months.

Additional provisions in occupation orders made under s 33, s 35 or s 36 (s 40)

Section 40 enables the court when making an occupation order under either s 33, s 35 or s 36 to make an ancillary order dealing with such matters as the payment of the mortgage or other outgoings and payment for repair and maintenance of the home. The court can also order the occupying party to pay the excluded party rent where the excluded party would (but for the occupation order) have a right to occupy the home. In addition, the court can grant either party use of the furniture or other contents of the home and order either party to take reasonable care of the furniture or other contents. In deciding whether to make such an ancillary order and in what terms, the court shall have regard to all circumstances of the case, including the financial needs, resources and obligations of the parties. Any ancillary order made will last for the same length of time as the occupation order itself.

Flowchart

The flowchart set out below explains who can apply for occupation orders and the appropriate section of the FLA 1996 to use.

Occupation Orders – who can apply?

Is applicant 'associated with' respondent? → NO → no right to apply

YES

Is or has the property been occupied by both the applicant and the respondent as their home? → NO → no right to apply

YES

Does applicant have a right to occupy the home? → YES → apply under s 33

NO

Is applicant spouse? → YES → apply under s 33 *or s 37 in rare event that a spouse would not have FLA rights.*

NO

Is applicant *former* spouse? → YES → does R have a right to occupy the home?
- NO → apply under s 37
- YES → apply under s 35

NO

Is applicant cohabitant *or* former cohabitant? → YES → does R have a right to occupy the home?
- NO → apply under s 38
- YES → apply under s 36

NO

no right to apply

14.2.5 Emergency applications (s 45)

In urgent cases, it may be possible for the solicitor to protect an applicant or child on the same day that she comes to see him or at least on the next day. Under s 45 of FLA 1996, the court can make both non-molestation and occupation orders without notice to the respondent (or 'ex parte') where it considers that it is 'just and convenient' to do so. In deciding whether to allow an application to proceed without notice, the court will take into account all circumstances including:

(a) any risk of significant harm to the applicant or child if the order is not made immediately;

(b) whether it is likely that the applicant will be deterred or prevented from pursuing the application if the order is not made immediately; and

(c) whether there is reason to believe that the respondent is evading service and delay in effecting service will seriously prejudice the applicant or child.

However, the courts are generally reluctant to grant orders where the respondent has been given no notice. Therefore, where it is not possible to give the respondent the full 2 clear days' notice required, the applicant's solicitor should consider whether to apply to abridge the notice period instead of applying without notice. Where the respondent has been given some notice (however short), he may be able to attend court to give his version of events. This will mean that the court will be in a better position to assess the situation and may therefore be persuaded to grant more wide-ranging relief than where the respondent has been given no notice at all. However, if the respondent has not had an opportunity to instruct a solicitor then the court is likely to make an interim (rather than final) order to allow the respondent time to seek legal advice before the final hearing.

Occupation orders will rarely be granted without notice, especially where they would involve ousting the respondent from his home.

It must be stressed that any order obtained without notice will be temporary only (an interim order). During the few days that the interim order is in force, the solicitor must obtain a hearing date for the final hearing and give the respondent the required notice.

14.2.6 Undertakings (section 46)

In the past, the necessity for a full hearing was often avoided by the respondent offering to give an undertaking, ie a promise to the court on similar terms to the proposed order. This avoided a court order being made against the respondent. The applicant was often prepared to accept the undertaking since, as it was made voluntarily, it was more likely to be complied with.

Under s 46 of FLA 1996, the court may still accept an undertaking in any case where it has power to make an occupation or non-molestation order. However, no power of arrest can be attached to an undertaking and the court will not accept an undertaking in a case where it would otherwise attach a power of arrest to the order. As it would appear that powers of arrest will be attached far more frequently than in the past (see **14.2.9**), undertakings are likely to become much rarer than before.

14.2.7 Procedure

(a) Which court?

One of the innovations of Part IV of FLA 1996 was to introduce a unified system of courts to deal with domestic violence applications. This means that the applicant's solicitor generally has a free choice whether to make the application in the county court or in the family proceedings court.

The family proceedings court has no power to deal with disputes between the applicant and the respondent over the applicant's right to occupy the home (s 59 of FLA 1996). A family proceedings court can only make an order in such a case where it is unnecessary to determine the ownership dispute in order to do so. Thus, any proceedings involving such a dispute should sensibly be commenced in the county court. However, where such proceedings are commenced in the family proceedings court and the court decides that it cannot deal with the application it has the power to transfer the application to a county court.

Applications in the county court can only be made in divorce county courts or family hearing centres. Where proceedings are already pending in a particular court (eg divorce proceedings), the application should generally be made in those proceedings. Any application to extend, vary or discharge an order should be made to the court which originally made the order.

Finally, any application made by an applicant who is under 18 must be commenced in the High Court.

(b) Transfer of cases

Irrespective of where a case started, it can be transferred to a more appropriate court. This will depend, amongst other things, upon whether the case raises a difficult point of law or a question of general public interest and the need to consolidate it with proceedings which may have been started in another court (see Family Law Act 1996 (Part IV) (Allocation of Proceedings) Order 1997, SI 1997/1896).

Cases can be transferred either vertically or horizontally and between any level of court. Thus it would be possible, for example, for the High Court to transfer proceedings to a family proceedings court.

(c) Public funding

Provided that the client is eligible, initial advice and assistance will be covered by Legal Help. Generally, the normal 2-hour limit will apply, after which time it will be necessary to extend the limit. If proceedings are taken ancillary to divorce, and the applicant is the petitioner in the divorce, then the initial limit is 3 hours. However, this covers the undefended divorce procedure too and so an extension may be needed.

Once the decision has been taken to bring proceedings for a non-molestation order and/or an occupation order, Legal Representation should be applied for immediately. Note that where the Legal Services Commission considers that it would be appropriate to write a warning letter to the respondent and/or to try and enlist the assistance of the police, it will not grant funding until these steps have been taken and proved ineffective. In addition, funding is likely to be refused unless the conduct complained of took place within the last 2 to 3 weeks or if the conduct complained of is not likely to be repeated or is of a 'trivial nature'.

In most cases, it will also be necessary to apply for Emergency Legal Representation. Family solicitors can themselves grant Emergency Legal Representation under the terms of their franchise. The solicitor will need to complete the appropriate section in Form CLSAPP3 and satisfy himself that the client is likely to be financially eligible. The solicitor must then submit an application to the regional office of the Legal Services Commission for both Emergency and Full Legal Representation within 5 working days of the grant of Emergency Legal Representation.

The procedure set out below assumes that the applicant is entitled to public funding. For a privately paying client, simply omit all steps relating to public funding and remember that a court fee must be paid.

(d) Obtaining an order without notice (ex parte)

(1) Grant Emergency Legal Representation.

(2) Telephone the court to make an appointment before the judge or magistrate. In the family proceedings court, the clerk or the court must give leave to make an application without notice.

(3) Telephone a process server so that he can be at court at the end of the hearing to collect the without notice order to serve it on the respondent. The order must be served personally and it is not usually thought wise for the solicitor to do this.

(4) Draft notice of issue of Emergency Legal Representation, the application and a statement in support. The application is on standard Form FL401. In the county court, the statement in support must be signed by the applicant and sworn to be true. In the family proceedings court, it must be signed and declared to be true. Alternatively, the family proceedings court may give leave to allow oral evidence instead of a written statement. Any written statement must give details of the respondent's behaviour and both parties' housing needs and financial resources. It should also explain why the application is made without notice.

(5) It is not essential to draft the order sought. Generally, however, the court would find it helpful to have a draft and so, if time permits, draft the without notice order on Form FL404.

(6) File at court notice of issue of Emergency Legal Representation, the application and the statement in support and obtain a date for the on-notice hearing. If the applicant is not publicly funded a fee must be paid. On filing, the court fixes a hearing date which will be inserted in a notice of proceedings (Form FL402). The respondent must be given 2 clear days' notice of this date.

(7) Attend the hearing before the judge, district judge or magistrate (in the family proceedings court an application without notice can be heard by a single magistrate, on-notice applications must be heard by a panel – see below). The magistrate, judge or district judge will read the statement in support and listen to the applicant's oral evidence. Hand any draft order to the magistrate, judge or district judge. If the order is granted it will be sealed by a court officer. A record of the hearing will be made on Form FL405.

(8) Hand the process server the without notice order, sealed copy application, copy statement in support, notice of proceedings and notice of issue of Emergency Legal Representation. Ask the process server to serve these documents on the respondent personally and then to swear an affidavit of service.

(9) If the court has made an occupation order, serve a copy of the application and the order on any mortgagee or landlord together with a notice in Form FL416 informing him that he has a right to make representations in writing or at any hearing. These documents should be served by first-class post.

Remember that any hearing without notice must be followed by a hearing on notice so that the respondent has an opportunity to put his side of the story.

(e) Obtaining a non-molestation or an occupation order on notice

If a without notice order has been obtained, many of these steps may already have been completed:

(1) Grant Emergency Legal Representation.
(2) Draft the following:
    (a) application in Form FL401;
    (b) statement in support. In the county court, this statement must be signed by the applicant and sworn to be true. In the family proceedings court, it must be signed and declared to be true. Alternatively, the family proceedings court may give leave to allow oral evidence instead of a written statement. Any written statement must give details of the respondent's behaviour and both parties' housing needs and financial resources. Where a without notice order has been obtained, the statement will probably already have been drafted. The same statement is generally used for both without notice and on-notice hearings. However, where further instances of violence have occurred, or the initial statement has been hurriedly drafted, a further statement should be drafted;
    (c) notice of issue of Legal Representation;
    (d) where the application is ancillary to a divorce under Legal Help, a notice of acting (for the reasons mentioned at **9.6.1**).
(3) File the application in duplicate, statement, notice of issue of Legal Representation, notice of acting and Emergency Legal Representation certificate (where appropriate). If the applicant is not publicly funded a fee must be paid.
(4) On filing, the court fixes a hearing date which will be inserted in a notice of proceedings (Form FL402). The respondent must be given 2 clear days' notice of this date. Hand to a process server sealed copy application, copy statement in support, notice of hearing, notice of issue of Emergency Legal Representation and notice of acting (where appropriate). Ask him to serve these documents on the respondent personally and to swear an affidavit to confirm service.
(5) If the FL401 includes an application for an occupation order, serve any mortgagee or landlord with a copy of the application and a notice in Form FL416 informing him that he has a right to make representations in writing or at the hearing. These documents should be served by first-class post.
(6) Once the respondent (and mortgagee/landlord) have been served, file a statement confirming that this has been done in Form FL415.
(7) Prepare the draft order required on Form FL404. This is not essential, but the court will find it useful.
(8) Attend the hearing before the judge or the district judge in chambers or panel of magistrates. In the family proceedings court, the hearing will take place before the domestic panel. This is a panel of magistrates who have received special training in family proceedings. The panel should consist of at least two magistrates, and should preferably include one man and one woman. The hearing will be in private. If the respondent fails to attend, service can be proved using the affidavit. The court can then make an order in the absence of the respondent.
    Hand any order drafted to the judge, district judge or magistrates. The judge, district judge or magistrates will read any statements filed by the parties and

may hear oral evidence from the applicant and respondent. If either of the parties has witnesses (eg a neighbour or relative) they may then give evidence.

If an order is granted it will be sealed by a court officer. A record of the hearing will be made on Form FL405. The court may direct a further hearing to hear representations from any mortgagee or landlord.

(9)   The respondent must be served personally with the order (even if he was present when it was made). Again, this is usually done by a process server who should swear an affidavit of service.

(10) If the court has attached a power of arrest to the order (see **14.2.9**), take a copy of the power of arrest to the police station nearest to where the applicant lives. The police will not be prepared to exercise any power of arrest until they have notice of it. Many breaches of orders occur shortly after they are made, so it is best to give the police notice of their power of arrest as soon as possible.

14.2.8 Procedural checklist

A checklist of the appropriate procedure may be helpful. One is set out below.

ON NOTICE PROCEDURE CHECKLIST

> OBTAIN LEGAL REPRESENTATION IF RELEVANT

> *FILE*:
> (i) Application (Form FL 401) in duplicate
> (ii) Statement in support
> (iii) Legal Representation Certificate and Notice of Issue *or* Fee
> [(iv) Notice of Acting (if client in divorce under Legal Help)]

> *SERVE ON R:*
> (i) Copy Application
> (ii) Copy Statement
> [(iii) Notice of Issue of LR Certificate]
> (iv) Notice of Hearing
> [(v) Copy Notice of Acting]
> [Give 2 clear days' notice]

> *SERVE ON MORTGAGEE/LANDLORD:*
> Notice in Form FL 416

> *FILE*:
> Statement of Service

> ATTEND HEARING
> Present case
> Produce draft order (if drafted)
> (Form FL404)

> SERVE order on R and mortgagee/landlord
> LODGE copy at police station if power of arrest

14.2.9 Enforcement

The basic method of enforcement where the respondent has breached a non-molestation or occupation order is committal for contempt of court. How the respondent comes before the court to decide on his punishment will generally depend upon whether or not the order had a power of arrest attached to it.

Power of arrest

Under s 47 of FLA 1996, where the court makes either a non-molestation or an occupation order and it appears to the court that the respondent has used or threatened violence against the applicant or a child, then it *shall* attach a power of arrest to one or more provisions of the order. The only exception to this is where the court is satisfied that the applicant or child will be adequately protected without such a power of arrest. Therefore, it would seem that the majority of final orders will have a power of arrest attached. As mentioned above, this will probably mean that undertakings will be less common than in the past, and will not be granted where there has been violence unless the applicant is willing to accept the undertaking and can persuade the court that she will be adequately protected by it.

In addition, a power of arrest should be attached wherever there has been use or a threat of violence towards *any* associated person and not just a spouse or cohabitant. A power of arrest can also be attached to one or more provisions of an interim order, but only where it appears to the court that the respondent has used or threatened violence against the applicant or child and that there is a risk of significant harm to the applicant or child if the power of arrest is not attached immediately.

The court can attach a power of arrest to one or more provisions of the order. It is, however, unlikely to attach a power of arrest to a provision restraining pestering only rather than violence. Any power of arrest will be drafted on Form FL406 which will set out which provisions the power of arrest will apply to.

Any power of arrest granted should be expressed to last for the same period as the provisions of the order to which it is attached. This period can be extended any number of times.

A police officer will have the power to arrest the respondent without warrant if he has reasonable cause to suspect the respondent of being in breach of any of the terms of the order set out in the power of arrest. Once arrested, the respondent must be brought before a judge, district judge or magistrate within 24 hours.

Warrant of arrest

Where the court has not attached a power of arrest or the respondent's breach is not covered by the power of arrest, or the police decide not to exercise their power of arrest, or an undertaking is breached, the applicant may apply for a warrant of arrest. The applicant will need to give evidence on oath to satisfy the judge, district judge or magistrate that there are reasonable grounds for believing that the respondent has breached the order. The judge, district judge or magistrate can then issue a warrant of arrest.

Penalty

The penalty available will depend upon whether the respondent is brought before a judge in the county court or a magistrate in the family proceedings court. In the county court, the judge can commit the respondent for up to 2 years (and/or impose an unlimited fine). In the family proceedings court, the respondent can be fined up to £5,000 or committed for up to 2 months.

In both courts, immediate committal is a remedy of last resort and is unlikely to be ordered save in exceptional situations. For example, in *Brewer v Brewer* [1989] 2 FLR 251, the Court of Appeal upheld an immediate committal for 2 months after the respondent entered the home, damaged property and made threats in public, including threats to kill the applicant. He later showed no remorse for what he had done. Alternatively, and more usually, a suspended committal order will be made. Indeed, the court should consider making a suspended order in any case where immediate committal is contemplated. General guidelines on committal were given by the Court of Appeal in *Hale v Tanner* (2000) LTL, 20 July, and reference should be made to that case for further detail. Finally, if the order had no power of arrest attached, the judge or magistrate may attach a power of arrest.

14.3 THE HUMAN RIGHTS ACT 1998

Non-molestation or occupation orders may raise issues under Article 6 of the European Convention on Human Rights. Public funding is often denied to respondents to such orders who may be advised to give undertakings on the basis of no admissions. Consideration may have to be given as to whether public funding should be provided given that undertakings can be the first step in committal proceedings which may result in imprisonment or a fine. One of the Article 6 guarantees is that the proceedings are fair and that each party has 'equality of arms' with the other. Yet if a respondent is not represented on an application, can he be said to have 'equality of arms'?

Occupation orders may also raise issues under Article 8 (the right to respect for family life and home). Interference with this right must be necessary and proportionate. Courts must therefore give careful consideration to the duration and scope of such orders.

14.4 PROTECTION FROM HARASSMENT ACT 1997

In the past, when an applicant did not come within the ambit of the relevant domestic violence legislation, for example if she was the partner of the abuser but they had not cohabited, she would have to bring an action for an appropriate tort, for example, assault. However, until recently, there was no tort of harassment, so protection could be obtained only where the conduct complained of amounted to an established tort (see, eg, *Burris v Azadani* [1995] 4 All ER 802).

The Protection from Harassment Act 1997 (PHA 1997) is intended to plug this gap in the law. Section 3 of PHA 1997 creates a statutory tort where a person pursues a course of conduct which amounts to harassment of another and which he knows or ought to know amounts to harassment of the other. There is no definition of harassment, save that PHA 1997 states that this includes 'alarming the person or causing them distress' (s 7). A 'course of conduct' must include conduct on at least two occasions.

Section 3 provides that where the statutory tort has been committed or is apprehended, the victim may claim damages and/or an injunction. Should the injunction be breached, then the victim may apply for a warrant of arrest in the same way as under FLA 1996.

PHA 1997 also creates two new criminal offences, criminal harassment and the more serious offence of putting someone in fear of violence (ss 2 and 4 respectively). In addition, s 5 gives the criminal courts power to make restraining orders prohibiting the perpetrator from engaging in further harassment.

14.5 CHAPTER SUMMARY

(1) In cases of domestic violence, a solicitor will have to decide whether to take action in the civil courts or whether other remedies, for example, writing a warning letter, involving the police, or removing the victim to a safe environment may be more appropriate.

(2) FLA 1996 allows applicants to apply for two main types of relief:

- non-molestation orders;
- occupation orders.

(3) Non-molestation orders can be obtained by a wide range of 'associated persons'.

(4) Occupation orders can be applied for by a more limited range of people. Whether a person has a right to occupy the home or is a former spouse, cohabitant or former cohabitant will determine whether they can apply at all and the relief they can obtain.

(5) In urgent cases, it may be possible to obtain orders under the FLA 1996 without notice.

(6) The respondent may give an undertaking instead of having an order made against him. However, the court will not accept an undertaking where it would otherwise attach a power of arrest to any order made.

(7) A power of arrest must generally be attached to an order unless the court is satisfied that the applicant will be adequately protected without it.

(8) Where an injunction is breached it can be enforced by applying for committal of the respondent for contempt of court.

(9) PHA 1997 creates a new statutory tort of harassment which may be used where the applicant does not fall within the provisions of FLA 1996.

14.6 FURTHER READING

Bird *Domestic Violence and Protection from Harrassment* 3rd edn (Family Law, 2001)

Clout *The Matrimonial Solicitor – A Guide to Good Practice* (Family Law, 1992)

Emergency Remedies in the Family Courts (Family Law, looseleaf)

Lawson-Cruttenden and Addison *Blackstones Guide to the Protection from Harassment Act 1997* (Blackstone Press, 1997)

Chapter 15

THE UNMARRIED FAMILY

15.1 INTRODUCTION

The number of unmarried couples who are living together has dramatically increased in recent years and over one-third of births are outside marriage. Family lawyers have traditionally been consulted by such couples when their relationship breaks down but, increasingly nowadays, they are being instructed by couples who want advice on setting up home together. To date, English law has developed piecemeal to deal with the problems of unmarried couples. However, The Law Commission is now expected to produce a consultation paper on cohabitation (and home sharing, in particular). Others, such as The Law Society and the Solicitors Family Law Association, are also actively considering the question of a comprehensive reform of this area of the law. The Solicitors Family Law Association's proposals include a new statute, under which cohabitants (including same-sex couples) may apply to the court for lump sum and property adjustment orders, and short-term financial support, for a period of not more than three years. In order to apply, the cohabitation must have continued for a minimum of two years, unless there are children of the family, in which case there should be no minimum period. It is also proposed that cohabitants should have the right to 'opt-out' of the new regime by means of a cohabitant contract. It remains to be seen what The Law Commission's proposals for reform of property law will be.

This chapter summarises the current legal position both during the time when the couple are living together, including advice on how to avoid problems in the first place, and when the relationship breaks down.

15.2 SETTING UP HOME TOGETHER

15.2.1 Ownership of the home

Duty of the buyers' solicitor

When a solicitor acts for joint buyers, he has a duty to advise on the relative merits of owning as joint tenants and tenants in common and may be sued in negligence if he fails to do this (see *Walker v Hall* [1984] FLR 126, *Taylor and Harmen v Warners* (1987) LS Gaz, 29 June).

It is also important to consider when advising joint buyers whether there is any conflict, or potential conflict, of interest between them, in which case a solicitor should not act for both of them.

Declaration as to beneficial interests

An effective way to clarify beneficial interests in a jointly owned property is by using a declaration of trust. The Law of Property Act 1925, s 53(1)(b) requires that a declaration must be in writing signed by the buyers. This will generally be conclusive evidence as to the ownership (*Pettit v Pettit* [1970] AC 777). Since there is no equivalent to MCA 1973, s 25 for an unmarried couple, the arrangement cannot be undone by the court at a later stage. Therefore, the buyers must both understand the position and be in agreement as to their respective shares at the time of purchase.

The declaration can either be included in the purchase deed, or be contained in a separate deed. On balance, it is preferable to prepare a separate document, especially if the property is registered because the Land Registry will not return the transfer after registration.

A further advantage is that some other important matters can be dealt with in a separate document, for example, division of outgoings such as repairs, insurance and the mortgage repayments; circumstances in which a sale may take place or be postponed; and, if necessary, provisions giving one party an option to buy the other's share.

15.2.2 Life insurance

It is important that couples living together make provision for life insurance to cover each of them against the financial consequences of the death of the other.

There is a legal requirement that provides that the person for whom the benefit of a life assurance policy is made must have an insurable interest in the life of the assured, otherwise the policy will be void and illegal (Life Assurance Act 1774, s 1). This interest must be of a financial nature. This can be a problem because, whilst marriage is recognised as giving the parties an insurable interest in each others' lives without the need to prove financial loss, cohabitation is not so recognised. It is therefore essential that where couples are living together, mutual financial support can be shown.

Most couples are concerned with life insurance in relation to an endowment or repayment mortgage upon their home. Clear advice must be given to them on the validity of the policy and the consequences if they split up. Insurance is also relevant in the guise of death benefit paid as part of an employment contract. Often the employee can nominate to whom the money should be paid by giving instructions to the trustees of the scheme.

15.2.3 Wills

The vast majority of people die intestate. This is not advisable especially for an unmarried couple (see **15.6.2**). When a couple decide to live together, they should discuss whether provisions should be made for the survivor if one of them should die. Wills that contain complementary provisions could then be made. A solicitor acting on a house purchase can explain the problems and encourage the buyers to make a will. A will might appoint a guardian for any children and deal with the division of assets.

15.2.4 Cohabitation agreements

An unmarried couple can enter into an agreement setting out arrangements which will apply while they are living together as well as establishing rights on the breakdown of the relationship. This is a developing area of the law and as yet there is no modern decision on the validity of such agreements. However, it is clear that solicitors are increasingly being asked to advise and draft agreements in this field.

There are several books of precedents now available, which are included in the further reading section at the end of this chapter (see **15.7**).

Validity of cohabitation agreements

In the absence of modern authority, cohabitation agreements are governed by general principles of the law of contract. The following issues could therefore be relevant.

ILLEGALITY ON GROUNDS OF PUBLIC POLICY

To avoid challenge on the ground of illegality on grounds of public policy an agreement must avoid any implication that cohabitation is part of the obligations of the agreement. It is, therefore, safer to enter into the agreement after, rather than before, the couple have started living together.

UNDUE INFLUENCE

Undue influence may arise if the agreement is unduly favourable to one party and that party cannot show that it was entered into freely or following independent advice (see *Zamet v Hyman* [1961] 3 All ER 793). A related issue for a solicitor is to bear in mind that it may be impossible to act for both parties due to the potential conflict of interest. This situation could arise where one party is contributing all the finance for a house purchase which would mean that the other party, in agreeing to this in a cohabitation agreement, would give up any chance of obtaining a share if the relationship broke down.

INTENTION TO CREATE LEGAL RELATIONS

In domestic circumstances there is a rebuttable presumption that the parties did not intend to enter into a contract. Where the couple have a written agreement, especially if they received separate legal advice upon it, it should not be difficult to rebut the presumption (see *Balfour v Balfour* [1919] 2 KB 571 and *Merritt v Merritt* [1970] 1 WLR 1121).

CERTAINTY

Any arrangements proposed must be set out clearly; otherwise the agreement may fail through lack of certainty.

CONSIDERATION

Any potential problem arising from a failure of consideration can be avoided by making the agreement a deed.

Matters to be covered in a cohabitation agreement

The main issues which could usefully be covered in a cohabitation agreement are as follows:

(1) ownership of real and personal property (see **15.2.1**);
(2) finances, for example, how to divide bills and resolve ownership of joint accounts;
(3) children, for example, their maintenance, surnames. Any agreement made in relation to children will be limited by CA 1989 and CSA 1991 and will be open to review by the court (see **15.4**);

(4) other matters: here it is important not to include matters which are too trivial, or personal matters, for example, housework or division of chores because this could make it more likely that a court would hold that the parties did not intend to create legal relations.

Enforcement of cohabitation agreements

The general rules of contract will apply to the enforcement of cohabitation agreements. It might also be advisable to include an arbitration clause in the agreement for dealing with disputes between the parties. The Family Law Bar Association Conciliation Board's conciliation procedure is available to unmarried couples who have lived together.

15.3 BREAKING UP

When unmarried couples split up, neither party has any right to claim maintenance from the other. Maintenance can nevertheless be claimed for children of the relationship (see **15.4.2**). Major disputes are therefore likely to centre around the ownership or occupation of their home. It is possible to bring the dispute before the court by seeking a declaration of ownership of the home under the Trusts of Land and Appointment of Trustees Act, s 14.

If the couple were engaged within 3 years before the dispute, it might be possible to use the Married Women's Property Act 1882, s 17. This Act enables property disputes to be determined summarily by the county court; generally it is used only by married couples. The Act confers no jurisdiction to vary property rights and so the court's powers are purely declaratory (*Mossop v Mossop* [1988] 2 All ER 20).

15.3.1 Ownership of the home

Jointly owned property

If the correct procedure was adopted when the property was purchased, the couple's intentions as to ownership should be clear. If the couple purchased as joint tenants, either could apply to the court for an order of sale under the Trusts of Land and Appointment of Trustees Act 1996, s 14 and the proceeds would then be divided equally. If the couple purchased as tenants in common, or if the joint tenancy was severed, only a declaration of trust made by them will be decisive (see **15.2.1**).

If the couple purchased as tenants in common and no declaration as to ownership has been made, it will be presumed that both parties have a beneficial interest in the property to the extent of their contributions (*Bernard v Josephs* [1982] Ch 391). Alternatively, if the tenancy in common was created by severance, then it will be presumed they own equal shares.

It is open to one partner to buy out the other's interest. If this is done, the prior permission of any lender must be sought. In contrast to divorcing couples, any transfer will be liable to stamp duty on the consideration paid plus the amount of any mortgage debt assumed (see Stamp Act 1891, s 57, Inland Revenue SP 27 April 1990, Finance Act 1985, s 83(1) and Stamp Duty (Exempt Instruments) Regulations 1987, SI 1987/516, Category H).

Legal estate in one name only

If a property is in the sole legal ownership of one party, the presumption is that that party also owns all the beneficial interest. In this situation the other party will have to establish a claim in equity. This will involve establishing a resulting, or constructive trust.

If an action is successful and a trust is established, the non-legal owner will be entitled to a share in the property equal to his beneficial interest as determined by the court in accordance with land law principles. The court cannot alter an unmarried partner's share to reflect MCA, s 25 principles as they are able to do with a married couple.

Judgments in this area have frequently not distinguished the various types of trust that can arise. However, interests based on direct contributions, for example, to the purchase price of a property are dealt with under resulting trusts; interests founded on wider equitable principles, for example, on the basis that it is just and equitable, are clearly constructive trusts.

In *Lloyds Bank plc v Rosset* [1990] 1 All ER 1111, [1990] 2 WLR 867, the House of Lords considered the law in this area in detail and the case contains a clear analysis of the circumstances where equity will impose a trust on the legal owner. They are as follows.

EVIDENCE OF AN AGREEMENT TO SHARE THE PROPERTY BENEFICIALLY PLUS ACTING
TO DETRIMENT IN RELIANCE ON THE AGREEMENT

The first situation in which a trust can be established depends on the non-owning party proving that not only did the owner intend to share the property beneficially with her but also that she acted to her detriment or significantly altered her position in reliance on the agreement. In *H v M (Property: Beneficial Interest)* [1992] 1 FLR 229, the parties lived together for 11 years, had two children, but never married. The assets included two bungalows in Essex and a property in Spain, all in the legal ownership of the man. The woman claimed a beneficial interest in the property. The court looked very closely at exactly what had been said by the parties as to how any assets would be divided. The man had said to the woman 'Don't worry about the future because when we are married it will be half yours anyway and I'll always look after you and the boy'. The man also made an excuse that the property was in his name alone for 'tax reasons'. In the light of this the woman had to show only that she had acted on this to her detriment. The court accepted that her detrimental action was the execution of a mortgage deed by her 'as occupier' postponing any rights she might have to the lender, thus prejudicing her domestic security. On this basis, the court awarded her an equal share in the English property, but dismissed her claim for a share of the Spanish house as no similar conversation had taken place.

The court will generally find a trust from discussions in the course of which the legal owner gives an excuse why legal ownership is not to be shared. In *Eves v Eves* [1975] WLR 1338, a man told the woman that the property was only in his name as she was under 21 years of age. Subsequently, she worked on various structural alterations to it. She was held to be entitled to a 25 per cent share (see also *Grant v Edwards* [1986] Ch 638). However, in addition there must be detrimental reliance. The court appears to take a wide view of this as illustrated above in *H v M*. Nevertheless, in *Midland Bank v Dobson and Dobson* [1986] 1 FLR 171, CA, the performance by the woman of normal household duties and the purchase by her of household items were 'quite consistent with the man's absolute ownership of the house'. Unless followed by conduct of a sacrificial nature, the expression of intention was at best an unenforceable declaration of trust lacking the written evidence required by the Law of Property Act 1925, s 53(1)(b).

NO EVIDENCE OF AN AGREEMENT, BUT CONDUCT OF THE PARTIES SUCH THAT COURT INFERS A COMMON INTENTION TO SHARE THE PROPERTY BENEFICIALLY

Here, direct contributions to the purchase price by the partner who is not the legal owner, whether initially or by payment of mortgage instalments, will be generally recognised as conduct that will justify the inference necessary to create a resulting trust.

However, a direct contribution to the purchase price will not establish a trust if given by way of gift or loan (see *Sekhon v Alissa* [1989] 2 FLR 94).

Contributions by labour may also count. In *Cooke v Head* [1972] 1 WLR 518, the woman non-legal owner made a small contribution to the mortgage payments as well as contributions by manual labour in helping to build a bungalow on land owned by the man. She was entitled to a one-third share for their 'joint efforts'. However, in the *Lloyds Bank* case it was pointed out that a common intention by the parties to renovate a house as a joint venture did not throw any light on their intentions with respect to the beneficial ownership of the property. The work done by the wife in supervising and helping with work and decorating was not enough on its own in this case to justify the inference of a common intention to share.

Finally, contributions to household expenses other than the mortgage are unlikely to establish a trust. In *Burns v Burns* [1984] Ch 317, CA, an unmarried couple with two children occupied for 17 years a house bought in the man's name. The woman made no contribution towards deposit or mortgage repayments, but fully performed the tasks expected of a wife and mother and, when able to return to work, was content to meet the household expenses out of her earnings. At no time did he depend on her financial help. It was held that the necessary common intention could not be inferred from her natural concern with the well-being of the household.

15.3.2 Occupation of home

If a non-legal owner does not have any beneficial interest in the property under the principles discussed above, he or she will have no right to remain there and may be excluded by the owner at any time on giving reasonable notice. However, in these circumstances the following ways of protecting the non-legal owner must be considered:

(1) contractual licence;
(2) licence by estoppel;
(3) Family Law Act 1996, Part IV;
(4) Children Act 1989, s 15 and Sch 1.

Contractual licence

It is necessary to establish the existence of a contract creating a licence. This means that a party will have to show that there was an intention to create legal relations, offer and acceptance and consideration.

In *Tanner v Tanner* [1975] 3 All ER 776, CA, a woman gave up a rent-controlled flat to occupy a house bought by the man, in which she brought up their children. The court found a licence for her to occupy the property did exist which would last until the children grew up.

Each case must depend on the particular circumstances and often the necessary elements for a contract will not be established (see *Coombes v Smith* [1986] 1 WLR 808).

Licence by estoppel

If there is insufficient evidence to establish a contract, the doctrine of estoppel has sometimes been invoked to give rise to rights of occupation rather than ownership.

Three elements are required:

(1) assurance of the right to occupy;
(2) reliance on that assurance;
(3) detriment suffered as a result.

In *Greasley v Cooke* [1980] 3 All ER 710, the woman was engaged initially as a maid but subsequently cohabited with the son of the family for 30 years. The woman looked after the children and was led to believe she could remain in the property for as long as she wished. The court held that an equity had been raised that could only be satisfied by allowing her to remain in the house for as long as she wished (see also *Maharaj v Chand* [1986] AC 898).

Family Law Act 1996 (FLA 1996)

Provided the man and woman are cohabitants or former cohabitants, an unmarried partner may obtain an order under FLA 1996 either to protect her and any children living with her from further violence from her partner, or in certain circumstances, an order to remove her partner from the home (see Chapter 14).

Even if FLA 1996 is used, it will provide only short-term protection as the order will give no long-term right to remain in the home.

The only alternative ways to obtain protection are using the protection given by the police using the Protection from Harassment Act 1997 (if this applies to the circumstances), a civil action (eg in tort for assault) or obtaining alternative accommodation. Reference should be made to the Housing Act 1996 (see **6.10**) to establish whether the local authority has any duty to provide alternative housing.

Children Act 1989, s 15 and Sch 1

An unmarried parent could apply on behalf of a child for financial orders from the other parent (see **12.10.4**). The orders that can be obtained include a property adjustment order or a settlement. It would be possible for a child to be granted a transfer of property order (which will include a tenancy) or a *Mesher* order to provide the child with a home until he is no longer dependent. The non-owning partner looking after the child would, therefore, be able to occupy the property as he would be looking after the child (see *J v J (A Minor: Property Transfer)* [1993] 2 FLR 56).

15.3.3 Sale of the property

If the property is jointly owned or if it is established that a trust of land does exist by virtue of a resulting or constructive trust, one partner can apply to the court for an order to deal with any dispute. The most likely dispute is that one partner will want to sell the house and the other will wish to remain living there. The application will now be made under the Trusts of Land and Appointment of Trustees Act 1996 (TLATA 1996).

TLATA 1996, ss 14 and 15 give the court wide powers to deal with any disputes concerning land subject to a trust. TLATA 1996, s 14 gives the court power to make an order that reflects the underlying nature and purpose of the trust. TLATA 1996, s 15 sets out the matters to which the court must have regard in determining any application for an order under s 14. They include:

(a)   the intention of the person or persons who created the trust;
(b)   the purpose for which the property subject to the trust is held;
(c)   the welfare of any minor who occupies or might reasonably be expected to occupy any trust property as his home; and
(d)   the interests of any secured creditor (eg a mortgagee) of any beneficiary.

If the court finds that the home is still needed as a family home it will delay a sale. This could be until the children grow up. Even where there are no children, the court could postpone the sale of the house for a specified period, for example to give the occupier time to buy out the non-occupier or until the occupier finds alternative accommodation. This will only be a postponement for a few months at the most.

The effect of the TLATA 1996 is to combine the old legal provisions in LPA 1925, s 30 and the existing case-law under that section (*Re Evers Trust* [1980] 1 WLR 1327, CA, and *Bernard v Josephs* [1983] FLR 178) to ensure that the court has broad and flexible powers.

If the client is publicly funded, the statutory charge will apply to proceedings under TLATA 1996, s 14. However, the Legal Services Commission has power, at its discretion, to postpone enforcement of the statutory charge in any case where the home is recovered or preserved under s 14 proceedings, or the proceedings result in the payment of a lump sum to the applicant which is to be used to purchase a home.

15.3.4 Tenancies

FLA 1996 has altered the position of cohabitants in relation to certain tenancies. The basic position before the Act (which will still be the position if FLA 1996 does not apply) is that if a tenancy is in the name of one partner, the other has no protection and will be a bare licensee who can be evicted on 'reasonable notice'. An occupation order may give protection under FLA 1996 for a limited period (see Chapter 14). If the couple are joint tenants, both will be entitled to occupy the property. If one gives up occupation, the other's continued occupation ensures the continuance of the tenancy.

FLA 1996, Sch 7 (in force from October 1997) introduces for the first time the right, in some circumstances, for a cohabitant to obtain a tenancy transfer order in relation to certain tenancies. The right to apply for a transfer order will apply irrespective of whether the tenancy is held jointly by the couple or by one of them alone and will only be available on separation where the tenancy was of a dwelling house the couple occupied together as husband and wife. The court's powers are available only in relation to tenancies specified in the Act, including protected and statutory tenancies within the Rent Act 1977, some agricultural tenancies, a secure tenancy (s 79 of the Housing Act 1985) and an assured tenancy (Part VII of the Housing Act 1988).

When deciding whether to make a tenancy transfer order the court must have regard to all the circumstances of the case: the circumstances in which the tenancy was granted or in which either became the tenant, similar factors to those relevant when granting occupation orders (see Chapter 14) and the suitability of the parties as tenants. Schedule 7 contains detailed provisions specifying the transfer orders that can be made and also gives the court a discretion to award compensation to the transferor. Orders under Sch 7 take effect without the need for any further document transferring the tenancy. The power to transfer tenancies could, therefore, be used as an alternative to an occupation order.

15.4 CHILDREN

There are an increasing number of children born each year to parents who are not married to each other. This makes no difference to the day-to-day care of the child while they are cohabiting, but there are legal differences which will alter the legal position if the parents separate. This section looks at the differences in the legal position where a child's parents are not married.

15.4.1 Parental responsibility

Where the parents of a child are not married at the time of the child's birth, the mother will have sole parental responsibility for the child (CA 1989, s 2(2)(a)). The father will not have parental responsibility unless he acquires it in accordance with the provisions of the Act. Strictly, only the mother will have the right to sign a form of consent to an operation, decide where the child should be educated, or appoint a guardian for the child.

Not having parental responsibility does not cut the father off completely because the Act allows a father even without parental responsibility to apply for any s 8 order without leave as he will come within the definition of 'parent' for the purposes of the Act. So, if he is unhappy about any aspect of the child's upbringing, he could apply for a specific issue order to determine the dispute with the mother. He could also apply for a residence order so the child could live with him. If his child is in care, he can apply for contact with the child (CA 1989, s 34). However, in any event he may still prefer formally to share parental responsibility. This could be reassuring for him if, for example, the child's mother has religious objections to blood transfusions and parental responsibility will give him more rights if the child is taken into care or put up for adoption.

The ways in which an unmarried father can acquire parental responsibility for his child are as follows:

Parental responsibility order (CA 1989, s 4(1)(a))

If the father wants to share parental responsibility with the mother and she is not willing to agree to this, the father can apply to court for a parental responsibility order. Such an order will give him joint parental responsibility with the mother and place him in virtually the same position legally as if he were married. Since the parents may not be living with each other when this order is made, he may wish to apply at the same time for a contact order (*Re H (A Minor) (Parental Responsibility)* [1993] 1 FLR 484).

The first thing to establish is paternity. If there is a dispute, the Family Law Reform Act 1969, s 20(1) can be used to obtain a court direction that there be blood tests. The court has a discretion to give such a direction (*Re F (A Minor)(Blood Tests)* [1993] 3 All ER 596, CA).

In deciding whether to grant the parental responsibility order, the court will use the welfare principle (but not, specifically, the statutory checklist). The court will also have regard to the non-intervention principle, although it will generally be necessary to intervene when this order is sought as the parents will be in dispute. In *Re H (Minors) (Local Authority: Parental Rights) (No 3)* [1991] 2 WLR 763, the court looked at which factors would be important in this situation and concluded that it was important to look at the father's degree of commitment to the child, the state of the father's current relationship with the child and his reasons for making the application. The court will not automatically refuse an order just because at the present time there is no likelihood of the order resulting in the father being able to exercise any of his responsibilities. A committed father could be granted the order if it would ultimately be in the welfare of the child to make it (*Re C (Minors)(Parental Rights)* [1992] 1 FLR 1). In *Re A (Minors)(Parental Responsibility)* [1993] Fam Law 464, the father, who had lived with the mother, was present at the child's birth and whose name was entered on the birth certificate, was granted a parental responsibility order (despite the mother's resistance and the fact that he had not seen the child for one year) as he had shown considerable commitment.

A series of recent cases has shown that the court is willing to make a parental responsibility order to give a father a recognised legal status and objections, such as a mother's hostility to a father's involvement in the child's life, or that the court refuses to grant the father a contact order, do not necessarily prevent the parental responsibility order being made (*Re G (A Minor) (Parental Responsibility Order)* [1994] 1 FLR 504, CA). However, the court may still refuse a parental responsibility order where the father has shown a high degree of commitment if it is clear that the father may abuse his parental responsibility. Thus in *Re P (Parental Responsibility)* [1998] 2 FLR 96, the Court of Appeal refused to grant a parental responsibility order where the father had been very critical of the mother's care and made it clear that he would use his parental responsibility order as an excuse to monitor the arrangements for the child's care. In another case, *M v M (Parental Responsibility)* [1999] 2 FLR 737, the court declined to make a parental responsibility order where the unmarried father had been involved in an accident, resulting in serious, permanent brain injuries. Although there had been a significant degree of commitment and attachment to the child, the father was incapable of exercising parental responsibility (and, in fact, required something akin to parental responsibility to be exercised by others over himself).

A parental responsibility order, once made, will end automatically on the following events:

(1) the majority of the child;

(2) the marriage of the father to the mother during the minority of the child. The marriage will give the father parental responsibility for his child;

(3) a court order discharging the parental responsibility order. An application to discharge the original order can be made by anyone who has parental responsibility for the child, for example the mother, or by the child himself

provided the court is satisfied that the child has sufficient understanding to make the application.

The application for a parental responsibility order can be made in the family proceedings court, High Court or county court. There is a standard application form which sets out details of the child and the applicant, including his reasons for applying. Figures available show that, in 1996, over 5,500 parental responsibility orders were made, the majority in the family proceedings court.

Residence order

If a father obtains a residence order in his favour, the court must at the same time grant him a separate parental responsibility order. If the residence order is subsequently changed, the parental responsibility order will not automatically end. This is in contrast to anyone else who loses a residence order, for example, a grandparent, who will also lose parental responsibility.

Parental responsibility agreement

Many unmarried parents will be living together and will be happy to acknowledge their shared responsibility for their children. In this case, they are able to enter into an agreement which will give the father joint parental responsibility with the mother. It will put them into the same position as if a parental responsibility order had been made.

Regulations provide that the agreement must be in a prescribed form, signatures of the parents must be witnessed by a JP, a justices' clerk or a county court officer (not by a solicitor) and the agreement must be recorded by sending it together with two copies to the Principal Registry of the Family Division. No fee is payable. The Registry will seal the copies and send one to the mother and one to the father. Agreements are open to public inspection (Parental Responsibility Agreement Regulations 1991, SI 1991/1478).

Even though a parental responsibility agreement was entered into with the agreement of the parents, it cannot be ended by agreement. It will end only when the child reaches 18 years of age, unless a court order has been obtained either on the application of anyone with parental responsibility or the child (with leave).

Figures available show that, in 1996, only 3,000 agreements were registered, which represents a tiny proportion of children born outside marriage. It appears that either lack of information about these agreements, the formalities involved or the reluctance of mothers to sign them is discouraging parents from entering into parental responsibility agreements.

Guardianship (CA 1989, s 5)

A mother with sole parental responsibility could appoint the father as a guardian in her will. On her death, the father would then acquire parental responsibility because he was guardian even if he had never obtained it during the mother's lifetime. If the mother had not appointed a guardian on her death, the court has the power to appoint a guardian and it could decide to appoint the father. Alternatively, in these circumstances the father could apply to the court to be appointed guardian (CA 1989, s 5(1)(a)).

If a mother with sole parental responsibility has appointed someone other than the child's father as guardian this appointment will take effect on her death and give the guardian sole parental responsibility, which the father could challenge only by applying for a residence order and/or a parental responsibility order (CA 1989).

If the father has acquired parental responsibility during the mother's lifetime any appointment by her of a guardian will be postponed while the surviving parent has parental responsibility. The only way a mother in this situation could ensure that the appointment of a guardian had immediate effect would be for her to seek a residence order in her own favour. In this case, on her death, the guardian and the father would share parental responsibility. This could be of great importance to a mother who is no longer cohabiting with the father of her child and who is anxious to safeguard a child after her death by making, for example, her mother a joint guardian with the father.

Marriage

If the child's parents marry, this will automatically give the father joint parental responsibility with the mother for any of his children.

Human Rights Act 1998

The fact that unmarried fathers (currently) have to apply for parental responsibility, unlike all mothers and married fathers, has not been found to violate their rights under the Human Rights Act 1998. In the Scottish case of *McMichael v UK* (1995) Series A, No 307-B; 19 EHRR 139, the child of unmarried parents was placed in care and then freed for adoption. The parents were denied access to essential documents and the mother brought a successful complaint under Article 6. The father complained that, as an unmarried father without parental rights, he was discriminated against as he had no right to the legal custody of his son or to participate in the care proceedings. The European Court held that the relevant legislation which distinguished between married and unmarried fathers had the legitimate aim of providing a mechanism for identifying meritorious fathers. The conditions imposed on natural fathers for obtaining recognition of their parental rights were proportionate to that aim.

What is of perhaps greater concern is the fact that the court can remove parental responsibility from unmarried fathers but not from mothers or married fathers. In *Smallwood v UK* (1992) EHRLR 221, a father whose contact order had been revoked then lost parental responsibility after the court considered that he would use it to disrupt the children. The father's application to the Commission was declared inadmissible on the basis that differences in treatment between married and unmarried men had an objective and reasonable justification. The Commission also said it was compatible with the Convention to have a system whereby the rights of unmarried fathers concerning care or custody over their children were more limited than those of the mother.

Removal of parental responsibility is clearly a serious interference with a father's right to family life under Article 8. Yet, on the basis of Convention cases, it seems likely that applications under the Human Rights Act 1998 may similarly fail on the basis that interference with this particular Convention right is justifiable and necessary.

In addition, there are other areas of potential disadvantage to unmarried fathers without parental responsibility where they may be able to argue a breach of Article 8 and Article 14 (the right not to be discriminated against in the delivery of Convention rights). For example, a child may not be removed from the jurisdiction without either the consent of everyone with parental responsibility or the leave of the court which means that an unmarried father without parental responsibility has no right to object.

The Government has proposed that joint parental responsibility should be automatic where unmarried parents jointly register their child's birth (which is in over 75 per cent of all cases). (See the 'Consultation Paper on Court Procedures for the Determination of Paternity and the Law on Parental Responsibility for Unmarried Fathers' (Lord Chancellor's Department, March 1998).) However, it should be noted that there is no present intention to change the provisions relating to the removal of parental responsibility from unmarried fathers.

15.4.2 Financial provision and property orders

The ways of applying for maintenance and property orders for the benefit of children of unmarried parents are much more limited than those available for children of married parents (see Chapter 12). The two methods available are first, to apply for maintenance using CSA 1991 (this Act applies to all absent parents irrespective of their marital status); and, secondly, to apply under CA 1989.

CA 1989 expressly provides that a father's obligation to maintain his children does not depend on his having parental responsibility. The financial provisions contained in CA 1989, s 15 and Sch 1 apply to both married and unmarried parents. The most useful provisions for an unmarried parent are those enabling lump sum orders and property transfer and settlement orders (see **12.10.4** and **15.3.2**).

15.5 BANKRUPTCY

15.5.1 Owner occupied home

The interest of a bankrupt in his home will form part of his estate and will vest in the trustee in bankruptcy automatically as soon as he is appointed. A partner left in the home can delay the sale only if there are minor children living with her in the home and then only for a period of 12 months. A spouse in this situation would be able to delay the sale for the same period if she had a matrimonial home right under FLA 1996, even if there were no children.

15.5.2 Jointly owned home

If the property was owned by the partners jointly, the bankrupt partner's beneficial interest will vest in the trustee in bankruptcy. The trustee will generally want to sell the property and can apply under the TLATA 1996, s 14 for possession and an order for sale. Any such application is likely to be successful as it was under LPA 1925, s 30 (see *Re Citro (A Bankrupt)* [1990] 3 All ER 952). The court may postpone the sale to enable the other partner to buy the interest of the trustee in bankruptcy.

15.6 DEATH

15.6.1 Ownership rights

If the home was jointly owned as beneficial joint tenants, on the death of one party the survivor will become the sole owner. If the home was jointly owned as beneficial tenants in common, the deceased's share will pass in accordance with his will or under the intestacy rules. In both cases there are inheritance tax problems because, as the parties were not married, the spouse exemption does not apply.

The sole legal owner of the home may die without leaving it by will to the other partner. If the survivor wishes to obtain a share, he will have to establish, either that he had a beneficial interest in the property, or successfully bring a claim under the Inheritance (Provision for Family and Dependants) Act 1975 (I(PFD)A 1975) (see **15.6.3**). If the survivor is not successful, he will be a bare licensee. The licence can be terminated by the deceased's personal representatives on giving notice to the surviving partner.

If the survivor was the sole legal owner, there could still be complications if the deceased had a beneficial interest in the property which has passed by his will or intestacy to someone other than the survivor.

15.6.2 Intestacy

The intestacy rules do not make any provision for an unmarried partner. However, any children of the couple will have rights on their parents' intestacy. It is, therefore, essential that an unmarried couple make wills.

15.6.3 Family provision

If the survivor can establish that, before the deceased's death, he was being maintained by the deceased, he is likely to be able to bring an action under I(PFD)A 1975. Periodical payments, lump sum and transfer or settlement of property orders can be made by the court.

A change to I(PFD)A 1975 introduced by the Law Reform (Succession) Act 1995 has extended the circumstances in which a claim can be made. It is now possible for an unmarried cohabitant to claim financial provision out of the deceased partner's estate if he or she lived with the deceased as husband and wife throughout a period of 2 years prior to the death, irrespective of whether he or she was financially dependent upon the deceased. This change applies to people dying intestate on or after 1 January 1996. In addition to the common guidelines (I(PFD)A 1975, s 3) there are special guidelines for the court to consider in an application by an unmarried partner. The court must have regard to the age of the applicant, the length of the cohabitation with the deceased and the contributions made by the applicant to the welfare of the family of the deceased, including contributions made by looking after the home or caring for the family.

Despite these changes, an unmarried partner is still not treated as generously as a surviving spouse. First, the court can only award an unmarried partner such financial provision as it would be reasonable to receive for maintenance. A surviving spouse can be awarded such financial provision as it would be reasonable to receive whether or not the provision is required for maintenance. Secondly, on an application by a spouse, the court will have regard to the provision that would have been awarded had the marriage ended with a divorce rather than with death. There is no similar provision for unmarried partners.

15.7 CHAPTER SUMMARY

(1) When unmarried couples decide to cohabit the following issues should be clarified:

- how any property (especially the home) is owned as between the couple;
- life insurance cover;
- wills.

The couple should be advised to enter into a cohabitation agreement.

(2) When an unmarried couple split up:

- neither party can claim maintenance from the other;
- maintenance for any children of the relationship can usually be claimed from the Child Support Agency;
- ownership of the home will be determined by land law principles and an order for sale may be obtained;
- occupation of the home may be obtained by establishing a contractual licence or by obtaining a property order in favour of a child under CA 1989 or, temporarily, by obtaining an occupation order under FLA 1996.
- transfer of tenancy orders can be made in some circumstances under FLA 1996.
- children of an unmarried couple:
  - mother has sole parental responsibility;
  - father can obtain parental responsibility by:
    - court order;
    - residence order;
    - parental responsibility agreement;
    - guardianship;
    - marriage to mother;
- if partner is bankrupt, sale of home can be delayed only if there are dependent children, and then only for 12 months;
- if unmarried partner dies intestate there is no provision under the intestacy rules for the other partner to obtain any part of the estate. Any children of the couple will have a claim;
- I(PFD)A 1975 may be available to an unmarried partner;

The Law Commission is considering reform of the law relating to unmarried couples.

15.8 FURTHER READING

Barlow *Cohabitants and the Law* (Butterworths, 1997)
Parry *The Law Relating to Cohabitation* 3rd edn (Sweet & Maxwell, 1993)
Priest *Families Outside Marriage* 2nd edn (Family Law, 1993)
Bowler, Jackson and Loghridge *Living Together Precedents* (Sweet & Maxwell)
Lush *Cohabitation and Co-ownership Precedents* (Family Law, 1993)
Mee *The Property Rights of Cohabitees* (Oxford: Hart Publishing, 1999)

APPENDIX

CODE OF PRACTICE FOR SOLICITORS FAMILY LAW ASSOCIATION (SFLA)

INTRODUCTION

SFLA solicitors believe in using an approach which is sensitive, constructive, cost-effective and most likely to result in an agreement. To achieve this, SFLA members follow this Code of Practice.

The Association was created in 1982 when there was widespread concern that solicitors an court procedures were adding to the distress and anger that can arise when family relationships break down. Our members believe that solicitors should deal with matters in a way designed to preserve people's dignity and encourage them to reach agreement. The result will often be to achieve the same or more satisfactory solutions than going to court but at less cost – in terms of emotion and money.

Most importantly, this approach is more likely to encourage family members to deal with each other in a civilised way. For example, it helps parents to put their own differences aside and to agree arrangements what are best for their children. Experience shows that agreed solutions are more likely to work in the long term than arrangements imposed by a court. Even when proceedings are necessary, it is best for the whole family if the proceedings are conducted in a constructive and realistic way rather than as if in the midst of a war zone.

What is the SFLA?

- We are an association of over [4,500] solicitors who agree to follow this Code of Practice. The Law Society recommends that all solicitors practising family law should follow this Code. Our members should explain the Code to their clients, as it will form the basis of the approach that they adopt.
- We are actively involved in law reform, both initiating improvements and responding to proposals for change.
- We provide education for our members to equip them to deal with both the legal and practical issues of family breakdown and its emotional consequences. We encourage mediation and counselling where appropriate.
- Our members vary from newly-qualified solicitors to those with many years of experience. However, membership is not a guarantee of excellence or legal ability.
- We produce guidance on good practice in specific areas of family law work.
- Keeping to the Code is not a sign of weakness. It does not expose the client to disadvantage. The approach the solicitor adopts should be firm and fair. Solicitors are not prevented from taking immediate and decisive action where necessary. Even when there are ongoing discussions, court proceedings may be started and continue at the same time in case negotiations do not produce an agreement.
- The Code is not a straitjacket. Its guidelines cannot be absolute rules. It may be necessary to depart from the Code if professional rules or duties require it.

GENERAL

1. At an early stage, you should explain to your client the approach you adopt in family law work.
2. You should encourage your client to see the advantages to the family of a constructive and non-confrontational approach as a way of resolving differences. You should advise, negotiate and conduct matters as to help the family members settle their differences as quickly as possible and reach agreement, while allowing them time to reflect, consider and come to terms with their new situation.
3. You should make sure that your client understands that the best interests of the child should be put first. You should explain that where a child is involved, your client's attitude to the other family members will affect the family as a whole and the child's relationship with his or her parents.
4. You should encourage the attitude that a family dispute is not a contest in which there is a winner and a loser, but rather that it is a search for fair solutions. You should avoid using words or phrases that suggest or cause a dispute when there is no serious dispute.
5. Emotions are often intense in family disputes. You should avoid inflaming them in any way.
6. You should take great care when considering the effect your correspondence could have on other family members and your own client. Your letters should be clearly understandable and free of jargon. Remember that clients may see assertive letters between solicitors as aggressive declarations of war. Your correspondence should aim to resolve issues and to settle the matter, not to further inflame emotions or to antagonise.
7. You should stress the need for your client to be open and honest in all aspects of the case. You must explain what could happen if your client in not open and honest.

RELATIONSHIP WITH A CLIENT

8. You should make sure that you are objective and do not allow your own emotions or personal opinions to influence your advice.
9. You must give advice and explain all options to your client. The client must understand the consequences of any decisions they have to make. The decision is to be made by your client, you cannot decide for your client.
10. You must make your client aware of the legal costs at all stages. The benefits and merits of any step must be balanced against the costs.
11. You should make sure that your client knows about other available services (such as mediation and counselling) which may bring about a settlement, help your client, the possibility of a reconciliation and, where appropriate, give every encouragement.

DEALING WITH OTHER SOLICITORS

12. In all dealings with other solicitors, you should show courtesy and try to maintain a good working relationship.

13. You should try to avoid criticising the other solicitors involved in a case.

DEALING WITH A PERSON WHO DOES NOT HAVE A SOLICITOR

14. When you are dealing with someone who is not represented by a solicitor, you should take even greater care to communicate clearly and try to avoid any technical language or jargon which is not easily understood.
15. You should strongly recommend an unrepresented person to consult an SFLA solicitor in the interests of the family.

COURT PROCEEDINGS

16. When taking any step in the proceedings, the long-term effect on your client and other family members must be balanced with the likely short-term benefit to the case.
17. If the purpose to taking a particular step in proceedings may be misunderstood or appear hostile, you should consider explaining it, as soon as possible, to the others involved in the case.
18. Before filing a petition, you and your client should consider whether the other party or his or her solicitor should be contacted in advance about the petition, the 'facts' on which the petition is to be based and the particulars, with a view to coming to an agreement and minimising misunderstanding.
19. When you or your client receive a Petition or Statement of Arrangements for approval, unless there are exceptional circumstances, you should advise your client not to start their own proceedings without giving the other party at least 7 days' notice, in writing, of the intention to do so.
20. You should discourage your client from naming a co-respondent unless there are very good reasons to do so.

CHILDREN

21. You should encourage both your client and other family members to put the child's welfare first.
22. You should encourage parents to co-operate when making decisions concerning the child, and advise parents that it is often better to make arrangements for the child between themselves, through their solicitors or through a mediator rather than through a court hearing.
23. In any letters you write, you should keep disputes about arrangements for the child separate from disputes about money. They should usually be referred to in separate letters.
24. You must remember that the interests of the child may not reflect those of either parent. In exceptional cases it may be appropriate for the child to be represented separately by the Official Solicitor, a panel guardian (in specified proceedings) or, in the case of a 'mature' child, by another solicitor.

WHEN THE CLIENT IS A CHILD

25. You should only accept instructions from a child if you have the necessary training and expertise in this field.
26. You must continually assess the child's ability to give instructions.
27. You should make sure that the child has enough information to make informed decisions. The solicitor should advise and give information in a clear and understandable way and be aware that certain information may be harmful to the child.
28. You should not show favour towards either parent, the local authority or any other person involved in the court proceedings.
29. Detailed guidelines for solicitors acting for children have been drawn up by the SFLA. Copies are available from Mary I'Anson, Administrative Director, SFLA, PO Box 302, Orpington, BR6 8QX.

If you would like a list of local SFLA members please send a stamped addressed envelope to the SFLA office, address above.

If you would like to know more about the SFLA, please contact SFLA, PO Box 302, Orpington BR6 8QX Telephone 01689 850227 or visit their website at http://sfla.org.uk.

INDEX

References are to paragraph numbers.